TOWARD A PEOPLE'S ART

TOWARD A PEOPLE'S ART

THE CONTEMPORARY MURAL MOVEMENT

Eva Cockcroft, John Weber, and Jim Cockcroft

Foreword by Jean Charlot

E. P. DUTTON & CO., INC. | NEW YORK

10 9 8 7 6 5 4 3 2 1

Library of Congress Catalog Card Number: 76–10038

ISBN 0-525-22165-4 (Cloth) ISBN 0-525-47426-9 (Paper)

Published simultaneously in Canada by Clarke, Irwin & Company Limited,
Toronto and Vancouver.

Contents

List of Illustrations

A. Plates

B. Figures

Photograph Credits

Note: This list gratefully acknowledges the many photographers whose work is illustrated in this book. The figures following each name indicate the number of the illustrations, and the color plates are identified as such. All photographs not credited to a specific individual have been provided by the authors.

Harold Allen, color plate 5
Alvarado School–Community Art Program (photo by Allen Nomura), 58
John Bright, 20
Esther Charbit, 39
Cityarts Workshop, 67
  Nestor Cortijo photo, 68
  Kenneth Golden photos, 34, 66, 70, color plate 11
  Cami Homann photos, 48, 49, 50
  Esther Lewittes, 40
  Alan Okada photos, 38, 69, color plate 12
Tim Drescher, 7, 19
David Garlovsky, 55
Dave Gess, 51
Bob Hennessey, 37
Institute of Contemporary Art (photo by Edwin Child), color plate 2
David Kahn, color plate 7
Lucy Mahler, 24
Michael Mauney, 56

North Country Art Center (photo by Janet Van Zee), 42, 43
Ray Patlán, 45, 46, 98
Philadelphia Museum of Art, Department of Urban Outreach (photo by Patrick Radebaugh), 12
Public Art Workshop (photo by Tom Dorsey), 99
Felicity Rainnie, 23
Gary A. Rickson, 3
Gilberto Romero, 77, 78, 79, 80, 81, 91
Julie Smith, 71, 72, 73, 75, 76, color plate 14
Daniel del Solar, 84, 85
Robert Sommer, 18
Keith Swinden, 30, 31
Edgar Torres, 33
Rev. Thomas, Stranger Home M. B. Church, 87, 88
Caryl Yasko, 59

Our former projects are located on streets in working-class communities—our patrons, critics, and new art-lovers are those living in the neighborhoods surrounding these mural sites. We work with the support of local community groups, and are aided by the community residents. They have never asked for our credentials or the prestige of a "name." They demand only that the artist bring respect, commitment, and vision to his work. Ultimately, it is the community residents and passers-by who most greatly appreciate the involvement of the artist. Unless one is actually witness to the enthusiasm, curiosity, and serious discussions of these newly involved art-lovers, one does not realize the vitality and the potential of the mural as a public art form.

We are dedicated to becoming artists for the people, entering into a living relationship with this vast audience, drawing on the people's boundless potential for creativity . . .

—William Walker, Eugene Eda, John Weber, and Mark Rogovin, *The Artists' Statement.*

Foreword

How could a foreword written by a veteran of the Mexican mural renaissance add anything worthwhile to this vibrant recital of the present deeds of American muralists? What we wrought in faith and hope happened half a century ago, long before the atom was split or men landed on the moon. Meaning at first to decline, I was genuinely moved, as I scanned these pages, by the undeniable zest of youth, the bloom of surprise at one's own achievements, the articulate faith in a future promising even more than the dynamic present. Such enthusiasm is heady. I accepted the task.

We too started on a crusade bent on toppling ivory towers once and for all. We too disdained the twin myths of personality and art for art. We would, through communal effort, create anonymous masterpieces beamed to the people at large. Selfless workers were we, busy at our self-imposed task, our schedule more exacting than any employer would dare impose, and that for the most meager of reward. Our youthful dread—and, as I gather, yours also—was that, come a potbellied middle age, some of us would weaken, shed anonymity, meekly take their place in the stable of artists of some art dealer.

Your book records the birth of a mural renaissance similar in many ways to ours, dissimilar in its locale, the multiracial Babylons of the United States. In Mexico, in the 1920s, we emerged from within the turmoil of a revolution, ostracized by cultured circles, unnoticed by military chieftains playing a game of musical chairs, its prize the presidential one and, for stakes, their very lives.

We were so few to begin with that, for a roll call of comrades, a finger count sufficed. We were so young that those of us who had reached their thirties received the homage due to age and wisdom. A happy fluke found us facing walls to paint on, the majestic walls of ancient palaces, a task that should have filled us with awe but did not. Up went our scaffolds. Up went masons and painters, troweling, frescoing, desecrating these hallowed places—or so opined men of taste. The revolution, even before the end of the shooting affray, had found its image.

Fifty years later it is bracing to watch a group of men and women, as young, as poor, as dedicated and assured as we were, experiencing for themselves the heady feel of painting murals, on walls far from palatial this time. The scale that these plebeian walls dictate often equals that giant one chosen by Michelangelo for the Sistine Chapel. Instead of serried ranks of red-robed cardinals, your audience is plucked out of milling street crowds, quick to react to what your murals have to say.

The story told in these pages is not yet history. It concerns a renaissance in the making and comes close to being a journal jotted as the work proceeds. How then could the authors attempt to generalize, to summarize, and even less to moralize, things that, as a rule, we expect from histories of art and funeral orations.

Both our groups violently broke loose from orthodox modern styles. In our day that was Cubism. The Mexicans were well versed in it, but a different language had to be forged to plead Mexico's case before the world. It took a touch of heroism to swap the much that Paris had to offer for a totally uncertain future. Our refusal to toe the line angered critics. Adolfo Venturi wrote: "It was unfortunate that the vogue for murals was started by Mexican painters like Rivera and Orozco, both academicians. They introduced a rather mechanical form and a social content, both foreign to art. Modern art may be symbolized by the picture of apples . . . If you compel a painter to fill some hundreds of feet of wall space with hundreds of figures he cannot find his form as he did after consideration of a single apple."

In truth, in that place and at that time, bullets were of more concern to us than apples. Those who criticize in retrospect our acceptance of official commissions lack in historical perspective. The last official world, that of dictator Porfirio Díaz, had disintegrated. President succeeded president as moving silhouettes in a shooting gallery. If hallowed walls were given to us to do with as we wished, it was in a spirit not unlike that of a chieftain rewarding his ragged troops with villages to sack and women to rape. The few reactionaries still on their feet raged at this desecration of cultural shrines. If Rivera ostentatiously hung from the upright of his scaffold close at hand a pistol in its unbuckled holster, it was no idle gesture.

I now realize that neither one of our mural movements could dissociate itself as thoroughly as it wished from contemporary fashions. Parisian Cubism remains at the core of our murals, its angles softened mostly by the deep respect in which we held the taste of our own brand of street critics, mostly Indian villagers come to the capital to sell their hand-made wares.

The official art you are reacting against is quite unlike the one we knew. New York has now replaced Paris, so it is said, as the navel of the art world. Splashes and blobs are "in." Sophisticated Happenings partake of the ballet. Meant for an even shorter span of life, Jean Tinguely's contraptions self-destruct. This thinning of the boundaries between the fine arts and the performing arts plays a role in your apparently casual concern as regards the preservation of your murals.

As does a time capsule, fine arts are crafted to project into the future. Gothic cathedrals were communal anonymous achievements. Call them propaganda art if you wish, but they were tuned so finely to the concerns of the masses that neighbors, in their desire to partake, harnessed themselves to the wagons that brought tree trunks from the forest, chunks of stone from the quarry, and—the locale being France—casks of wine to cheer the builders. Today the medieval fires of faith are mostly embers, but cathedrals remain as living witnesses to that faith.

A parallel occurs as Mexican murals enter history in their turn.

Present-day Mexico, oil rich and politically stable, could easily look with disdain on the Mexico we knew and loved, crisscrossed by illiterate chieftains leading unwashed peasants to slaughter. Were it not that our painted walls document this yearning for justice that made today's Mexico a reality.

Clear though your motives are to yourselves, a time may come when onlookers will have lost the key to their meaning. For the very reason that your murals document strictly contemporary attitudes, they deserve to last and enter history, as medieval shrines did, as Mexican murals do.

JEAN CHARLOT

Preface

In this preface, we should like to provide a few precautionary words about what this book tries to do, what it does not do, and why we have written it. We do not consider ourselves writers. Two of us are artists who have become muralists, and the third is a political sociologist. We have been participants in the community-based mural movement.

This vital movement, which has been variously called the public art movement, the contemporary mural renaissance, people's art, or simply street art, has produced hundreds upon hundreds of large-scale wall paintings in less than a decade. They are concentrated in a dozen major cities of the United States and Canada, but almost every city has seen a few being created. We have participated in the design and execution of a few dozen of the new murals, and we have personally witnessed the execution of several dozen more. We have been actively involved in two of the groups that have played an important role in the mural movement. These are the Chicago Mural Group (John Weber) and People's Painters of New Brunswick, New Jersey (Eva and Jim Cockcroft). Special chapters on Cityarts Workshop of New York City's Lower East Side and Artes Guadalupanos de Aztlán of the Santa Fe area have been contributed by founding members of those groups: Susan Shapiro-Kiok and Geronimo Garduño respectively.

Like most other muralists today, we did not become muralists by learning classical methods in controlled studio courses; mural painting was hardly mentioned in the art-history courses we attended. We learned it in the streets by doing it. Like most of our fellow muralists, at first we simply did large paintings on walls. Only later, as we went on, did we come to analyze and study mural painting as an art form. We did not realize all that was involved in our undertaking. We got into mural painting as a response to the times—to the developing social movements around us—out of a felt need to break out of the isolation of the studio, to make direct contact as artists with the oppressed, to make a public statement as artists in the only forum that then seemed viable: the streets.

We were hardly aware of the demands community mural painting would place on us: not only the strenuous physical labor and long hours when actually working on a project, but also the necessity of becoming a teacher, group leader, organizer, public speaker. In between each project have been months of preparation; planning; endless meetings (sometimes several in one day); discussions with landlords, with community groups of every conceivable type, and with other muralists. Then there have been fund-raising proposals to draft and reports to write. It has been totally absorbing for the last few years, each of us talking, eating, sleeping, breathing community mural painting. We have been transformed by this intense experience, not only into mural painters, but also transformed in our view of ourselves and our neighbors, of art and of the artist's place in society.

We write out of this lived experience and the thinking that has been part of it. This book is, in the first place, an attempt to assess and sum up our own experience and that of our friends in the mural movement. We hope that by sharing our perceptions in written form we may in some way be useful to others in the mural movement, and that we might help interpret the community-mural phenomenon to other interested artists, community workers, political activists, and progressive people at large. We hope the book will contribute some insights and stimulate further discussion and research. In brief, we hope that our writing will help bring an understanding and appreciation of murals and of the contemporary mural movement to a mass audience of those who are generally interested in art and social change.

The book is deliberately more analytical than descriptive. For that very reason it is in the form of a reflection upon experience. The mural movement has been a unique experiment in the possibility of a democratic mass culture that is public, authentic, and activist, in opposition to the manipulative culture of alienated spectator-consumers produced by the commercial bourgeois media and the equally alienated obscurantist "high" culture of the elite institutions. We believe that correct ideas do not fall from the skies, nor can they simply be appropriated from scholastic studies. Correct ideas emerge from, are tested and proven in, social practice. As our practice is incomplete, so are our conclusions, for theory can only solve those problems that arise in practical work. Nonetheless, we offer our modest contribution toward a revolutionary program in art.

We felt obligated to write in order to break through the near blackout of critical attention. Aside from extensive spot or human interest coverage in local papers, the entire literature on contemporary murals consists of some dozen magazine articles, a few pamphlets, chapters in a few books, and a methods manual.[1] Despite the artistic richness and social significance of the mural movement, only a handful of established art critics have given the community murals attention: in particular, Harold Haydon, Lawrence Alloway, Robert Taylor, and Elizabeth Stevens. The literature on public art in general is scanty, reflecting the privatistic focus of the art market; the nature of public art is little understood, outside of the mural neighborhoods. Few critics are prepared to deal with the aesthetic, art-historical, or social issues involved in discussing public art forms.

The mural movement itself is largely responsible for the rebirth of interest in mural art and socially committed art in the universities, art schools, and in publishing. Where only a few years ago Mexican mural painting was rarely even mentioned in art-history courses, now a number of schools offer courses in mural painting, the history

[1] There is one recent short book: Robert Sommer, *Street Art* (San Francisco: Quick Fox, 1975).

of murals, or the social history of art. Books have been published on the Works Progress Administration (WPA), and a number of people are researching the contemporary movement. Muralists who started in the 1930s, some of whom continue to paint murals today, have helped keep alive the mural form and have supported the new muralists. If we identify and clarify some of the strengths, problems, and issues of the contemporary mural movement, we will have contributed to this burgeoning discussion. Words, however, will not settle these questions, for in the field of art, as in life, the ideological struggle is resolved only by deeds, by works of art, and ultimately by the people.

The vitality of the contemporary mural movement casts a new light on the central problem of twentieth-century art. This central problem is not the destruction of the collectible art object by nonsalability, by environmental scale, or by participatory creation, all of which are characteristics that the new murals share with Minimal and kinetic art, Conceptual art and Happenings, etc. It is the problem of the audience. Despite the promotion of art as spectacle, status symbol, and hobby, visual art has persistently lacked a true audience in this country. A visual art for and with the masses, understood and supported by them, is something our country has not previously seen. The very possibility of it is denied by many—a denial that is one of the premises of much that has passed through the galleries in recent decades. Can there be a fully developed art based essentially on the working classes and expressing their values and vision?

That the murals have had an audience from the beginning is beyond doubt. It is the response and support of the community audience that has sustained us and that has shaped our development. It has been a measure and touchstone. Through the murals, the people have reappropriated art as visual expression. From the outset the murals have had an audience; community residents have celebrated, loved, and protected them because they have had a part in them. They have seen images of their humanity reflected in the murals. The murals have told the people's own story, their history and struggles, their dignity and hopes. When we write of people's art, we are referring to this community audience, including the oppressed national groups and minorities, the working class; the "lower middle class" of service professionals, the tradesmen and students, the small owners and local merchants; the street youth and the pensioners; all the masses of working-class and ethnic neighborhoods, who are in no way part of "the art world" or of the bourgeois art-buying public.

The identification of the artists with the audience and the audience with the murals has often made it seem as if the mural movement were a spontaneous outpouring of expression from the working class. Brian O'Doherty, director of Visual Arts Program for the National Endowment for the Arts, writes in this vein: "Equally important has been the recognition of the inner city mural phenomenon, which was carried through in an irrefutable sweep of feeling not by a single artist, but by groups of artists, and not just by artists, but by an entire class, one that is usually far removed from privilege. . . . its search [was] not for an audience, but for an arena to display the values of its audience. . . ."[2]

This relationship with the multinational working-class audience is the heart of the mural phenomenon and its most revolutionary aspect. Accordingly, the human process of community murals is a major focus of this book. We hope we have been able to illustrate and bring to life the basis of these assertions by describing the concrete human reality of painting on the street.

The quality of the murals "as art" has been questioned more often than has their authenticity of expression. This skepticism is in part natural. The murals are recent, diverse, scattered, only semipermanent, and of variable quality. It is, in fact, hard to gain enough of an overview to judge. At the same time, some of this critical silence represents social prejudice and ignorance of the aesthetics of murals. Too often the spokesmen of the official art world conveniently pigeonhole the new murals as "protest art," as "minority art," as "poor art for poor people," in order to dismiss them from serious consideration. Murals, however, are not only protests, nor are they

[2] "Public Art and the Government: A Progress Report," *Art in America* (May–June 1974): 48.

simply large paintings on walls; they are painting wedded to architecture, public art conceived in a given space, art rooted in a specific human context. They are an art form in their own right, a rediscovered and rapidly developing one, which we attempt to explain in some depth in our chapter on aesthetics (chapter 11). The mural artists are also developing rapidly; at least a dozen have achieved a mature, personal idiom in the mural form. Serious criticism (and major commissions) are already long overdue.

Groups have played a highly significant role in the mural movement. Quite naturally, this book concentrates on the mural groups we know best, the ones in which we participate. We sketch their development and methods, their internal life and problems. Each of the four groups discussed is representative of certain types of community-mural activity, of a certain range of styles and methods, and of a distinctive form of artist organization.

In the introductory chapters, we try to provide a historical and conceptual framework for the murals. We briefly sketch the origins of the movement and give an overview of the diversity and geographic distribution of contemporary mural painting. We cannot claim to make a complete survey of all the murals; they are springing up too fast. Even to attempt such a complete survey would require a book in itself, or several books. There certainly is a need to document fully irreplaceable works, masterpieces that will fade or disappear within a decade, as well as the less magnificent ones. But we cannot pretend to do that here. Rather, we offer a sampling and a typology of current murals to indicate the range of the phenomenon and to provide a background against which we examine in some detail the experience of a few mural groups.

This book, then, is neither a thorough and proper history of the entire movement nor even of the groups to which we belong and which we know best. It is neither a collection of monographs on individual muralists nor an instruction manual on how to paint murals. Others more qualified by temperament and training have taken up or will, we are confident, take up these tasks. The establishment of accurate chronology, the tracing of influences, a *cata-*

logue raisonné of murals, will not, however, capture the fascinatingly complex process by which the artists and the movement have grown. The mural idea has spread by word of mouth and by occasional newspaper articles; murals and mural groups have appeared seemingly spontaneously in different cities without apparent contact with the earlier projects in Chicago, New York, or Boston. But we have been aware of a fragile network of communication and cross-influences between cities, energized by the sense of participating in something large and dynamic. The writers of this book met through the informal process of contacts that has characterized the spread of the movement from the beginning. From the outside, the artists have often been anonymous to the point of seeming invisible (nonwhite and women artists have often been invisible); and this anonymity has often been deliberately chosen by mural directors who have seen their role as that of a medium through which a community can express its own message. But from the inside, we have lived a very intense life of sharing, of learning from one another in collective projects, of discussion and debate.

We have often doubted if the uniqueness of community-mural work on the street could be communicated to those who have not shared in it. In remembering so many late-night discussions between black, Latin, Asian, and white muralists, between muralists and community supporters, we think of what Braque once said of his years spent creating Cubism with Picasso—that what they had said to one another would never be said again. Those conversations, rich with colloquial eloquence at times, informed by a shared sense of responsibility for an enterprise of far-reaching revolutionary implications, would be worth more than this book. The happenstance encounters; the changes of plan that led to mural projects; the day-to-day byplay on the street of people's reactions to the artists, to the painting; the human drama of growth seen in young members of a painting team—we try to transmit some of the flavor of all this while realizing the impossibility of reproducing the real process of having lived it.

Therefore, we apologize in advance for all errors and omissions that may be found in this book. We apologize for any misstatements concerning priority in the early years of the movement, for any errors concerning authorship and sponsorship of murals, and for any unintended distortion of meaning resulting from misquotes or quotes out of context. We apologize to the many mural artists whose contributions deserve fuller treatment. We hope that other artists and close observers of the mural movement will supplement and correct our writing with their own. The opinions expressed here are solely ours and do not represent the views of any other artists or groups of artists, including those groups in which we have participated.

We hope that the artists concerned will judge our intent generously, bearing in mind that we are fellow artists. In those cases outside of our personal knowledge, we have relied on fragmentary press materials, word of mouth, and, whenever possible, exchanges of letters and photographs. We are indebted to all the muralists and friends of the mural movement who have provided us material, photographs, narratives of mural experiences, and who have taken us to see murals in various cities. Many of their names appear in the text, but we should also like to pay special thanks to Joan Brigham, Rupert Garcia, Shifra M. Goldman, David Kahn, Nancy Schaefer, Daniel del Solar, and Robert Sommer. For his generous help in providing information, photographs, and criticism, we thank Tim Drescher.

There is a special significance to participants writing about any event or process; in art this is exceedingly rare. The Bauhaus artists were perhaps the last to do this extensively—and also, coincidentally, the last group of artists in a Western industrialized nation to participate in a collective endeavor that projected a vision of art's social role. For a long time after this book was first proposed, it was conceived as a combination manual and anthology of mural-movement documents, manifestos, and narrative reports. We hope to assist in the preparation of such a documentary mural reader in the future, but we decided that the immediate need was for a more expository and analytical statement, summing up our experience and what we have learned. This forces us to establish certain categories and generalizations and to project a certain patterning of complex realities—a difficult task when we know the story behind so many murals personally in detail, each one different, and when, on the other hand, our knowledge of many other murals, their context and circumstances of creation, is fragmentary or blank. We do not pretend, in doing so, to be objective. We write from a point of view; we are unashamedly subjective and partisan. We want a sense of our own experience to permeate this work. And that experience more than anything else has been a process of learning. We hope that a sense of that will be transmitted.

This book was in part made possible by a sabbatical leave (1974/75) provided John Weber by Elmhurst College, Elmhurst, Illinois, and by a critics' grant to Eva Cockcroft (1975/76) from the National Endowment for the Arts. To help finance the painting of more murals, all royalties from this edition will go directly to the four mural groups discussed in special chapters. Royalties from the second printing will go to cover expenses incurred by the authors in the writing of the book. Royalties from all subsequent editions will go to set up a fund to help support community-based public art.

For her editorial assistance, typing, criticism, and forbearance, we are deeply grateful to Elsa Weber. We want to thank Matthew Baigell, Jean Charlot, Shari Gruhn Lewis, and Francis V. O'Connor for their encouragement. Coming through on short notice, Dee Sloboda did a superb typing job on the final manuscript. We also want to thank our children, who proved very understanding.

Finally, we should like to apologize for not recognizing by name the many community people and nonprofessionals, old and young, whose support and participation make the murals possible. This book is, nonetheless, about your efforts and for you.

E. C., J. W., J. C.

Chicago
May 1, 1975

1

Beginnings

> No one asked for the "Wall of Respect." It just had to be painted. It made a direct statement to the Black community and the statement came directly out of the community through its artists.
>
> —Harold Haydon, *Chicago Sun-Times,* December 13, 1970.

In early spring 1967, a group of some twenty black artists started painting on a semiabandoned two-story building on the southeast corner of Forty-third and Langley streets. It was in the center of Chicago's old "black belt" South Side, an area scheduled for demolition to make way for urban renewal. The project began without fanfare, unnoticed by the press; but it gathered around it a festival of the arts for black people. Photographs were added to the paintings and poems inscribed among the portraits. Musicians came to play jazz sets, poets to read poems. Uncommissioned, without patronage or manifestos, it was a self-determined effort of community-conscious artists. The *Wall of Respect* was the beginning (pl. 1).

Most of the participating artists were members of the Organization for Black American Culture, or OBAC (pronounced *obasi,* the Yoruba word for chieftain). At that time, OBAC included not only painters, but writers, poets, actors, playwrights, and others, organized into three workshops: literary, visual arts, and community. OBAC's statement of purposes was definitive: "We want to provide a new context for the Black Artist in which he can work out his problems and pursue his aims unhampered and uninhibited by the prejudices and dictates of the 'mainstream.'"[1] The artists found a "new context" in the community itself, which soon claimed the *Wall of Respect* as its own.

Some sections of the *Wall of Respect* were painted directly on the brick, others on panels. Few of the artists had done exterior artwork before, and much of their work peeled badly after a year or two. Some sections simply grouped rows of portraits and photos, whereas others were filled with fully developed compositions. To facilitate the work, figures were grouped by fields of accomplishment: statesmanship, athletics, music, literature, religion, etc. Silvia Abernathy divided up the wall, laying it out in formal rectangular areas corresponding to the natural rhythmic divisions in the wall determined by doors, moldings, boarded-up windows, and window bays. Mirna Weaver painted the sports section, Eliot Hunter and Jeff Donaldson the jazz section. Edward Christmas and another artist painted the literature section, including the poem "Calling All Black People" by LeRoi Jones (Imamu Amiri Baraka). William Walker, assigned with other artists to the religious-leaders section, which was to include Dr. Martin Luther King, Jr., Nat Turner, etc., painted a march led by Elijah Muhammed, called "The Messenger." Carolyn Lawrence painted the adjacent newsstand with silhouette dance figures. Other artists involved included Roy Lewis, Norman Perris, Wadsworth Jarrel, Wyatt T. Walker, Will Hancock, Florence Hawkins, Barbara Jones, and Darryl Colror. Billy Abernathy, Jr., and Bobby Sengestacke contributed photographs. Curly Elison, a sign painter, did the lettering, and Lenore Franklin, a community activist, assisted the artists.

It was not exactly a mural, nor was it simply a gallery in the streets. Its purpose was not to bring aesthetic enlightenment to an area too poor to support even a nominal art fair, but to use art

[1] "Wall of Respect," *Ebony* (December 1967): 49.

publicly to express the experience of a people. It was a collective act, an event.

The wall proclaimed that black people have the right to define black culture and black history for themselves, to name their own heroes. In the words of Bill Walker, "the main idea was to come forth with the spirit of giving unselfishly." Painting about black heroes was "to overshadow the worst examples having to do with human entrapment. We had a responsibility to make an impression on the little ones. The artists had no concern with winning the approval of the establishment or attracting notice from the establishment—which would have contradicted what they were about."[2]

The *Wall of Respect* embodied a unique moment—the moment when a large group of black artists in different media could collaborate publicly in direct contact with the community on the basis of being black. Distinctions between poster and easel painting, poems and photos, were submerged in the sense of the absolute necessity of public communication of black pride, accomplishment, and self-respect. "This Wall was created to Honor our Black Heroes, and to Beautify our Community," the wall's inscription stated. Political lines between various shades of nationalism—between mysticism, reform, or revolution—were blurred or had not yet been drawn. The *Wall of Respect* coincided with the year that James Foreman called "the high-tide of Black resistance." The action of the masses seemed to be running ahead of the ideologies and tactics of any and all leaders. The artists were, in a sense, swimming with that tide.

Like anything else that evolves in time, the wall's character was altered and molded by the pressure of events. As the summer progressed, the community responded, insisting on impressing their own stamp on the work. Many opposed the inclusion of Dr. King, demanding Stokely Carmichael instead. Walker, Weaver, Franklin, and others continued working on the wall. Eugene Eda joined the group and painted a giant fist, flanked by portraits of Malcolm X, Stokely, and H. Rap Brown. The fist initiated a change from por-

[2] William Walker, interview with Eva Cockcroft, 1975.

traits to statements about conditions in the community, a shift of direction that was fundamental to later developments. Walker painted over "The Messenger" with a composition entitled "See, Listen, and Learn," which showed Nat Turner preaching to a dense crowd of people.

The police watched the activity around the wall with suspicion. The artists were threatened, and there were anonymous attempts to bribe local gangs to deface the wall. The street gangs, however, supported the project. The street, which earlier had been the scene of a shoot-out, became neutral ground for the rival P. Stones and Disciples. The Main 21, leaders of the Almighty P. Stone Nation, met with the artists and offered to help secure materials. Congressman Ralph Metcalfe promised to ensure noninterference by the police.

In August, local civil-rights leaders called for a mass demonstration on Forty-third Street near the wall. A street permit was denied, but on a hot afternoon, angry people filled the streets from every direction. Police with shotguns waited on the rooftops. In the midst of this sea of protesters, Curly Elison, with permission from the demonstration leaders, calmly lettered *Wall of Respect* under the figure of Muhammed Ali. Walker held the ladder and passed up the paint. He remembers it was "an hour of high tension—the air was so thick, so heavy."[3]

The wall was dedicated later that month, on August 27. The street was again filled with people; but this time the atmosphere was festive, and vibrant with music. Gwendolyn Brooks and Don L. Lee read poems dedicated to the wall and Val Ward, founder of the Kuumba Theatre Workshop, recited. Historian Lerone Bennett declared, "The Wall is home and a way Home."[4]

The wall rapidly became an undeclared landmark. Its fame spread by word of mouth. For a quarter, children would offer to explain "our" wall to the growing number of visitors, naming each portrait and symbol. Johnny Ray, the "chairman" of the wall, would

[3] *Ibid.*
[4] "Wall of Respect," *Ebony* (December 1967): 49.

come out of his television-repair shop, the last operating business on the block, to talk about it. Walker especially remembers one young man who, after studying the wall for a long time, said simply, "I'm gaining my strength."

The significance of this historic beginning was fully recognized by at least one of the participating artists. William Walker, who had obtained permission from the owner to paint on the wall, originally proposed the idea of the *Wall of Respect* to its sponsors, OBAC and the Forty-third Street Community Organization. Walker later recalled how for fifteen years, while working as a sign painter and decorator, he had been waiting for a rebirth of public art, for a chance to address his people directly in paint. Raised in Birmingham, Alabama, Walker had done his military service in the Air Force and then had enrolled in the Columbus Gallery of Fine Arts, where he studied under Emerson Burckhart, Joseph Kanzani, Samella Lewis, and Edmund Kuehn. His first painting projects had been in Memphis and Nashville, Tennessee. "It was in Memphis," Walker recalled, "that I first became aware of the fact that Black people had no appreciation for art or artists—they were too busy just struggling to survive. . . . In questioning myself as to how I could best give my art to Black people, I came to the realization that art must belong to ALL people—that is when I first began to think of public art."[5]

Later, Walker was recognized by many of us as the founder of the mural movement, not only because of his role in the *Wall of Respect,* but also because his commitment to public art went far beyond the event in which the wall was born and beyond the historical period that it embodied. Throughout the difficult early years, Walker persevered. The force of his personal example and clear vision of the importance of public art helped draw other artists into the movement. For many, he was the teacher.

The significance of the *Wall of Respect* extended beyond Chicago. In 1968, the *East Side Voice* invited Walker, Eda, Hunter, and Christmas to Detroit. There they executed the *Wall of Dignity* on

[5] From *The Artists' Statement,* Chicago Museum of Contemporary Art, 1971.

1. William Walker, Eugene Eda, Eliot Hunter, and Edward Christmas: *Wall of Dignity*. 1968. Detroit.

2. William Walker, Eugene Eda, and others: *Wall of Truth*. 1969. Chicago.

Mack Avenue, a few blocks from the Chrysler plant, and worked with several Detroit artists on the Grace Episcopal Church on Twelfth Street, close to the burned-out area that had been the center of the recent riots. In December 1968, at the invitation of Rev. Thomas Kerwin of Saint Bernard's Church (across the street from the *Wall of Dignity*), Eda and Walker began work on masonite panels for the front of the church. After completing this *Harriet Tubman Memorial Wall,* they returned to Chicago.

In 1969, Walker and Eda renewed the *Wall of Respect*, covering the fist and portraits of Stokely and Rap Brown with panels that dramatized police repression, and replacing "See, Listen, and Learn" with the composition "Peace and Salvation." Then, across the street, on the boarded-up doorways of a burned-out tenement, they began the *Wall of Truth*. Again, panels were combined with sections of direct painting, but this time almost all of the sections were related to the themes of oppression, unity, and confrontation. In one section Walker combined collaged real posters with painting. Over the title a panel was hung with the following inscription:

> We the People
> Of this community
> Claim this building in order
> To preserve what is ours.

The walls had become a visible rallying point for the community.

The more famous the walls became, the more they were an embarrassment and obstacle to the city administration, which found its urban-renewal plans for clearing the area now frustrated by the presence of the paintings and the community's pride in "its" walls. At least twice in 1969 and 1970 mass rallies at the walls forced the city to delay scheduled demolition. A counterplan was put forward: that the buildings be rehabilitated and given to the community for an art center. The city insisted the structures were unsafe but promised an art center after demolition. Urban renewal was stalemated.

The people refused to abandon the walls, and the artists continued to work on them, creating new panels, which spread around the corner. Eventually, it was hard to tell just where the *Wall of Truth* ended. It was on a street that already had various hand-painted signs, including a Christ carrying the cross on a storefront church, and a group of musicians gracing the front of Pepper's Hall of Greats, a well-known blues club.

Photos of the *Wall of Respect* graced the cover and inside pages of the Summer–Fall 1968 issue of *Arts in Society,* an issue devoted to "the Arts and the Black Revolution." *Ebony* magazine ran a feature article on the wall in December 1967. The wall captured the imagination of artists in other cities. In 1968 similar walls were painted in black communities in Boston, Saint Louis, and Philadelphia. Wall of Respect became a generic term for these new black murals. Dana Chandler, one of the original Boston muralists, recalls: "We wanted to do some Walls of Respect in the black community like the one that was done in Chicago. The difference was that, unlike the wall in Chicago, where, as I remember, the money did not come from the city, but people got together and raised the money to put it up, we did go to the city and ask them for money."[6]

As the idea of outdoor murals spread throughout the nation, the first wall was remembered. In 1973, when Caryl Yasko (a white artist) met with local gang members to discuss a mural for Forty-seventh Street on Chicago's South Side, the reaction was: "Wow! Now we'll have our own Wall of Respect, and nothing will ever happen to it."

> I think that that wall in Chicago was the pivotal wall for influencing the erection of Walls of Respect around the country—they started it for everybody, blacks, whites, Puerto Ricans, everybody. . . .[7]

In a sense, the news of the wall was like a single spark setting off a prairie fire. By 1970, Chicano, white, and Asian artists were directing mural projects in at least a dozen major cities and a number of smaller towns. The year 1970 may be taken as marking the time when inner-city wall painting emerged from isolated events and

[6] Dana Chandler, interview with Eva Cockcroft, 1974.
[7] *Ibid.*

3. Gary A. Rickson: *Segregation, A.D.*, and Dana C. Chandler, Jr. (Akin Duro): *Stokely and Rap: Freedom and Self-Defense*. 1968. Boston.

4. Mario Castillo and neighborhood youths: *Metafísica*. 1968. Chicago.

individual gestures to become a conscious multinational movement of artists who now began to call themselves muralists.

Once again, the events that marked the transition occurred in Chicago. The year 1970 was one of tremendous growth for mural painting in Chicago and other cities. Some thirty murals, directed by black, white, Chicano, and Asian artists, were painted in Chicago alone; even more were painted in Boston (pl. 2). Federal, state, and local grants made it possible for muralists to work on a much larger scale. It was also in 1970 that the mural movement's first manifesto was written: *The Artists' Statement,* by William Walker, Eugene Eda, John Weber, and Mark Rogovin. The occasion for the manifesto was the "Murals for the People" exhibition at the Chicago Museum of Contemporary Art, February–March 1971.

Because of the museum exhibition, efforts to preserve the first walls were revived, and alternative plans were discussed. The artists pledged to contribute new panels to the Walls of Respect and Truth in order to revive interest in them, many of the original artists having moved away. In early 1971, when Walker, Eda, Weber, and Rogovin were just beginning on their panels in the museum's basement, the women's board of the museum toured the *Wall of Respect* and the *Wall of Truth.* It was the ultimate recognition by white respectability. If the artists thought, however, that this bit of slum tourism might help ensure the preservation of the walls, they were soon disabused. Less than a month later, while they were still working in the museum, a fire "of unknown origin" was set in the rear of Johnny Ray's shop, and it spread to the entire building. The fire destroyed most of the paintings, although people did manage to remove some of the panels. Once the wall was dismantled, the city proceeded with demolition of the remaining buildings in the area, four years behind schedule. The few remaining panel sections, mostly from the *Wall of Truth,* were eventually installed under Eda's supervision outside of Malcolm X College on the near West Side.

The *Wall of Respect* was gone, but the movement it had sparked was very much alive. This movement has several elements relatively new to art in America. These new elements include:

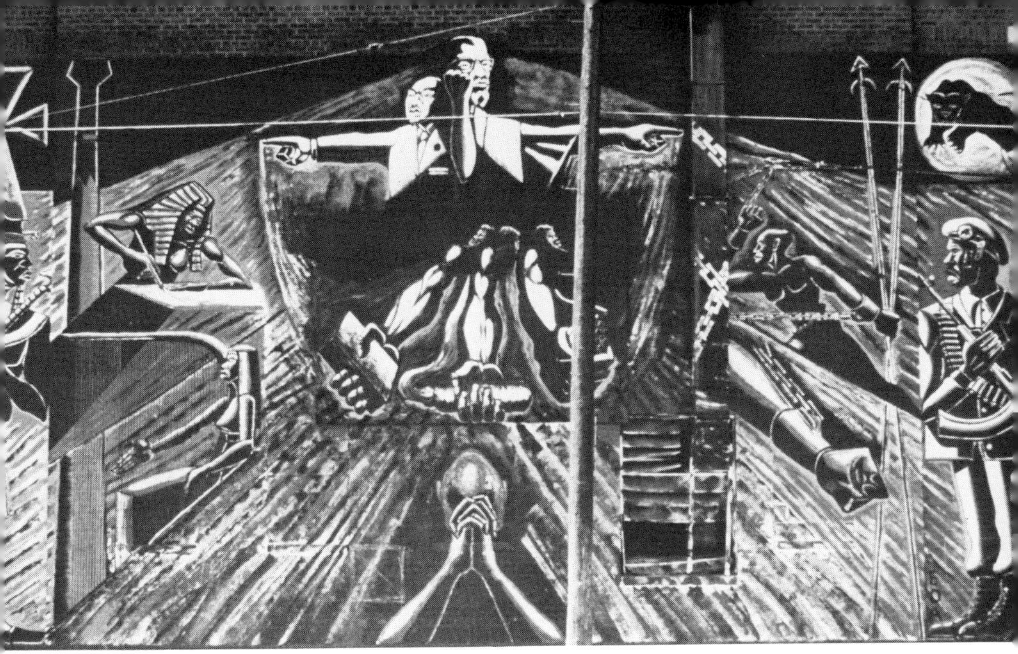

5. Eugene Eda: *Wall of Meditation.* 1970. Chicago.

- the locations, outdoors and in "neglected sites," in working-class and minority neighborhoods, rather than inside government buildings.
- the initiative of artists. Groups of artists rather than politicians or professional administrators continue to administer several of the mural programs.
- the leading role of black artists and in general of artists belonging to oppressed groups traditionally excluded from the established art world (blacks, Chicanos, other Latins, Asians, and women).
- community support and involvement (financial sponsorship, discussion of theme, practical support, inaugural celebrations, and people's protection of the murals). The first walls in Chicago, Santa Fe, Detroit, etc., were entirely sponsored by the local community. Although subsequently government did get involved in sponsoring some murals through municipal departments of cultural affairs, state arts councils, and especially through the Na-

tional Endowment for the Arts, official funding was never more than partial, usually on a "matching" basis. Involvement of the local community base continues to give the murals a distinctive character and role.

- a collective character. The murals are often executed by groups of artists or are designed and executed by nonprofessional local residents led by an artist.

Naturally, these elements are not completely new. They occurred *episodically* in the work of the WPA and the Mexican mural movement. But they *characterize* the contemporary mural movement.

2

Historical Background

Our murals will continue to speak of the liberation struggles of Black and Third World peoples; they will record history, speak of today, and project toward the future. They will speak of an end to war, racism, and repression; of love, of beauty, of life. We want to restore an image of full humanity to the people, to place art into its true context—into life.

—William Walker, Eugene Eda, John Weber, and Mark Rogovin, *The Artists' Statement.*

Sociopolitical Context

Starting with the civil-rights movement, waves of protest and grass-roots organizing spread across the nation, engulfing more and more sections of the population in self-examination, conflict, and struggle. The Indochina War, the crisis of the cities, and a growing alienation from traditional American values came to constitute the critical issues of the 1960s. There simultaneously occurred a wide range of local organizing activities that shared a general thrust toward attempting a positive grass-roots reconstruction of society. The early murals were strongly related to these national issues and to the efforts of community and neighborhood organizations.

The overarching context of these movements for social change was the gradual decline of imperialism, most starkly represented in the controversial engulfment in Vietnam and the neglect of the cities. The costs of imperialism ran high: fifty thousand young Americans killed in Indochina, $140 billion for a war with no end in sight, inflation at home, decline of the dollar abroad, and immeasurable "social costs" from widespread alienation and disillusionment with the ideology of "melting pot" America.

During and after World War II, millions of blacks from the South had poured into the northern and western cities seeking employment in the booming arms plants, automotive and steel industries, and other centers of industrial production. Contrary to popular myth, from 1960 to 1966 this black migration to the big cities did not slacken. Overcrowding in rat-infested tenements represented a serious threat to life and health. Urban schooling, housing, medical care, and other services deteriorated. But instead of reform, there occurred corporate disinvestment from many urban industrial areas. Assembly plants moved to the suburbs, and available city jobs declined, particularly for youth. The urban landscape became increasingly marked by poverty, racial tension, drug addiction, and revolt. The costs of the Vietnam war were draining monies and energies away from much-needed social services in the cities.

In their alarm at these crises, society's ruling circles became sharply divided over the relative merits of reform or repression, and rival cliques contended for power. (This contention was reflected in the disarray of the Democratic Party in 1968 and in the internecine struggles leading up to Watergate.) The National Advisory Report on Civil Disorder of 1968 bluntly told Americans that social unrest would continue to increase unless actions were taken to remedy the underlying causes of the problem. The report recommended not only a centralization and strengthening of police forces, but also a number of positive-action programs. By 1968, money began to flow in unprecedented sums into the inner cities for "cool-out" programs of various kinds. Innumerable public-funding programs were established, building on earlier pilot projects and ranging from the Office of Economic Opportunity (OEO) to Head Start. Some of these were short-lived and poorly planned.

Residents of urban slum communities themselves helped develop community organizing and self-help programs aimed toward positive goals. This nonfunded community organizing was led by a wide range of political organizations, such as the Congress of Racial Equality (CORE), Rent Strike, and the Black Panther Party; student organizations, such as Students for a Democratic Society (SDS); and politicized youth organizations, such as the Puerto Ricans' Young Lords, the southern white migrants' Young Patriots, and the Chicanos' La Raza and Brown Berets. Social clubs, ethnic-studies departments in colleges, clinics, food co-ops, welfare-rights unions, tenants' organizations, youth centers, and various storefront operations were established. These and similar groups began to develop cultural, economic, and political programs within their own communities. (Churches, block clubs, and neighborhood organizations sponsored most of the early murals.)

A critical factor underlying the intensity of local organizing and national mass protests was the historic impact of the civil-rights movement. Essentially a struggle for democratic rights, it had affected many strata of society and had developed many economic, political, and cultural demands. It had spread rapidly, involving millions of people and giving examples of mass protests and local organizing. It had gained limited but substantive victories in legislation for voting rights and equal economic opportunity. The songs, linked arms, work with school children, experiments in street theatre, reintroduction of the mimeograph machine as a weapon of free speech, underground press, use of militant art images—all had manifested a new sense of cultural freedom. This new cultural ambience, and the issues of protest and positive alternatives that came to fill it, created the possibilities and space in which a mural movement could emerge and grow.

The civil-rights movement's struggle for democratic rights was pregnant with a larger struggle for economic equity, cultural expression, and, ultimately, revolutionary demands. The spread of the black movement from the rural South to the urban South and North, the shift from integrationism to "Black Liberation," and the increased emphasis on empowerment all reflected new tendencies.

The rapid evolution of the Student Nonviolent Coordinating Committee (SNCC) is one example of how the black-people's movement went from civil rights to ever larger circles of demands. In the beginnings, more than any other group, SNCC made the call for black power its slogan in voter-registration drives such as that in Lowndes County, Mississippi. SNCC also was one of the first groups to raise the issue of the Vietnam war with its indignant chant of "Hell no! We won't go!" SNCC also exemplified, in its philosophy and practice, a New Left type of radicalism. Unlike most other civil-rights organizations, SNCC was people centered rather than leader centered. It opposed both the Republican and Democratic parties, and it viewed itself as less centralized, sectarian, and regimented than the older leftist parties. As James Forman has recalled, SNCC also "fought against the American value system of making money and paid its staff only subsistence. . . . It believed in sending its staff to work with the most wretched of the earth while some of the organizations thought this was a waste of time. . . . It argued for a basic revolution in American society, while others always advocated change within the present system."[1]

Working-class militancy, with ups and downs, generally rose after the mid-1960s, among both blacks and whites. Martin Luther King's personal evolution reflected the broader trend, as he cast his lot in the last months of his life with the working class (e.g. striking sanitation workers in Memphis, Tennessee). Workers came increasingly to voice their discontent with speedups, unsafe working conditions, polluted neighborhoods, loss of life in Vietnam, and war-related inflation. The diffusion of protest throughout society was occasionally symbolized even in the names of groups—e.g. "Black Panthers," "White Panthers," "Grey Panthers" (elderly people). Growing segments of the white working class and petite bourgeoisie were becoming disgruntled with the government. They observed the concessions made to blacks as indicative of what protest activity might win, even as some of them found their antiblack feelings aggravated. The long-term trend seemed to be a kind of

[1] "Black America, Organize and Struggle," *Guardian,* July 24, 1974.

dialectic between the diffusion of social protest and limited concessions on the one hand, and a combination of co-optation, repression, and racism on the other. The overall effect was unmistakable; growing alienation from traditional values and the status quo, disaffection from the government, and the growth of movements for social change to multiracial proportions.

The shift away from integrationism and reformism toward empowerment and radicalism touched a vibrant chord in many people. The electrifying impact of the cries for black power and "Power to the People" necessarily affected artists and intellectuals as well. The black-power movement, for example, attempted to redefine the self-image of black people and searched for the historical and cultural heritage for that identity in a way that involved the sympathy and emotions of almost every minority person in the country. People everywhere sought to establish their sense of selfhood, their cultural identity, their own image, their own heritage. People wanted to control their own media, their own schools, their own lives. This mass quality of the cultural quest for identity necessarily brought great pressure to bear on nonwhite artists and intellectuals, as well as on their more socially conscious white counterparts, to join in the struggle. They became aware that they could play a very meaningful role in the rising tide of popular struggle through the talents and skills they had developed, rather than with their marching feet alone. As the myth of melting-pot America was laid to rest, not just blacks, but others—Chicanos, Puerto Ricans, Asians, women, Native Americans, white ethnics—joined in rediscovering their cultural heritage and with it a new pride and dignity in themselves.

The struggles and cultures of other nations had an energizing impact on those now in movement. A strong sense of identification with liberation struggles abroad began to influence significant sectors of the antiwar and black-empowerment movements. The politics and cultures of countries like Algeria, Ghana, Tanzania, Cuba, China, North Korea, Vietnam itself, became a subject of study and sometimes of rather strained and posturing emulation. People came to recognize their historic links with other countries and to sense new possibilities for affecting revolutionary change. The student movement saw itself as having international dimensions, as 1968 became known around the world, even in Eastern Europe, as the year of international student revolt. Growing numbers of oppressed people took on an analysis of their own struggles "within the belly of the monster" as parallel to Third World struggles against imperialism.

As the anti-imperialist analysis gained strength, a new commonality began to emerge between the struggle of the Vietnamese against aggression in Southeast Asia, and the struggle of groups at home, which tended toward a unification between the largely white antiwar movement and the movements of oppressed minorities. King came out for the antiwar movement in 1967. Black and white GIs in Vietnam and elsewhere began to unify in ever larger numbers against their situation in the service. Soon thereafter, Vietnam veterans against the war moved to the forefront of the antiwar movement. The population as a whole shifted more and more toward an antiwar position. Rank-and-file workers' caucuses sprang up as wildcat strikes spread in unprecedented numbers. The National Guard was called out to quell rebellions in city after city between 1965 and 1968, and the nation's leading politicians spoke of the "dangerous unraveling of the social fabric."

In retrospect, it can be seen that the victories won by the civil-rights movement effectively blew the lid off the McCarthyite era of silence and opened the way for expanding a struggle for democratic rights into a class struggle. Out of the ensuing ferment and the many organizing activities, there emerged a growing number of neighborhood murals. These murals spread across the nation as part of the general creative outburst accompanying the various community organizing efforts and community-development programs. Community arts overlapped with local legal struggles, direct-action movements, self-defense efforts, rising community militancy. From this human potential there developed the contemporary mural movement, one of many steps in the long march down the road of reappropriation of art and culture by the people.

Art-World Context

The mural movement coincided with the desire of artists to move out from the museums. Much of the avant-garde felt a need to expand the ever-shrinking audience for visual art and to regain a sense of relevant interaction with society. The social upheavals of the 1960s only accentuated these needs.

The art scene of the late 1960s was characterized by a bewildering succession of styles, accompanied by solemn pronouncements of "the death of painting," "the exhaustion of formalism," etc. In the space of a few years, painting went from Pop to Op to Minimal, from hard edge to stain. Some artists gave up painting altogether and moved to stronger stimuli: mixed media and audience-participation art, environmental art, Happenings, disposable art. Some dabbled with scientism and technologism, producing kinetic art, computer art, light art, and machine art. Each of these had its season in New York City and was as quickly passé.

Artworks, however avant-garde, were consumed like other merchandise. The more avant-garde, the better. Even those artworks that appeared to be unsalable because there was no art object to buy or sell, as in the earthworks and other Conceptual art, were sold and exhibited. This seemingly infinite capacity of the art world to commercialize even the most "avant" of avant-garde art only evoked further rebellion in the ranks of artists. They expressed their anger at this co-optation of even antiart works during demonstrations against the Dada exhibition at The Museum of Modern Art in New York City, March 1968. Artists objected to the museum's co-opting an "anarchic revolutionary movement" and "reducing it to no more than a collection of boutique objects."[2]

Art critics, gallery owners, museum spokesmen, collectors, professors, art students, seized on each innovation as they tried to forecast the next step in the history of art. According to the ideological

[2] Therese M. Schwartz, "The Politicalization of the Avant-Garde," *Art in America* (November–December 1971): 100.

legacy of the "embattled avant-garde," new and rebellious art forms should be initially misunderstood and rejected by society and the established art institutions. But the avant-garde had become the academy. For economic reasons, most well-known artists taught at university or professional art schools. The institutions of the art world, the art schools and the museums, had taken on many of the avant-garde values, institutionalized them, taught them, and vied for who could produce or show the newest advance.

Artists suffered from instability in the international art market and speculation by collectors in styles. For example, 1968 was the year of the Minimal in art. This was certified by two important events: The Museum of Modern Art's show of Minimal art, the "Art of the Real," and the decision by Documenta IV, an important international art show, to devote their exhibition exclusively to two styles, Minimal and Op. These two shows served to guarantee investments in those styles by providing international certification of their importance. They also placed great pressure on artists to conform, at least to some extent, with these movements. Since only "in" styles were exhibited by important shows in any one season, even the established "stars" of the art world were under some pressure to conform to the current trends if they wished to be seen.

By maintaining at least a partial monopoly of style each year, investors could be assured that the works they bought would have their place in art history and thereby gain a secure value. This type of marketing led to pressure on artists to specialize and produce a kind of "trademark" art that could be bought and sold with some assurance. The owner of, for example, a Larry Bell cube or a black painting by Ad Reinhardt, while he had an original one-of-a-kind object, also had bought a trademark item.

The artist of conviction, of course, refused to be influenced by marketing considerations. However, even when well-known and respected, he was confronted by his own powerlessness in the face of this type of manipulation by museums and exhibitions. Avant-garde artists rebelling against this situation found their interests coinciding, at least temporarily, with those on the fringes of the art world, e.g. women and black artists, who were attempting to use the impetus and tools of the social rebellions to break open a niche for themselves in the museum world. From this uneasy alliance came the demonstrations for artists' rights; picketing of museums; boycotting of international shows; formation of artist coalitions, cooperatives, or unions; and the establishment of workshop galleries, women's art centers, etc.

For those artists whose personal convictions propelled them beyond artists' rights toward participation in the movements against the war in Southeast Asia or for one of the national liberation struggles in the United States, the situation was far more complex. Even within the highly permissive avant-garde aesthetic, there remained one taboo: the insertion of social content into an artwork. As antiwar artist Abe Ajay, one of the signers of the 1965 artists' statement against the war, put it: "I believe the fine artist should sign strong statements against evil at every opportunity and keep his legs in shape for long marches on the Pentagon. As a strict constructivist, however, I believe an artist's work should be clean as a hound's tooth of politics and social protest imagery."[3]

The ability of some avant-garde artists to live this split existence is perhaps most apparent in the case of Donald Judd, who was an antiwar activist and at the same time a leader of the Minimal-art movement. However, others found this kind of split existence schizophrenic and searched for some way to unify their politics and their art. In the next major antiwar action by artists, the Los Angeles Peace Tower of 1966, the physical presence of artists was still more important than their artistic endeavor, even though artwork was included as part of the action. The importance of the Peace Tower lay in its construction and defense, and in the publicity generated by the bodily presence and participation of well-known artists. The tower included 418 two-foot-square paintings in every conceivable style hung as a decorative band well above eye level. The placement of these small paintings so far from view re-

[3] *Ibid.*

flected their function. They were meant to symbolize artistic involvement, but they were not to be seen or studied for themselves.

The Angry Arts Week of 1967 seemed to provide a more serious attempt to use art itself rather than the signatures or bodies of the artists for protest. As part of the New York week, there was a *Collage of Indignation,* which included among its makers many leaders of the avant-garde. But, for the most part, these artists found themselves unable to contribute art. Instead, as a way out of the dilemma, they scrawled graffiti, expletives, or their names. The movement toward Happenings and other forms that used the artist's body provided a limited avenue toward protest art within the mainstream art world. Occasional individuals, like environmentalist-sculptor Edward Kienholz or some of the Pop artists, created an undercurrent of socially critical art acceptable in the art world; but for most artists, there seemed to exist no viable way within established norms to breach the purist barrier in the more traditional artistic media.

To those on the fringes of the art scene (students and aspiring artists) as well as those artists who had never been "in" (women, blacks, and Latins), the futility of these isolated gestures was clear. Those unwilling to choose between art and activism or to reconcile themselves to a schizophrenic existence in which their art and their politics had to remain totally distinct came to question the basic assumptions of the avant-garde ideology and practice as such.

For many artists, this led to a new analysis of the role of art and the artist in bourgeois society. A new awareness of the ideological role of abstract art and its relationship to the existing social structure came to the fore simultaneously with the questioning of "objectivity" and the alleged "end of ideology" in other contexts. As "value-free" social science was seen to epitomize white male values, so too "value-free" art was recognized as containing certain values and an ideology of its own. The social isolation of the artist, and the tendency of much art to appear as a luxury unrelated to masses of people, were not accidental phenomena. They were rooted in the rise of capitalism, the demise of traditional patronage systems, and the growing separation between the worker and his product.

Under industrial capitalism, the artist, like other marginal small producers, is squeezed by the forces of market competition. At the mercy of middlemen, dealers, and gallery owners, the artist receives only the first price for his work and retains little control over its use after it has left his studio. Although he regards himself as part of the intellectual and professional stratum of the petite bourgeoisie, the artist is often worse off economically than a common laborer. Only by becoming famous through the system of publicity that surrounds the marketing of art and having his work become an object of speculation can the artist raise his prices, gain access to private patrons, and begin to rise from his economically lumpen position. Art may be respected, but the artist is misunderstood, isolated, or ignored. The practical bourgeois has no respect for the artist because he is poor, while the working class thinks he is crazy.

This marginal and anomalous position of the artist is rationalized by romantic ideas of misunderstood genius: the elitist ideology of the avant-garde. The roots of avant-gardism are in the nineteenth century, when artists began to produce with new freedom but in a social vacuum for an anonymous audience, their work a commodity in a market economy. To the bourgeoisie, art is increasingly a non-essential luxury, an object of conspicuous consumption, a status symbol, as well as an object of speculation and a means of investing surplus capital. To maintain their tenuous social position and their self-respect, many artists began to create works that were both anti-masses and antibourgeois: art for the artist and his select circle, "art for art's sake."

The glossing over of the antibourgeois intention or content of much avant-garde art was aided by the tendency of formalist criticism to isolate the object from its context. This was reinforced by the individualist character of the artworks, which made it necessary for critics and museum spokesmen to explain the work to the public. John Berger, the English critic, defines mystification as "the process of explaining away what might otherwise be evident."[4] Formalist criticism, by discussing the work of art in purely visual terms and the history of art as a series of formal innovations, art breeding art,

[4] *Ways of Seeing* (London: Penguin Books & BBC, 1973), pp. 15–16.

serves as the perfect vehicle for this mystification. When social context, historical conditions, and even statements of intent by the artist are considered basically extraneous to an understanding of the artwork, its antibourgeois aspects are disregarded or ignored. The object of artistic endeavor becomes essentially the successful resolution of certain formal problems, and the connoisseur can enjoy any artwork, from any culture, equally—and with total disregard for its original meaning.

This type of criticism, dominant in America until the very recent resurgence of a more socially oriented point of view, was important in making avant-garde works acceptable. The eminent critic Gregory Battcock defined the contemporary critic's role in his anthology of art criticism, *The New Art:*

> For art is not merely a question of understanding, but of acceptance and response. Since people have so much to lose by facing up to the challenge of art, they will not—cannot—do so. . . . The critic has, as it were, to paint the painting anew and make it more acceptable, less of a threat than it often is. It is scarcely an exaggeration to say that the art of our time could not exist without the efforts of the critic.[5]

In defining what this society considers to be "art," the critic works hand in hand with the museums. What the critic explains, the museum certifies. Through massive educational programs, museums attempt to convince the public of the excellence of the art they select to show. The message is: If you are educated and sensitive, you will like it. Yet museums represent only one class in a divided society. Founded, and for the most part still controlled, by individual wealthy families, museums are staffed by officials who are responsible to the boards of trustees rather than to city governments, representatives of artistic communities, or city residents. Although many people correctly sense the antipopular content of much of abstract art and reject it because it does not speak to them, museums seek to convince people that this art is universal and

[5] *The New Art: A Critical Anthology* (rev. ed.; New York: Dutton Paperbacks, 1973), p. xviii.

should be enjoyed by all. The mystification and confusion that result isolate culture from its human relevance, while reinforcing class divisions.

In U.S. society, the gap between the artist and the masses and the separation between art and society have reached their most extreme form. Some of the explanation for this lies in the particularity of American social development. Unlike the nations of Western Europe, the United States has had no aristocratic tradition of culture. With the exception of indigenous Indian civilizations, which were systematically eliminated or isolated, there existed no historical basis for a high respect for culture or artists. The American bourgeoisie did not sponsor the creation of an "American" high culture but simply attempted to import or appropriate European culture whole hog.

Those who were to become the mass of the American working-class population were conquered peoples and immigrants: Indians, African slaves, Chicanos, Puerto Ricans, Irish, Jews, Germans, Italians, etc. They were deprived of their native arts. (This was more true of visual arts, because of their nontransportability, than of other cultural forms, such as music, dance, cooking, or dress.) The melting-pot ideology pressured immigrants to abandon their ethnic and national heritages and to become "Americans." Through the homogenization of American culture, furthered by the monopolization of ownership of newspapers, radio, and television, a strong and uniform image of what constitutes "being American" is, and has been, constantly presented to the populace. Many of these American values reflect the Anglo-Saxon, Puritan view of art and all sensual forms of expression as wasteful or tainted by evil and decadence. This antiart attitude was compounded by the democratic ethos of the early settlers and immigrants, which rejected aristocratic forms and manners. These particularly American factors produced a greater alienation of the masses from art than in cultures with a different artistic heritage.

Thus, artists in America were more marginal and further removed from social acceptance than in older societies. This eventually led to even more extreme avant-gardism and antipopular attitudes among American artists than among those in Europe. At the same time, throughout the history of American art, there has been a strong counterthrust toward a more democratic art, represented by such artists as John Sloan, Winslow Homer, Ben Shahn, and Jacob Lawrence. The history of American art can be read as a dialectic of alternating currents between avant-gardism, usually tied to European movements and a total rejection of American materialism and culture, and attempts to create an American style: artists of the Ashcan school, regionalists and American scene painters, and some Pop artists, who have tried to integrate art with their society in some meaningful fashion.

Paradoxically, the capacity of American consumer society to consume and the insatiable appetite of the media for novelty in any form have created an openness to abstract styles within the general public. Advertising in the mass media, especially television, has integrated stylistic innovations from the art world into its commercials and has introduced the general public to complex visual-art styles. These visual styles, used, for example, as a background for 7-Up commercials, introduce people to abstract styles, although not to abstract art. Use by advertisers of complex visual styles and artistic innovations give to these forms a content and context (that of the product, social prestige, modernity, etc.) that are readily understandable. These ads show that people will accept any style, so long as they understand why it is being used and what its meaning is. In the mystifying world of the museums, however, where the context and content become art for art's sake, an expression of a kind of class solidarity of a select audience, these styles are rejected by the majority of the people.

In the late 1960s more than ever, the people were left with an art that refused to address them or the social realities of their lives. The process of deculturation of the masses, which had begun with the loss of their native arts through "Americanization" and had been magnified by the increasing elitism of avant-garde art that no longer made even a token attempt at communication, was compounded by the "education" policy of the museums and art institutions, which proclaimed a class-exclusive culture as universal. At the same time, the mass media bombarded the masses with a full complement of escapist entertainment that did not satisfy the need for a true culture.

The social upheavals of the 1960s, which affected both artists and the masses, left the socially conscious artist with few options. New demands for meaningful culture were being made by protest and liberation movements—demands that, within the accepted parameters of the art world, were unfulfillable. It was in this context that mural art reemerged as a realistically possible solution to the problem.

3

The Mural Scene: An Overview

As the "move to the walls" spread in the late 1960s, divergent motives and conflicting trends appeared. While some of the new murals, in the tradition of the *Wall of Respect,* reflected the drive of artists (mainly from oppressed groups) to relate to the mass movement, to express the people's heritage and experience, others were motivated primarily by the desire to involve alienated inner-city youth in visual expression. Other murals represented personal gestures, asserting an aesthetic presence in the midst of the realities of urban chaos; yet others sought to use abstract decorations as part of urban plans to salvage downtown areas. As early as June 1967, simultaneously with the *Wall of Respect,* the first "decorative" mural appeared, painted by Allan D'Arcangelo on the side of an East Ninth Street tenement in New York City. In 1968, the first photorealist murals were painted in Venice, California. Also in 1968, the first collective youth murals were done in Latin areas of Chicago and New York City.

In those early years, neither government support nor large-scale grants were necessary to initiate a mural project. In the case of the very first murals, either walls were taken over by the community, as in some areas of Chicago condemned for "urban renewal," or walls belonged to friendly community organizations, or walls were donated by sympathetic landlords (who sometimes helped to subsidize the mural). An artist, a group of artists, or a community group with limited funds wanting to do an outdoor wall could subsidize their own painting. As mural art became more diverse, large-scale, and sophisticated, however, the costs of doing murals came to add up well beyond the means of most artists and communities.

Within a few years, all the different forms of wall painting were organized either from above by municipal programs, such as Boston's Summerthing, or from below by artists and local community organizations. Municipal programs took two basic directions. Some sponsored wall-painting activity as simply one of several organized activities in response to local demand, or to "cool out" inner-city youth during the "long hot summer." Others involved commissions to artists of local reputation for large-scale decorations in downtown areas. In some cities, both types of programs coexisted. In several cities, however, the artists organized themselves to establish their own ongoing programs and to obtain funding. These artist-run programs took three basic forms: workshops offering training and collective expression to inner-city youth; coalitions or cooperatives of community-minded artists, formed to develop mural painting as an art form and to gain mutual support or joint funding; and collective groups based on the European "squad" or the Latin American "brigade" model. Each of these workshops, cooperatives, and collectives identified itself with one or the other of the two main directions in the new mural art: that of murals as social communication, or that of murals as personalistic or nonobjective decoration.

These two directions stem from opposing philosophical bases: a community-based orientation versus an urban-environmental one. The urban-environmentalist direction emphasizes making art available to the general public, improving the looks of the city, and supporting artists. Usually painted by white artists, urban-environmentalist murals are normally commissioned. Their style is frequently abstract or decorative. Their content purports to be nonideological. Artists working in this general direction often are not primarily muralists, nor do they intend to become full-time muralists.

Community-based murals, on the other hand, while also concerned with the environment, have a rationale of working for the local audience around issues that concern the immediate community, using art as a medium of expression of, for, and with the local audience. They involve artists with community issues, community organizing, and community response to their artwork. They are usually painted in neighborhoods of working-class and oppressed groups. Frequently, they are done by nonwhite artists indigenous to the neighborhood. Often in a figurative or expressionistic style, they almost always involve some form of local support. Although many community-based murals are essentially the visualization of a single person's conception (the many speaking through one), others are the result of distinct individuals working together to create a wall painting that reflects not one voice or one hand but many. This thrust toward communal modes of mural creation has led to the development by the community-based mural movement of techniques for working together in cooperative ways, of techniques for helping nonartists to conceive and create in artistic language, and to some unexpectedly fruitful experiments that seem to be leading toward the development of new mural forms. Finally, community-based murals tend to be painted by artists who become full-time muralists.

Naturally, murals that fit into one of these two general directions of the mural movement do not constitute "pure" examples, any more than do the directions themselves remain pure, simple, or separate. The nature of funding alone does not serve to distinguish between these two types, although decorative murals are generally better funded, and community-based murals usually rely on some local support. Once the practice of mural art caught on, outside funding, whether federal, state, county, municipal, or private, came to be involved (however niggardly) in almost all urban-environmentalist murals and many community-based ones as well.

Although any categorization of the variety of murals produced by the mural movement is somewhat arbitrary, a glance at the prevalent types of murals being painted will help familiarize the reader with the mural scene overall. Historically, the movement began with a type of mural that in some ways resembled a gallery in the streets. Two or more artists would work together on a single wall divided into separate sections. These distinct sections, wholly individual in style and execution, would usually be united by similar thematic material. Exemplified by the *Wall of Respect,* this type of mural has appeared frequently in the black communities of Boston, Philadelphia, Chicago, and Detroit. Artists' statements about the walls often emphasize the necessity of bringing art to the community and of serving popular struggles. As Eugene Eda asserted: "As a Black artist, I will work on the most conspicuous buildings in deprived areas. I will produce Black art. . . . I paint for and identify with the masses of Black people."[1] Dana Chandler, while painting a militant black-power mural in Boston's Roxbury in mid-1968, told a reporter: "There is no Black art in the Museum of Fine Arts, so we are going to utilize the facade of buildings in our community for our museum. . . . Black people [are] painting murals about themselves and their situation. . . . Black art is not a decoration. It's a revolutionary force."[2] More recently (1974), the public-gallery format has been used in the Chicano movement on the West Coast. San Diego's Toltecas en Aztlán muralized the round water tank in Balboa Park in this fashion (fig. 17). And as the pilot program for Los Angeles' Citywide Mural Project, Judy Baca coordinated the 450-foot two-block-long composite mural at Mott and Second streets.

Thematic murals continue to be the most widespread. Whether created individually or by a group, they constitute a unified statement of a particular theme. Their aim is social communication; their subject matter is chosen because of its relevance to the community audience. Many, perhaps most, community muralists have con-

[1] From *The Artists' Statement,* Chicago Museum of Contemporary Art, 1971.

[2] Thomas H. Shepard, "Exodus Building Hub Artists Canvas," *Citizen Item* (Allston-Brighton, Boston, Mass.), July 29, 1968, p. 1.

6. Varios Artistas de Aztlán: *Las Vistas Nuevas*. 1974. Los Angeles.

7. Michael Rios: MCO mural. 1972. San Francisco.

sciously adopted figurative styles, using painterly-sculptural modeling and "stage space." Some muralists, however, especially those dealing with ethnic identity themes, have chosen to work in abstract styles that emphasize African or pre-Columbian design, color, or symbols (fig. 4). On the West Coast, countercultural forms, comix, and psychedelia have been widely used as well. In San Francisco, several of the early Mission-district murals employ the underground-comix style and comic-book elements to make social statements. In Mike Rios's mural at the Neighborhood Legal Aid Building, for example, scenes from everyday life in the Mission appear: lining up for food stamps, being hassled by the police, facing a judge, sitting in jail, etc. The Mission residents are shown as moles (they lead an underground life), whereas the oppressors are shown as pigs, hound dogs, etc.

A broad variety of murals resemble posters in their function, style, or location. Poster-function murals are generally conceived of as intentionally impermanent and replaceable. Usually combining a written with a visual message, they are part of the search for alternative means of communication in times of social upheaval, or when it is felt that the ordinary media do not serve this need. Using walls for communicating specific messages about events or issues has a long tradition in Latin American countries, and this form of wall painting developed into a genuine mural movement during the Allende years in Chile when the Brigada Ramona Parra and others transformed Santiago into a painted city. It has also been used for many years in Puerto Rico. In the United States, experiments with poster-function murals have included giant painted billboards, handball courts, and portable murals. In Los Angeles, Mechicano Art Center sponsored a series of bus-bench murals that substituted people-oriented art for the advertisements usually found on the backs of benches where people wait for buses. A large number of murals use posterlike graphic techniques derived from serigraphy or photography that give them a "poster look."

Graffiti-spontaneous walls involve a number of people working more or less simultaneously. Unlike public-gallery walls, which in-

8. John Weber, Oscar Martinez, and team: *Defend the Bill of Rights.* 1973. Chicago.

9. Toltecas en Aztlán, coordinators: People's Park mural. 1973–74. San Diego, California.

volve the organized participation of a group of artists working in clearly defined areas, a graffiti-spontaneous mural is a relatively unplanned paint project involving a group of nonartist participants working side by side but individually on an area of wall without clearly defined boundaries. The result is a composite mural. An early example from the counterculture was the People's Park mural in Berkeley, California, where almost the only rule was not to paint over what someone else had done. Monsignor Robert Fox's Harlem block-cleanup projects in New York City in 1967–68 created numbers of folk murals of this type, containing peace symbols, flowers, children's drawings, etc., with a message such as "Viva la Calle 103!" In Los Angeles, where Chicano graffiti, like Chicano slang, is so highly developed and integral to the local culture, graffiti-mural projects with Chicano gang members have developed into an emergent art form. The social workers and artists working with the gangs have helped them to develop from dense and decorative pure graffiti walls to less random, more painterly and richer thematic statements that still retain graffiti as an element (pl. 8).

The urban-environmental muralists are responsible for most of the giant supergraphics that decorate walls in large urban centers. Painted in contemporary abstract styles, these murals are mammoth blowups of gallery art. Most often, they are painted by professional sign painters working from small designs identical in style to the artist's other studio work. Most commonly and successfully done in the form of hard-edge abstractions, successive bands of color, or modular patterns, they have sometimes been called "advertisements for art" and aim to bring the art of the museums outdoors (fig. 10).

In addition to the hard-edge abstractions or supergraphics, murals have also been painted in recent years in other gallery styles—especially pop, photo-realism, and California "funk-art" variants. Cincinnati is a center for the pop style with several humorous murals, including a huge cartoon-style dog painting with his tail, a gigantic King Kong "Kosherilla" on a downtown delicatessen, and a building that seems to be held together by a bolt and a wing nut.

The trompe-l'oeil superrealist murals of the Los Angeles Fine Arts Squad and Public Works, Inc., of Yellow Springs, Ohio, display a more ironic brand of visual wit (fig. 11).

Many recent big-city murals relate to the business of an area and have a commercial or identification function. Often these murals are painted on stores and may even serve as giant shop signs. Because they are supported by local business interests and, unlike the pure supergraphics, have an easily understood public dimension, commercial murals are sometimes used in city-sponsored projects for the revitalization of downtown areas. The psychedelic health-food–restaurant murals so common in California are counterculture variations of this trend. Boutiques, health-food stores, yoga palaces, record shops, bookstores, and theatres in hippie-artist areas from Haight Ashbury in San Francisco to Montréal generally have a variety of murals that reflect the commercial and cultural outlook of the residents. Occasionally there are politically motivated commercial murals as well. For example, serving a distinct political end is Paco's Tacos taco-stand mural in the Mission district, painted by the Mujeres Muralistas (a group of Chicano and Latin American women drawn from students of the San Francisco Art Institute and connected with the Galeria de la Raza, a cooperative Chicano gallery in the Mission district). Disturbed at the "cultural imperialism" implied by the planned opening of a McDonald's near a new BART subway station, the Mujeres Muralistas painted this richly colored mural to celebrate the Latin American cultural tradition. At the same time, it represents a call to Mission residents to support local ethnic businesses and eat tacos instead of Big Macs (pl. 6). Coincidentally, McDonald's has recently helped sponsor murals relating to community issues and ethnic heritage near their restaurants in Chicago.

Urban-Environmentalist Direction

Variously called decorative, cosmetic, environmental, etc., murals in this branch of the mural movement share much of the philosophical base of urban-renewal planners, architects, and engineers who advocate and practice efforts to renovate depressed downtown areas. Using the language of science and technology, these professionals talk about solving the "ills" of urban life by "cutting out the cancers" destroying "our" great cities. When encountering a problem area that they cannot simply eliminate because it is essential to the city's functioning, they often recommend another technique: that of camouflage or surface disguise. An excerpt from a book on urban design sponsored by the American Institute of Architects describes this option with ingenuous disdain for humanity:

> Perhaps the real defect of the gray zone is that we see too much of it. We pass by large extents of it on our new elevated auto expressways as we soar above the streets toward the center city. If the gray area is too frequently visible, too depressing because it is too much in our presence, perhaps we can arrange our major routes to avoid it, to bypass it, to give us views of the city we hold in higher esteem. Could we not do this on the larger scale of the city? Could we not conceal, or at least play down, that which distorts our central city's better self?[3]

The experts dealing with city problems from within the perspective of urban renewal generally see themselves as concerned with aesthetic rather than political problems. Their concern is the general welfare in a "total" environment that does not cater to sectarian interests. The political ramifications of their projects—and the objections raised by the people directly affected—often come as an unpleasant shock to them. Government and private agencies, together with urban planners, have made a big push to "brighten up the gray areas" by supporting large decorative mural projects—the so-called supergraphics.

This movement to redecorate the cities coincided with the desire of artists to enlarge the audience for abstract art through working directly in the urban environment. Because of the contemporary concern with process and change rather than permanence, the transitory nature of outdoor murals, which are highly vulnerable to

[3] Paul D. Spreiregen, *Urban Design: The Architecture of Cities and Towns* (New York: McGraw-Hill, 1965), p. 132, cited in Robert Goodman, *After the Planners* (New York: Simon & Schuster, Touchstone Books, 1971), p. 113.

destruction or deterioration, could now be viewed more positively. Painting on city walls was a logical extension of museum-scale environmental art. It possessed the sought-after quality of physical "presence" and partook of the nature of a Happening. In addition, there was a strong historical precedent for the use of abstract color in the urban environment in the aesthetic ideas introduced by the Constructivist movement and put into practice in certain works of Le Corbusier, Theo van Doesburg, Sophie Tauber-Arp, and Fernand Léger.

There were social motives as well. Many artists resented the commercialization of the art world and wished to alleviate social problems and bring art to the people. As Tania, one of the original City Walls (New York City's abstract mural group) muralists, put it: "A wall belongs to everybody—it can't be traded on the art market. . . . It's nobody's property and it's everybody's property, the way art should be."[4] City Walls' Jason Crum, the group's founder, has added: "City planning has been serving the needs of commerce instead of the citizens. . . . The minds of artists are wasted in our society when they are put to the making of precious objects for a few."[5]

New York City architects, city planners, and government officials responded favorably to professional artists seeking to paint outdoors. City planner David Bromberg encouraged and supported the first City Walls mural, Allan D'Arcangelo's 1967 Wall on East Ninth Street. Doris C. Freedman, then head of the city's Department of Cultural Affairs, offered strong support to City Walls artists, who incorporated as a nonprofit, tax-exempt organization in 1970. Eventually, Freedman left the department to become president and major spokeswoman for City Walls. Among the major financial backers of the group has been Mrs. Joan K. Davidson of the J. M. Kaplan Foundation, who served for two years as president of City Walls. Currently, Mrs. Davidson is director of the New York State Council for the Arts. Private benefactors of City Walls have

[4] *The New York Times,* October 20, 1970.
[5] *Ibid.*

included individuals like David Rockefeller, president of Chase Manhattan Bank, and William Bernhard, the philanthropist. Support has also been received from the National Endowment for the Arts and the New York and New Jersey state councils for the arts.

The scale of individual, foundation, and government largesse to City Walls and other environmental muralists dwarfs that received by the community-based mural movement. For example, the red, blue, and green abstraction designed by Robert Wiegand and painted by sign painters on the Lever Brothers Building at Park Avenue and Fifty-third Street in 1970 reportedly cost over $11,000, of which $4,000 went to the artist (*The New York Times,* October 20, 1970). In addition to the generous artist fees, the higher cost of City Walls–type murals is due to the use of professional sign painters to execute the designs.

The oft-stated aim of City Walls is to "bring light and color into a grimy city." An open letter by Jason and Margaret Crum circulated in 1970 expands on this. The letter states that City Walls murals serve "the dual purpose of bringing art to the people and transforming the derelict walls into a new art form." The Crums claim that the wall paintings sell "no bill of goods—for a government, a church, or a bottling company." The political significance of murals by City Walls, they state, "is simply in their existence."

Yet, the same letter makes a social comment pregnant with political import—and highly insensitive to the real problems of poor and working-class residents of the city. In the same gray (or, rather, antigray) spirit of the city planners fascinated with technology, the letter states: "In a grey environment, men have grey thoughts. We all need art in our lives. There exists now a large gap between our social condition and our technological condition. Things are bound to change as machines take over much of the drudgery that men formerly had to do. The wall-paintings are one way to provide a transition and a direction during this time." This faith in a technological solution, a political stance shared by much of the business and professional community, has little relevance for the urban poor until they receive a fairer distribution of the benefits of technology.

In terms of audience and content, the Crums make it clear that they have no intention of "talking down to the people."

The murals of City Walls, Inc., tend to look the same, irrespective of location. This occasionally leads to some stark contrasts. Some walls, like Jason Crum's bands of color in the run-down squatters' park in the Puerto Rican neighborhood at East Seventh Street between Avenues B and C stand out as painful symbols of their own irrelevance. Other City Walls murals in commercial areas of the city, such as midtown or the financial district, are more consonant with their environment. Even in these locations, however, they remain private images in a public space.

Noted art critic Lawrence Alloway, in a piece on City Walls, has pointed out: "Successive kin bands of color or modular patterns which echo systems of architectural construction in terms of decorative overlay do not have a public content. They embellish 'ugly' points in the city, but that merely reduces their content to being a symbol of sensitivity and control in a squalid or untidy environment."[6] In a second article, Alloway further elaborates a fundamental aesthetic problem involved with large supergraphics. After acknowledging that the history of abstract art has shown that abstract imagery is more than decoration and has an expressive content, Alloway states: "However, when geometric grids and color sequences are presented on walls, at an architectural scale, the decorative potential exceeds compensatory theories of expressiveness. Thus, City Walls has extended the role of the professional artists in the city, but *at the expense of* the aesthetics of Abstract art"[7] (emphasis added). The cosmetic function of such murals is closely related to their aesthetic character—that of a screen or tapestry of color hung across an offending reality.

City Walls, Inc., has provided the urban-environmentalist direction of the mural movement not only with its earliest but also with its best-known and most influential articulation. City Walls, Inc., acts as a kind of broker between artists and the business organiza-

[6] "Art," *The Nation*, September 21, 1970, p. 254.
[7] "Art," *The Nation*, September 25, 1972, pp. 252–253.

10. Jason Crum: *Tammuz.* 1969. New York.

tions that provide many of its commissions. Artists are usually chosen (or approved) by the financial sponsor. During its influential early period from 1967 to 1973, City Walls served as the strongest advocate of nonobjective decorative murals and espoused a policy of supporting only abstract artists. Recently, with the rise of photo-realism and figuration to a new popularity within the official art world, City Walls has sponsored some nonabstract murals. Most City Walls murals, however—there were over thirty-five by May 1974—have been pure hard-edge abstract patterns. These include eight murals by Jason Crum, two by Richard Anuszkiewicz, two by Nassos Daphnis, three by Tania, and five by Robert Wiegand. The works of Mel Pekarsky (five murals) and Allan D'Arcangelo (two murals), although consistent with the general abstract direction of the group, are tempered somewhat by the incorporation of landscape elements into the design. However, City Walls' influence has been as an exponent of purely abstract supergraphics of the Crum-Wiegand-Anuszkiewicz type.

Since 1971, City Walls, Inc., in addition to promoting murals in New York City, has been active as a consultant to business, government, and civic agencies in many other cities—including Detroit; Jersey City, New Jersey; Philadelphia; Syracuse, New York; Boston; Cincinnati; Atlanta; and Toronto. In helping develop supergraphic mural programs in other cities, City Walls, Inc., provides "expertise in dealing with city red tape"[8] and assists in the coordination of artists with sponsors.

Supergraphics are often commissioned by municipal arts councils or museums on the basis of design competitions. The Cleveland Area Arts Council calls its program "City Canvasses" and sells silkscreen copies of the designs, underlining the character of the work as blowup copies of current easel styles. In Detroit, in addition to a large number of abstract supergraphics, Alex Pollack's decor of chickens, watermelons, and other produce for the rejuvenated East Market area represents an example of the successful use of graphics in urban planning. Chicago's Sachio Yamashita has put forward a number of proposals to paint the city in rainbow stripes. Excluding New York City, the largest collection of supergraphic walls probably consists of those murals in Montréal sponsored by Benson and Hedges on the eve of the Universal and International Exhibition (Expo 67).[9]

There are many variants within the urban-environmentalist direction of the mural movement. A number of murals painted spontaneously by individual artists in their own neighborhoods derive from

[8] From public letter by Doris C. Freedman, What Is City Walls, Inc.?: A Brief History, May 14, 1974.

[9] The Expo murals also exemplify the hidden politics of such art: in the social cause of their being commissioned, in the corporate nature of their funding, and in the "cool-out" function they helped serve by providing salaries to dissident Québecois youth. Benson and Hedges has gone on to sponsor supergraphics in other Canadian cities.

an urban-environmentalist viewpoint. These murals, mainly by unknown artists and often with countercultural overtones, appeared in hippie strongholds like Haight Ashbury and Berkeley in the late 1960s. They represented a chance for the struggling artist to be seen, as well as to help alter the quality of life in one's own neighborhood. The desire of artists to decorate their neighborhoods has not been limited to bohemian white areas. Saint Elmo's Village in Los Angeles is an example of black artists and neighborhood residents' use of decorative outdoor painting—on sidewalks, walls, doors—to transform their environment into a genuine community art center.

The murals in Venice, California, grew out of this same kind of direct action by local artists. In 1969 two young men in Venice, Terry Schoonhoven and Vic Henderson who later were to be known as the Los Angeles Fine Arts Squad, decided one day to walk outside their studio and paint the exterior wall with a photographic image of the street on which it stood (*Brooks Street Scene*). Another Venice artist, Wayne Holwick, painted black-and-white photographic images outside his house (e.g. *Groupie*, 1968). The kinky superrealist images of these artists caught on, and the Fine Arts Squad was commissioned to paint other, larger walls—e.g. a mural of California falling into the sea, commissioned for $20,000. Although other spontaneous individual efforts by artists in their own neighborhoods generally ended up being one-shot or two-shot affairs, the success of the Fine Arts Squad's giant superrealist painting with a surrealist edge led to their being commissioned to do murals elsewhere, including Paris, France (1973). Other photographic superrealists, such as Kent Twitchell, have "made it" with murals in the Los Angeles area, which has a kind of tradition for this type of work (e.g. the mammoth mural begun in 1957 and still going at the Clougherty–Farmer John packing plant in Vernon).

The urban-environmentalist direction includes fewer nonwhite artists than does the community-based mural movement, but it does not exclude blacks. A number of black mainstream artists have done murals. For example, William T. Williams became involved briefly

11. Los Angeles Fine Arts Squad: *Brooks Street Scene*. 1968. Venice, California.

with mural art in the mid-1960s. Williams was a member of an interracial, multifaceted cultural group, Smokehouse Associates, that was trying to bridge the gap between art and audience. Williams painted several abstract murals in East Harlem. However, troubled by graffiti defacements and the feeling that "most of the murals painted to date are too studio-oriented and decorative," Williams and Smokehouse dropped out of the mural movement.[10]

Some artists who proclaim the philosophy of environmentalism also have a direct community orientation. Noteworthy in this regard is the Philadelphia Museum's Department of Urban Outreach (DUO) mural program. Environmental artists Don Kaiser and Clarence Wood of DUO consider themselves consultants or technicians, who try to provide community groups and organizations with

[10] *The New York Times,* October 20, 1970.

12. Clarence Wood with West Philadelphia artists: James Rhoads School mural. 1973. Philadelphia.

assistance in painting the kinds of murals (on walls or other surfaces like buses or roadways) that the community wants. The murals they have helped to sponsor, designed by themselves or other artists or community people, have ranged from decorative abstracts to figurative social protests, such as that in Chinatown protesting the construction of a freeway.

In various cases in Philadelphia and elsewhere, community youths have chosen to design in abstract idioms. A mural designed and painted by youths from three separate gangs on Broad Street in downtown Philadelphia, under Don Kaiser's supervision, is a colorful abstraction with subtle, formal variations between the black and Puerto Rican sections of the wall. In other cases, supergraphic design has been used as the framework for scenes or portraits. The mural at the James Rhoads School in West Philadelphia is an example of a very large project of this type. Clarence Wood and a team of eight artists worked with students and neighborhood youth on the painting, each artist supervising ten nonartists.

Community-based Direction

The largest concentration of community-based murals is in Chicago, where the movement toward people's art has progressed furthest in theory, practice, and durability over time. Historically, even as New York City has been the center for the American abstractionist school of art, so Chicago has been the principal location for socially oriented art and literature. An industrial city with a long history of labor protest dating back to the Haymarket riot, Chicago has been a center for socially conscious culture from the days of Upton Sinclair and Carl Sandburg to those of expressionist painter Leon Golub and the "Chicago Monster school." Following the police rioting during the 1968 Democratic Convention, artists from around the nation held an exhibit in Chicago protesting the administration of Mayor Daley, police brutality, and related issues. Chicago has never been dominated by the museum-gallery success ethos to the degree that New York has. Moreover, Chicago was a center of social protest in the 1960s and the scene of numerous strong community-organizing efforts and innovations, from those of Saul Alinsky to those of the Black Panther Party, Young Lords, Young Patriots, and SDS. Compared to cities like Boston, New York, or Atlanta, Chicago is lacking in the thick, liberal veneer of corporate benevolence and governmental welfarism.

Consequently, from the very beginning, mural art in Chicago came from the independent efforts of socially concerned artists and communities working together. The Walls of Respect and Truth provided an inspiration for other Chicago artists and a model for working with local community organizations. This type of community-based mural painting spread from the predominantly black South Side to other working-class and ethnic neighborhoods of Chicago in 1968–70.

In the Spanish-speaking area around Eighteenth and Halsted streets, Mario Castillo, working with Chicano youths, painted two largely abstract murals using Mexican design motifs and color as the formal elements (fig. 4). The second of these murals combines the theme of cultural heritage with the issue of antiwar sentiment represented in the central image: the Y of the peace symbol made up of hands reaching out, palms up. In the same neighborhood, Ray Patlán, recently returned from military service in Vietnam where he had painted a mural in an Army chapel, began a series of murals in the auditorium of Casa Aztlán, a community center for day-care, medical, educational, and other services. Patlán's indoor mural depicts the history of his people from the Spanish Conquest to the present, concluding with images of hard-hat railroad workers, Cesar Chavez, and the Huelga's red-and-black flag (pl. 5). John Weber painted his first mural, *Power to the People,* with black teen-agers at Saint Dominic's Church near the Cabrini-Green housing project in 1969. That same year, Puerto Rican artists and youths painted figurative murals inside and outside "the People's Church," celebrating the heroes and heroines of Puerto Rico's struggle for independence. Don McIlvaine of the Art and Soul Workshop in Lawndale, Chi-

13. Don McIlvaine: *Black Man's Dilemma* (process shot). 1970. Chicago.

cago's West Side, worked with the conservative Vicelords (formerly a gang organization) to paint *Into the Mainstream* and *Black Man's Dilemma,* the first of a series of murals at and nearby the group's headquarters. Various paintings and sculptural works were incorporated into the project. Mitchell Caton painted a richly colorful mural down one side of an alley, calling it *Universal Alley* (pl. 4). Caton's mural, which blends the images of jazz, street culture, and cubistic African masks, includes a long verse dedicated to Fred Hampton (murdered Black Panther leader). Mark Rogovin directed black youths at the Christian Action Ministry (CAM) Center in West Chicago in the painting *Unity of the People,* a mural tribute to the heroes and heroines of black and working-class history. And, Eugene Eda completed a mural series in the basement of the DuSable Museum, incorporating cornices and ceiling to indict slavery in slashing strokes of red, black, white, yellow, and green.

Among other murals painted more or less spontaneously in Chicago at the same time were a railroad-embankment mural, *People's Handshake,* and the mysteriously beautiful elongated black dancers, arms upraised, in an alleyway off Fifth Avenue and Trumbull. By the end of the summer of 1970, there existed over thirty murals in Chicago.

It was at this time, in the combined contexts of established social-protest movements, community organizing, and advances in mural technique, scale, and expressiveness, that the established art world took notice of the murals. Both *Life* and *Time* magazines ran articles on the nationwide upsurge of murals in 1970. Harold Haydon, art critic of the *Chicago Sun-Times,* wrote two articles sympathetic to the murals in Chicago and, with foresight, warned of the dangers inherent in the kind of sudden establishment recognition the murals were attracting: "There is at least one danger in all this attention. Genuine people's wall painting, with its artist-to-people communication, could be neglected in the current move to decorate the city. It is easier and safer to sponsor exercises in abstract form and color."[11]

[11] Harold Haydon, "Showcase," *Chicago Sunday Sun-Times,* December 13, 1970.

Outside funding received in 1970, supplemented by local community monies, permitted artists who had helped originate Chicago's mural movement to work on a more imposing scale. That summer, Bill Walker painted his highly original, gigantic *Peace and Salvation, Wall of Understanding* (pl. 9); Eda his imposing *Wall of Meditation* (fig. 5); Weber his *Wall of Choices* (fig. 35); and Rogovin his *Protect the People's Homes.* The outside funding did not initiate a new movement, but it helped sustain an already productive and developing one. The muralists had already established a philosophy and practice of community involvement.

The number of murals in Chicago grew steadily after 1970, so that by the end of 1975 close to two hundred walls had been completed. In 1970, Eda, Walker, and Weber formed the Chicago Mural Group (CMG), which has since grown to include a dozen artists. In addition to the prolific work of CMG artists, numerous Chicago murals have also been done by separate workshops, community organizations, and individual artists. Rogovin set up the Public Art Workshop (PAW) as a mural painting and resource center in 1972. PAW provides community classes, a slide collection of U.S. and Mexican murals, slide talks, and other resource materials. With Marie Burton, Holly Highfill, and Tim Drescher, Rogovin compiled the *Mural Manual*[12] (first published by PAW, 1973), source of much excellent advice on how to paint community murals. Burton, formerly a teacher at Chicago's Saint Mary's Center for Learning, where she directed indoor and outdoor murals, is now leading her own program in Milwaukee. Highfill runs a program in Chicago's uptown area. José Gonzalez, Ricardo Alonzo, Mario Castillo, and a number of other muralists participate in Movimiento Artistico Chicano (MARCH). Walker, now independent, leads International Walls, Inc. Among Chicago's other muralists are Marcos Raya, Mario Galán and Bob Solari.

The gradual, steady growth, yet relative lack of outside financial support, of Chicago's mural movement from 1967 to 1971 contrasts with the rapid growth and decline of Boston's Summerthing mural program. From its inception, Boston's mural movement had the

12 (Boston: Beacon Press, 1975).

support of the mayor's office and the Institute of Contemporary Art. "Summerthing, Boston's Neighborhood Festival" was the major coordinating agency. Organized in 1968, Summerthing's mural program was the inspiration of Boston artist Adele Seronde (daughter of Christian A. Herter). Seronde directed the program during its formative years. Her proposal, "The City as a Museum," combined the environmentalist-abstract and political-figurative tendencies of the nascent mural movement, emphasizing in both a strong neighborhood orientation. "One of the things we just didn't want to do was to have artists doing it all. . . . The murals have been particularly valuable to the Black community as a kind of forum. As propaganda they're instructive, they make a sociological statement, but perhaps more importantly, they're yards and yards of metaphor for people who lack a real channel of expression."[13] This feeling was carried out in the distribution of murals around the city in the first two years of Summerthing, when half the mural projects were in predominantly black neighborhoods, in spite of the fact that blacks then constituted only fifteen to twenty percent of the population.

Summerthing's role was that of a middleman or broker between funding sources, communities, artists, and the city government, helping to find walls, funnel neighborhood requests to available artists, and secure equipment and materials. With an initial grant from the Massachusetts Council on the Arts, donations from the business community, and city support, Summerthing initiated a series of projects in both black and white inner-city neighborhoods. Besides a number of mural projects, Summerthing sponsored general social-reform projects, such as playground construction, benefit art shows, theatre festivals, and arts-and-crafts classes.

In spite of its fairly obvious "cool-out" dimension, the Summerthing program coincided with the desire of politically oriented black artists to paint Walls of Respect for their communities. When Kathy Kane, head of the Mayor's Office of Cultural Affairs, invited Dana Chandler and Gary Rickson to a meeting at the mayor's office in the

[13] Adele Seronde, interview, in Robert Taylor, "Wall-to-Wall Boston," *Boston Sunday Globe*, October 26, 1969.

14. Gary A. Rickson: *Africa Is the Beginning.* 1969. Roxbury YMCA, Boston.

spring of 1968 to discuss what kind of input black artists might want to contribute, the two artists attended, intending to obtain supplies and city assistance in getting permissions for painting on walls in Roxbury. Chandler and Rickson made it clear that the city was not to tell them what it was they could and could not paint.[14] The city accepted the artists' conditions. This pact of mutual convenience made possible the rapid development of powerful, militant mural statements in Roxbury and South End during 1968–69, which emphasized black culture, identity, and struggle.

A number of black artists painted outstanding murals dealing, in

14 Dana Chandler, interview with Eva Cockcroft, 1974.

different art styles, with black-awareness themes, and attracting considerable community approval and involvement. Al Smith's 1968 mural at the corner of Martin Luther King Boulevard and Humboldt Avenue was a complex symbolic-religious statement. Chuck Milles painted two powerfully designed, semicubist murals, one in Orchard Park (1968) and the other at the corner of Columbus and Dartmouth streets (1969). In 1968, Rickson and Chandler jointly painted two Walls of Respect, one in Roxbury and the other in South End (fig. 3). The Rickson-Chandler walls, with their strong black-power themes, had impact both locally and nationally (they were widely reported). In 1969, Rickson went on to paint the symbolic, mystical *Africa Is the Beginning* on the new YMCA building in Roxbury. And in South End, nineteen-year-old Roy Cato, Jr., painted his simple and moving mural *Black Awareness*.

A number of community-based murals of high artistic quality continued to be funded by Summerthing in 1970. In South End, Yantee Bell's Leonardoesque unity figure on a field of blue next to the "el" joins races and religions in a primeval unity; Sharon Dunn's *Black Women* integrates biological motifs with African origins and present-day figures in a modern figurative style (pl. 2). In Chinatown, Dan Hueng and Bob Uyeda created a crisp abstraction of a Chinese junk. And, although the number of socially concerned murals funded by Summerthing dropped drastically after 1970, in 1971 James Brown painted his anti–drug-abuse mural (fig. 96), on a former police station converted into a drug rehabilitation center, The Third Nail, at Roxbury Crossing. Very large and deceptively simple, Brown's mural "reads" clearly, and yet subtly, even when one passes it on the Amtrak train speeding into Boston.

The expansion of mural painting in Boston peaked in 1970, when signs of change in Summerthing policies also became evident. For the first time, Summerthing offered not only paint and scaffolding but also modest artist's fees. Among nineteen Summerthing mural projects, four were cosponsored with the Institute of Contemporary Art. ICA's "Project '70" funded specific public artworks with government and business support. It lasted only one year, but it sponsored nearly thirty projects, of which about half were murals; the others involved playgrounds, parks, and recreation centers. Also in 1970, Summerthing greatly expanded the number of neighborhoods, artists, and types of murals. Thirteen areas were affected, including Chinatown, Back Bay, Downtown, Dorchester, East Boston, Mattapan, and North End. Although only two of the original mural artists were supported, eighteen new artists worked on these wall-painting projects in 1970. Of these eighteen artists, only three went on to do other mural projects in the next two years.

In 1971–72, Summerthing shifted its emphasis toward environmentalism and artistic "purity." This shift was not unrelated to the temporary tailing off of social ferment that began in late 1970. A change in the content of community-based murals toward less aggressively violent statements occurred also in Chicago beginning in 1971. Mural themes generally became more positive, dealing with drug abuse, education, brotherhood, and the need for multinational unity (pl. 3). Nevertheless, most of the Summerthing murals painted in 1971–72, as *Boston Globe* art critic Robert Taylor has observed, reflected little social concern at all: "They demand to be viewed as 'pure' art."[15]

An interview with Jim Higgins about his Roslindale mural reflected this new emphasis: "I'm not trying to state any revolutionary or cultural theme or life standard. I think in the purity of art for art's sake all these statements are included."[16] The new orientation of Summerthing was further elaborated by Summerthing director, Barbara Morris, in 1972: "There is a basic need to improve the environment. . . . Public art . . . shows recognition towards artists, and hopefully creates more commissions for them while constantly improving the appearance of the city."[17] In traditional art-world fashion, 1972 Summerthing solicited projects from artists for

[15] "In Four Years, 72 Hub Public Murals," *Boston Sunday Globe,* August 13, 1972.

[16] *Boston Sunday Globe,* October 10, 1971.

[17] Susan Garber and Susan Miller, "An Historical Summary of Public Art In Boston," mimeographed (Boston: Institute of Contemporary Art, May 1974), p. 2.

15. Dana C. Chandler, Jr., and Nelson Stevens: *The Black Worker.* 1973. Boston.

a competition, "Other Walls, Other Spaces," that could range from "multimedia events, light sculpture, and found objects, to the sound of silence." It selected twelve projects, most of which were essentially private statements by artists in public spaces.

By 1972, the number of professional-artist murals in Boston had declined to the 1968 level, and by 1973, the Summerthing mural program was essentially over. Noting the seventy-two murals painted in Boston between 1968 and 1972, art critic Taylor had praised Summerthing as "the most vital public mural program of any city in the world."[18] Yet by autumn 1973, it was obvious that the vitality of the mural movement in Boston had been drained. To deal with the decline, the ICA sponsored an Arts Renewal Conference, May 1974, which stated as one of its aims the revitalization of Boston's mural movement. There was much talk but few concrete results.

With the decline of Summerthing support after 1970, the community-based mural movement in Boston continued, but on a smaller scale. The strongest artists—Chandler, Seronde, Rickson, etc.—are still painting murals in spite of the lack of city support.

[18] Taylor, "In Four Years, 72 Hub Public Murals."

What happened to the movement in Boston points out some of the dangers inherent in city-sponsored community mural movements, however good the intentions of city sponsors. Initially, under Seronde's strong leadership and under the pressure of the social ferment of the late 1960s, Summerthing served the needs of community artists very well—so well that they did not feel the necessity to organize into strong artist groups but were able to deal with the city individually. The lack of artist control furthered by this situation left the artists highly vulnerable to changes in administration or cutbacks in funding. When the political situation cooled down in the early 1970s, the money for inner-city murals with artistically strong social communication was reduced. The impressive expansion of the mural program in 1970 introduced new artists into mural art but made no provision for *developing* mural artists. Although it is important to spread a growing mural movement to other communities and encourage new artists to work in the field, it is also essential that this not be done at the expense of groups already working and of experienced muralists who, in the course of their experience, have brought the mural movement toward aesthetically stronger work. Rather than do this, Summerthing, with the cooperation of ICA, introduced museum-style control techniques such as competitions.

In 1974, Los Angeles established a new city-sponsored Citywide Mural Project (fig. 6) with a community orientation similar to Boston's Summerthing. Funded directly by the L.A. City Council, Citywide planned thirty-five community mural projects in diverse neighborhoods for its first year and set up a mural resource center to disseminate information on murals in the L.A. area. Citywide provides elaborate guidelines for community approval, involving several sets of sketches that must be approved by neighborhood meetings before a mural is begun. In addition to materials, modest commissions are offered the artists; youths working on the projects are also paid. Citywide emphasizes team murals with adolescents, children, and senior citizens, although it also funds individual murals. Not unlike Boston, the new Citywide project in L.A. is headed by a dedicated community muralist, Judy Baca.

16. Roberto Chavez: Untitled mural. 1972. Los Angeles.

However, the situation in Los Angeles in 1974 differed from that of Boston in 1968. City funding in Boston coincided with the beginnings of the mural movement, locally and nationally. Since 1971, when the Chicano murals began, Los Angeles has been a major center for community murals, with alternative forms of artist organization well developed. L.A.'s new Citywide program also is able to draw on the experience of the development of murals elsewhere.

Among the first Chicano murals in East Los Angeles were many coordinated and organized through the mural programs of Mechicano Art Center, a cooperative gallery and coordinating center set up by local artists in 1971. The gallery-center method of organization within the community-based mural movement is a not uncommon one and has several variants. In the case of Mechicano, the center provided paint and scaffolding, but not money, to artists who wished to do walls. In addition to the murals on Mechicano's building, located in the heart of the *barrio,* and to those painted in the immediate surroundings, Mechicano coordinated the ten murals completed by 1974 at Ramona Gardens housing project, one of the *barrio*'s most run-down areas. Mechicano artists gained entry to the housing project by first doing a mural with gang youths from the project on a nearby grocery store.

The high concentration of murals in housing projects, the "muralization of public housing," is unique to Los Angeles, and shows the transformation effect such concentration in a small space can have upon an environment. For example, the more than forty murals (of eighty planned) covering the walls and fences of Estrada Courts confront residents and visitors with a world of color, forms, and shapes, in distinct styles and expressing a multitude of themes. These murals have been coordinated by Charles "Gato" Felix of Goez Gallery, a private gallery for Chicano artists in East Los Angeles.

Much mural activity in East Los Angeles, where the majority of Chicano murals are concentrated, has involved a loose and informal type of gallery organization. The artists are socially conscious and paint in every conceivable style, including naturalistic landscape, supergraphic, figurative-heroic, surrealist, and graffiti-pop. In San Diego, California, as well, a gallery-center type of organization has served to consolidate the community-based mural movement. Housed in a remodeled water tank in Balboa Park, San Diego's

17. Toltecas en Aztlán: Centro Cultural de la Raza mural. 1974. Balboa Park, San Diego, California.

Centro Cultural de la Raza serves as a place for Chicano artists to meet and work. The city provides the space and salaries for the Centro staff. Besides the murals covering the Centro itself, murals in San Diego include those at the "people's park" at the base of Coronado Bridge, covering many of the bridge piers (fig. 9). Being close to the Mexican border, San Diego artists have developed close relations with Mexican artists. There are also good relations between San Diego's Centro group and East Los Angeles artists, and in at least one instance, artists from San Diego and L.A. have helped one another paint murals.

In San Francisco, a city funding and coordinating effort for all the arts was undertaken in the late 1960s. Called the Neighborhood Arts Program, its function is "to bring art to the neighborhoods," especially in the inner city. It facilitates fairs, theatre performances, workshops, etc. As in Los Angeles, the city program has worked closely with artists loosely organized around a gallery, Galeria de la Raza, whose director, René Yánez, cooperated with Neighborhood Arts staff member Eric Reuther in coordinating mural projects undertaken at schools, parks, and youth centers in the Mission district from 1971 to 1973. These murals include the comix-influenced

18. Ernie Palomino: Untitled mural. 1971. Tulare and F streets, Fresno, California.

cooperative walls at Mission Rebels and Horizons Unlimited (two youth centers); Mike Rios's controversial Neighborhood Legal Aid Building mural of Mission residents as moles facing pig justice; the three-artist Jamestown School and Recreation Center mural (fig. 100); and the Balmy Alley murals.

Most of California's Chicano murals have grown out of the larger political context of La Raza movement, which has epitomized the national-liberation struggle of Chicanos throughout the country, from Houston to Santa Fe, Denver to Chicago, city factories to farm fields. The entire Southwest has been caught up in a cultural renaissance for Chicanos. On the cultural scene, this movement has taken the form of political theatre groups like Teatro Campesino, poster workshops like La Raza silk-screen workshop, and Chicano artist organizations. San Francisco's Galeria de la Raza, for example, grew out of four other Bay Area art organizations: The Mexican American Liberation Art Front, Casa-Hispana de Bellas Artes, Artistas Latinos Americanos, and Artes 6.

As the mural movement in California has grown since its inception in 1971–72, and as many artists have come to feel a primary identification as muralists, there has begun a search for ways to unite Chicano mural artists throughout California into an organization that will serve their interests as a significant priority. The first statewide meeting of Chicano muralists was held in mid-September 1974 with the aim of providing better communication and cooperation among artists working throughout California. In addition, muralists of various ethnic backgrounds have begun meeting regularly in San Francisco. Some of the political muralists in Haight Ashbury have organized themselves into the Haight Ashbury Muralists. Among the murals some of these artists have done are the antiwar *Rainbow People* (1972, repainted 1974), and *Unity Eye* (1973). In 1974, murals also appeared in San Francisco's Chinatown as part of the battle to preserve the International Hotel, which houses many older Asian workers as well as community groups like the Asian Community Center and the Kearny Street Workshop (fig. 85).

19. Haight Ashbury Muralists: *Rainbow People* (new version). 1974; originally 1972. San Francisco.

Even more prevalent than the gallery-center type of mural coordination is the teaching workshop. Workshops and staff programs are the predominant form of organization for mural programs that attempt to help nonprofessionals express themselves in the mural form. Cityarts Workshop in New York City, founded in 1968 by Susan Shapiro-Kiok, has introduced techniques that have influenced other programs with a similar orientation. One is a mass-participation, cement-mosaic technique for a composite project, wherein the individual contributions and designs made by passersby and neighborhood residents are combined into a coherent and permanent whole (fig. 67). First tried in the Al Smith housing project, it was then implemented in Washington Square Park Plaza (750 participants), Hell's Kitchen Playground wall (50 participants), and the truly impressive Gaudiesque *Grant's Tomb Memorial Centennial Bench* (400–500 participants, pl. 13). The second technique, that of the opaque projector, revolutionized the making of figurative murals by nonartists by eliminating the need for extensive training in drawing and design.

One of the most successful of the graffiti-arts programs has been the Graffiti Alternatives Workshop (GAW) in Philadelphia, founded by Sandy Rubin and Bob Rivera in 1970. Participants, among whom have been many of Philadelphia's leading graffitists, work out their ideas on paper, on construction-site fences, and eventually on public buses and, as abstract murals, on housing-project walls. GAW's "non-directive" teaching has led mainly in the direction of abstract design. Some "graduates," like Carleton Baxter, have gone on to found their own community "graffiti" workshops, which continue to paint abstract murals of high quality.

Statements by ex-wall writers published in the GAW *Primer* are especially revealing:

> I wanted to create something, but I didn't know how and I had no connections. I found the Workshop, and there I was able to learn to put my ideas and talents into a painting program. I worked on projects and found it more fun than writing on walls, and a way of making some money. . . . [The Workshop's] helping the young kids get into a better life.
>
> —Cold Duck

> If you've noticed it or not, Cornbread, Cazz, Tity, Chewy, Cold Duck, Cool Earl, Kidd, Bobby Cool, Les, Dr. Cool, Turtle, Jason, Echo, Wine, Real Kill, Kool Aid, Sly, Ding and Neptune have either forgotten how to write or they've realized that we—as blacks—definitely must get ourselves together. A clean community is very together, if you can dig it! I don't want to hear the bull about there is nothing else to do. Nor do I want to hear all the other excuses we made up to tell our People about why we write. I'm not saying you shouldn't get known, I'm only saying the brothers can get a reputation with everyone digging on your constructive program. With all the names on walls throughout the city, that's enough potential and ability to make this a beautiful Philly if you do artistic work instead of writing . . .
>
> —Bingo[19]

Perhaps nowhere has work with gang and youth murals been so extensive as in Los Angeles (pl. 8) and San Diego (fig. 9). In murals executed there, part with a brush and part with spray cans, a

[19] Sandy Rubin and Bob Rivera, *A Primer for Community Graffiti Workshops* (Philadelphia: Graffiti Alternatives Workshop, 1972), pp. 22–23.

20. Gang members with artist Bill Butler: Lil' Valley mural. 1972. Los Angeles.

variety of folkloric images, portraits of heroes, emblems of the Chicano movement and of local gangs are tied together in a colorful, dense, overall mass of *placas* ("gang symbols") and graphisms. These are graffiti murals properly speaking and have their own aesthetic validity as well as sociological interest. Often these murals serve a commemorative or peace-pact function. For example, the Lil' Valley mural on Ken's Market at Sixth Avenue and Bonnie Brae Place in East Los Angeles, which marks the boundary between two gangs, commemorates the deaths of youths from both gangs. Assisted by artist Bill Butler, members of the Lil' Valley gang painted the mural as a symbolic peace settlement. Professional Chicano artists, such as "Los Four" (Charles Almaraz, Robert del la Rocha, Gilbert Lujan, and Frank Romero), have incorporated images from the *barrio* into their murals and have adopted graffitist techniques. In 1974, Los Four were given a show at the Los Angeles County Museum of Art, during which they brought the *barrio* into the museum and created a special spray-paint mural collectively.

More than sixteen L.A. gangs have been involved in mural painting in recent years. Among those working with gang youth, staff workers Sam Zepeda and David Kahn of Educational Participation in Communities (EPIC, sponsored by a consortium of colleges) have helped organize mural projects within the community agencies with which they work. One of Zepeda's projects with the "Arizona" gang is a commemorative Madonna at Casa Maravilla; it has become a religious icon before which residents present fresh flowers and plants. Kahn's mural project for the Ramona Gardens Dropout Prevention Center, completed under the direction of *barrio* artist William Herrón, is a depiction of the horrors of gang violence (pl. 7). Individual artists like John Rodríguez, who has painted nine murals with gangs in East Los Angeles, or Judy Baca, who painted murals with major gangs for two years before assuming the directorship of Citywide Mural Project, have also been influential in the development of gang murals in Los Angeles.

In addition to murals painted by gangs, a number of murals dealing with gang violence and closely related to gang structures have been painted by *barrio* artists. John Alvarez's mural at The Dip, a bar marking the corner boundary line between gangs, captures the street problems and oppression behind gang violence. Willie Herrón, himself a product of the East Los Angeles *barrio,* has painted a series of murals that deal with the problems of gang violence and include graffiti as part of their structure. Herrón considers the graffiti on the lower sections of his murals as a fundamental part of the artwork (some of the graffiti already on the wall is left untouched, more is added in the course of the painting). Without the graffiti, Herrón says, the wall is too untouched, too bare, and is not really a part of the neighborhood. Herrón treats the names with respect, and when a boy dies, he paints a cross over the name.[20]

Through the work of such workshops and artists teaching gang and other untrained youths, and through the techniques for group expression that they have helped develop, an avenue for creating

[20] Willie Herrón, interview with Eva Cockcroft, 1974.

21. William F. Herrón, Jr.: *The Wall That Cracked Open.* 1972. Los Angeles.

22. Clement Roach: Winchester Square wall. 1974. Springfield, Massachusetts.

new directions in the movement toward a people's art has been opened. This thrust from below, combined with the input of professionally trained artist-muralists, has established one more basis for the birth of a wholly new art derived from the people themselves. As more and more gang members abandon the subculture of drugs and fighting to become community artists, graffiti are replaced by murals that increasingly abandon the primitiveness patronized by romantic middle-class anarchists and join the mainstream of the contemporary mural movement. Clubs, whether Chicano, black, or white, are actively seeking assistance in converting their gang-roster walls to murals.

The community-oriented mural movement has spread to prisons and schools, which have a long though little publicized tradition of wall painting. Black artist Faith Ringgold has painted a women's mural in the Women's House of Detention at Riker's Island (New York City). At the Adult Correctional Institution and at the Boys

Training Center in Cranston, Rhode Island, Shelly Killien set up an innovative program involving both professional artists and prisoners in the creation of murals. Although successful with inmates, the program was eventually terminated by prison authorities. The mid-1960s saw a rebirth of children's murals, often done in permanent media—mosaic, ceramic tile, and cement. The renaissance in children's murals, which we examine in chapter 5, spread to several cities; for example, in Portland, Oregon, KOW Radio and the Arts and Crafts Society sponsored thirty-five children's murals. Increasing numbers of art teachers have shown interest in mural painting, a few becoming full-time mural facilitators. Most high school murals have been directed by teachers. San Francisco's Alvarado School-Community Art Program, initiated by parents at a multinational school in 1968, has brought community arts into the schools with tremendous success. Ruth Asawa, Nancy Thompson, and other artists have enabled children to create numerous lively murals there (fig. 58). On many college campuses the offices, lounges, and gateways to black-studies, Puerto Rican–studies, and other Third World departments have murals painted by groups of students almost as a direct carry-over from the community murals. And the process has become two-way. The black-studies program at the University of Massachusetts in Amherst, for example, has taken black art from the campus into the nearby industrial city of Springfield. A former Chicagoan, art professor Nelson Stevens has set up the university-sponsored program in which art students work for the community as summer mural painters. In 1974–75, over a dozen murals celebrating black women, music, culture, and the African heritage appeared inside and outside community centers, health clinics, a warehouse, a bar, and on other walls, transforming a ten-block downtown area.

In addition to the forms of organization already discussed, there are two others that are widespread: individual artists working on their own, and, at the other extreme, collectives. Some artists working alone relate to one or another community-development program or neighborhood, whereas others work simply as individuals, often with some link to, or identification with, the national movement. Dewey Crumpler, who has painted murals in the Hunter's Point district and at Washington High School in San Francisco, is one of various black artists working individually on murals with a community orientation. After painting an exterior mural with youths at Hunter's Point, Crumpler traveled in the United States studying murals and meeting other black muralists. His interest in developing his mural talents eventually took him to Mexico, where he studied for three months with David Alfaro Siqueiros and Pablo O'Higgins. With knowledge gained there, Crumpler undertook the Washington High School mural, in which he treats the special problems of perspective presented by works above eye level (fig. 33). This technical orientation derives from Crumpler's feeling, shared by most community-based muralists, that murals must be "not just commentary but also art, art of struggle."[21]

[21] Dewey Crumpler, presentation at meeting of San Francisco muralists, San Francisco Art Institute, September 28, 1974.

23. Arnold Belkin: *Against Domestic Colonialism*. 1972. New York.

Although there are many individual artists like Crumpler working to paint murals that attempt to speak to social issues, it is not possible here to mention more than a few. Arnold Belkin, who was trained in Mexico and worked for many years there, is now painting murals in the New York City area. Technically among the more advanced of American muralists, Belkin has shared his knowledge with younger artists working in the mural movement. The mural Belkin did in collaboration with Cityarts Workshop in a "vest-pocket park" at Forty-sixth Street between Ninth and Tenth avenues deals with the issue of urban renewal. Also working individually in New York is Lucy Mahler, whose mural on the exterior of Wright Brothers School in Manhattan's Upper West Side became a focus for community support. Other active muralists doing important work are: Jim Dong in San Francisco; Sergio O'Cadiz in Los

24. Lucy Mahler: *Let a People Loving Freedom Come to Growth.* 1973. New York.

Angeles; Leo Tanguma of Houston, Texas; Janet Henry of Jamaica Art Mobilization (JAM) in Jamaica, New York; and countless others.

There are various mural collectives that, like collectives in general, come and go with regularity. The collective idea, itself the direct expression of a political philosophy advanced by New Left organizations, came to the fore mainly with the student movement, the counterculture, and certain community organizations. One type of mural collective that grows directly from these sources is that which involves students or youths located at, or around, a college campus. People's Painters, whose first murals appeared at Livingston College in central New Jersey in 1972, provides an example of a student-based collective that operates at times like a brigade. As with collective experiments in revolutionary theatre and music (e.g. Teatro Campesino and El Grupo), People's Painters are composed of people whose primary commitment is political. More important in their work than either consistency, quality, or permanence are an ideological commitment to artistic anonymity, group effort, and political education and struggle through mural messages on current issues.

National or ethnic mural collectives are also common. Within the Chicano movement, which is sensitive to the many historical precedents for communalism in its Indian and Mexican heritage, the collective form has been a frequent mode of organization. Rather than at a university setting, the national or ethnic collective tends to work within the neighborhood of its people. Developing directly out of the local *barrio,* a collective like Artes Guadalupanos de Aztlán (Santa Fe, New Mexico) may remain local or may spread out. In the case of Artes, as the members became more political and tied to the general La Raza movement, they took their art out of Santa Fe and into other Chicano areas of New Mexico, as well as into Colorado and Arizona. Besides painting impressive murals, members of Artes involve themselves in other political organizing and in working to educate Chicano youth.

Both Artes and People's Painters work in a nonindividualistic manner, in which the designs and painting are undertaken as a group effort. The result is a single collective style, distinct from the individual styles of the group members. Although this submersion of individual styles in an effort to attain a group expression characterizes many mural collectives, it is not universally accepted as necessary. For example, San Francisco's Mujeres Muralistas work more in the manner of a musical ensemble. Within a general thematic and color schema, individuals in the group work each in her own style on separate sections of the mural (pl. 17). Group work of this kind, several individuals working together to do separate sections of a unified mural project, characterizes the early murals done by artists associated with Galeria de la Raza.

The group chapters that follow provide detailed accounts of the development of three different types of artist organizations: artist cooperative (Chicago Mural Group), workshop-staff program (Cityarts), and collective (People's Painters and Artes Guadalupanos). There, a more concrete and firsthand picture of the problems and aims of the community-based mural movement is given. This movement has already spread to practically every major city in the country, and a number of rural communities as well. Although regional communications among muralists have made significant gains, as in California, only in the mid-1970s did informal national networks begin to develop with lasting potential. The authors of this book are discovering each month new centers of vigorous growth in community murals—places like Milwaukee, Cincinnati, Sacramento, Denver, New Orleans, Washington, D.C., Baltimore, San Antonio, Houston, as well as London, Glasgow, Berlin, etc. Therefore, the examples of art style and artist organization provided in this chapter must be viewed as a limited, although representative, selection.

4

Mural Painting as a Human Process: The Community

The artist-to-people communication is the kind of relationship that would place the artist and his art in a position of respect, pride, and dignity, all of which the artist should have. These views are founded on the grounds of knowing from experience, of talking with people in a community during the time that the art project is in progress, of discussing the conditions of their problems and the world, and of realizing how art can become more relevant to the people of the world. . . .

People are now realizing that public art is essential because it is relevant to each of them. Art is a universal language, destroying the barriers that stand so firm before man.

—William Walker, from *The Artists' Statement,* Chicago Museum of Contemporary Art, 1971.

Community Is a Process

Just what do we mean by *community?* the sociologist asks, noting that we use the word over and over again in various ways. Do we mean a unit of urban geography? All, or only some of, the residents?

To whom was Santi Isrowuthakul referring in 1972 when he wrote: "The most important and meaningful thing is that these walls now belong to the community, and I have related my art to the people"?[1] The community people to whom Isrowuthakul referred are not anonymous. They are some three hundred individuals—young and old, Asian, Latin, and Anglo—who live within a block or two of the Sheridan Center Christian Fellowship Church on Chicago's North Side. They are the community "board," the restaurant owner who gave his wall, the more than forty young people who helped design and paint the walls, the members of the *conjunto* (musical group) and rock bands who played at the dedication, and the old woman who, to everyone's delight, danced at the dedication. Each of them has a name.

If we are to give *community* a functional meaning, it must be a group of people who share a sense of community—who share common interests, common values, and a sense of solidarity or trust based on these ties. This is conscious community. In our society, dominated by alienation and conflict, there is precious little of this community. Many urban areas seem not to be "neighborhoods" at all, but mere agglomerations of transient strangers. Most people live without any sense of rootedness or belonging. Therefore, in approaching a community arts project, a sense of community cannot be assumed. The artist often does not find a preexisting common ground to stand on. Community cannot be outlined on a map; rather, it is built, and it can be dispersed again. Community is a process of people coming together around common problems, discovering their common values, and developing their sense of solidarity. As Sue Shapiro-Kiok says, "Community art is art that builds community."

Murals do not magically start the community process and, in fact, cannot become part of that process until it has already begun. Murals can act as a catalyst, and make community stronger, more visible; but in order to do that, they must be a vehicle for the redefini-

[1] Chicago Mural Group Report to National Endowment for the Arts, 1972, unpaged.

tion, or reformulation, of common values. In many cases this calls for the revaluation of a history and heritage previously ignored or suppressed. Inevitably, community murals are controversial, for in a world of injustice, exploitation, war, and alienation, a formulation of values implies a criticism of that world and the projection of a possible alternative world. Community art becomes a form of symbolic social action and implies further social action.

In this chapter we examine how murals enter into this process of emerging community consciousness. The human process of murals cannot be contained in a compact summary of the interaction of social categories or classes, because when one becomes involved, one no longer perceives "the people" as a category, the anonymous "masses" without history or culture. During a mural project, the artist meets the working class and its children as flesh-and-blood individuals, with their own culture and personal histories that intersect with the "universal" history of "great individuals" and "great events" in fascinating ways. He or she discovers the previously hidden life and local history of a specific people.

It is the accounts of participants that give reality to our analysis. As the Chinese say, No participation, no correct observation. We structure this chapter around the stories of several murals, including a few artists' work reports. Unfortunately, for purposes of generalization, we draw most of these work reports from Chicago, where more complete documentation has been available, but muralists around the country have confirmed the process we describe. The first story is an example of how the community can be intimately involved in a mural even when the painting is done by a single artist.

Peace and Salvation, Wall of Understanding

The wall (pl. 9) is just east of the Cabrini Homes, a bleak, aging, all-black Chicago Housing Authority project. You can see it from the elevated train that runs nearby and separates the projects from the fashionable high rises to the east. On the next corner is Saint

Dominic's Church, where the story of this mural began. Saint Dominic's had only a scratch congregation but was a center of community activity. In the summer of 1969, neighborhood teen-agers had already decorated a retaining wall with militant imagery, and the following winter Keithen Carter had begun his cycle of religious murals in the church sanctuary. In June 1970, when Bill Walker proposed a monumental outdoor mural to the circle of community activists who frequented the church, they took up the idea. They introduced him to a meeting of The People's Organization (TPO), a small but active group of project residents who became the official local sponsors. Walker obtained permission for a wall near the church from Mrs. Hipps, owner of the building and proprietor of the dingy ground-floor grocery.

Walker continued meeting with TPO while problems with funding, insurance, and scaffolding dragged on. Meanwhile, dramatic events, later pictured in the wall, unfolded in the neighborhood. The months-long gang warfare between the Blacks and the Cobra Stones was brought to an end, largely through the efforts of TPO. This peace was again shattered when two white policemen were shot by snipers. Under cover of hysterical headlines, the entire housing project was virtually held hostage for days while an army of police ransacked hundreds of apartments, until the "suspects" turned themselves in.

There was a further delay, while the artists searched for a scaffolding contractor. Unable to find a contractor who would insure his own work, they finally put up the four and a half stories of sectional scaffolding themselves, with the help of a dozen community residents. Several unemployed youths and half a dozen members of the Cobra Stones helped hoist the sections. A neighbor experienced in construction work gave up his Saturday afternoon to set the top sections, and Brother Joachim set the tie-on bolts with equipment supplied by TPO. During the next week of scraping and priming the wall, Walker was assisted by Bougalou, a young resident, and a few other friends. When funding ran out, TPO somehow came up with money to allow Walker an extra two weeks on

25. William Walker: scaffolding for *Peace and Salvation, Wall of Understanding.* 1970. Chicago.

the scaffold and also hired the same construction worker to dismantle the massive scaffold, which he did single-handed in far less time than it had taken a dozen volunteers to put it up. Most of the costs were met by outside funding, but the support of TPO represented a generous effort for such a poor and small organization. The story of these events, relevant to understanding the context of the imagery of *Peace and Salvation,* is typical of many walls, not in its details, but in the length of time involved, often as much or more time than that actually spent painting.

Walker worked alone on the wall for two months, into the first frosts of October. Despite Walker's working alone on the actual painting, which reflected his concern that the professional role of the muralist be respected, his work with the community and impact on the community were most intense during this period. A much broader cross section of community residents, workers, and passersby became involved in discussion about the mural, as they viewed the spectacle of the blank wall gradually transformed before their eyes. Neighborhood regulars, intent not on panhandling but on offering their opinions, accosted passersby and visitors with interpretations of the painting in progress. From the symbolism of the wall, one idea led to another, and soon there would be a little group of men and women heatedly debating national and world politics, police repression, racial injustice, or the fate of the world. The group of street-corner regulars, unemployed men of various ages, was particularly impressed by Walker's forceful personality and the heroic scale of his task. They protected the wall by watching over it. The men who habitually sat facing the street on a sort of low wall at the southwest corner would now sit facing the mural, or would watch it from across the street until long after midnight. Walker left his supplies on the scaffold at night for more than two months without a single instance of theft, not even of a can of paint.

The community gathered around Walker, and he painted the community into the wall. He included the portraits of many local personalities in the lower portion along with nationally known leaders. And although the mural's meditation on violence and peace, unity and disunity, has a universal dimension, the hands firing at each other from buildings, the confrontation with police, the unity march including all the street clubs with their tams (club berets) and symbols—all were understood in a very current and local context. The mural's complexity is really for the residents of the immediate vicinity and for the pedestrian audience.

Walker involved community people in side projects of their own. He gave neighborhood children paints and brushes to decorate the concrete floor of the corner lot. Local residents, encouraged by Walker, who gave them supplies and instructions, painted two smaller murals. One of these satellite walls, on a religious theme, was painted directly across the street by John Robinson, a lay preacher, professional decorator, and self-taught artist who had already done a mural inside a nearby church. The other volunteer mural, a block away on a small, deserted brick garage, was painted by Vanita Green, a seventeen-year-old former dropout, on the

26. William Walker: dedication for *Peace and Salvation, Wall of Understanding*. 1970. Chicago.

theme of black women. She worked in a department store and, like Robinson, painted after getting off work until dark. The mural, her first, was naïve in style but charged with the conviction of her own personality. Another girl started a mural but got no farther than priming before cold weather.

The dedication ceremony for *Peace and Salvation, Wall of Understanding,* presided over by TPO president, John Stevens, on a chilly October 31, drew over a hundred people. Jesse Jackson, Lerone Bennett, and Margaret Burroughs spoke, followed by community artists and poets, local clergy, political candidates, and curiously enough, the district police commander. Walker gave an eloquent speech and was presented with a plaque. Cookies were distributed to the children, although a block party was out of the question so late in the fall.

Two weeks later, vandals threw bags of paint on Green's mural. Asked if she planned to restore it, she said: "No, it says more the way it is. Before it was just a bunch of pretty pictures. Now people have to stop and think. Why would anybody want to do that to that painting?"[2] She changed the name from *Black Women* to *Racism.* Robinson's mural was destroyed when the building was demolished in 1972.

Watched over day and night by the street-corner group, Walker's *Peace and Salvation* remained untouched. Walker returns each year to repaint sections damaged by the weathering of the crumbling brick. In 1972, a Republican candidate pasted a campaign poster over the painted posters in one corner. Walker retaliated by painting over it a large red, white, and blue sign reading, "Watergate, Watergate." In 1974, he changed the poster again to a portrait of Richard Nixon manipulating chess pieces bearing the heads of the conspirators. In 1975, he returned again, after police had sprayed "All black parasites" across the marching figures. Now the poster memorializes the dead in Vietnam and slain leaders.

Community Pride: The Prestige of Murals

The physical survival of the murals, which are so very vulnerable, exposed to the "direct action" criticism not only of the masses but of isolated eccentrics as well, is a testimony to the pride people take in their murals. Neighborhood people speak of the murals as "ours," rather than as the artist's. Pride is based on possession. Often, when a new mural is just finished in a neighborhood, people declare that their mural is definitely the *best*. One elderly Polish gentleman in Logan Square assured us this was so, adding, "It *must* be the best, even though I haven't seen the others."

In Cabrini-Green, as in other mural neighborhoods, residents bring their friends and relatives from other parts of the city to see the murals. More than a few Chicago residents, who perhaps have rarely been to the Art Institute, think nothing of going out of their way to see the latest murals in other neighborhoods or to attend a

[2] As quoted in Robbyelee, "It Makes You Stop and Think, The Way It Is Now," *Second City* 2, no. 12 (December 1970): 2.

mural dedication a few miles away. Correspondingly, there is a remarkable openness to outsiders visiting the murals. Chicago, like many other American cities, is made up of tight, racially segregated ethnic communities, but visitors to the murals encounter few problems. Identifying their mission is the password that dispels all hostility, as if the very presence of a mural created a privileged area of sanctuary.

The attention given the murals by visitors and by local press certainly reinforces local pride in the walls. At first the visitors were a small number of individual mural enthusiasts, community artists from other neighborhoods and cities, older artists with memories of Mexico, a few journalists from local papers and from faraway places—England, Germany, and France. Later, when the murals were better publicized, occasional busloads of college students and club women came from the suburbs, a curious sort of inner-city tourism that was accepted with good grace by the somewhat surprised and bemused local residents. Tours also came from other city neighborhoods—children, adolescents, and adults, studying the walls to gain inspiration in planning their own murals.

Proof certain of the prestige of mural painting in working-class areas is the frequency of false claims to authorship of various murals. It is not hard to meet young black men who claim to have participated in the *Wall of Respect*—there must be hundreds—and perhaps a few of them did in some way. One went so far as to claim sole responsibility in a book (since corrected). In 1975, John Weber spent a morning listening to an unemployed house painter named Skip explain the many poems he had written to embellish the murals in Universal Alley on Fiftieth Street in Chicago. Although the poems were in fact written by Siddha, Skip had assisted Mitchell Caton in preparing the wall. Skip's boasting was really a tribute to the mural, his explanations fine examples of the poetic speech cultivated in the area.

Pride in Action: Community Defense

Pride and identification go beyond verbal expressions or individually felt emotions to include concrete acts of defense of the mural, the muralist, and the muralist's materials. Eugene Eda recalls that the scaffolding for his 1970 *Wall of Meditation* (fig. 5) had been set up a couple of weeks before he could actually begin work on the wall:

> So it stayed up about a week or two weeks, or three, and parts of the scaffolding start disappearing, and—you know—after I came back early in the summer they had to go back to the scaffold people and get the missing materials, and they had to pay for the stolen parts. As I began to work, sketch, and paint on the wall, parts of the scaffolding were "rediscovered." A couple of people would bring me a wheel back, or bring me a part, and say, "This is yours, isn't it?" Well, I'd say, "Yeah."[3]

The Gary Rickson–Dana Chandler Wall of Respect at Columbus and Massachusetts avenues in Boston caused a furor because of its direct political statements (fig. 3). Chandler's section included the image of Stokely Carmichael shining out rays into the bodies of two slaves breaking their chains. The right-hand side showed H. Rap Brown with a Molotov cocktail. In front of the wall, South End Neighborhood Action Program (SNAP) built a playground with the help of community teen-agers. The Boston Redevelopment Authority, responding to what it claimed were complaints from whites traveling through the neighborhood on their way to work, threatened to paint over the mural. In defense of their mural and the playground, a group of community youths went down to the Redevelopment Authority's offices and told the authorities, "If you change that mural, we will pull your office apart." Summerthing also backed the artists. The Redevelopment Authority ceased its threats.[4]

[3] Interview with Eva and Jim Cockcroft, 1971.
[4] Dana Chandler, interview with Eva Cockcroft, 1974.

The building on which the mural was painted was scheduled for demolition and is now gone, but on its site a recreation center named after Harriet Tubman has been built.

Community residents protect their murals from defacement, and there has been very little graffiti added to community murals anywhere in the country. The reason is quite simple: There is no motive for adding graffiti to walls if the mural itself serves the same purposes of group assertion, expression, and identity—in a grander, more impressive, and effective way. Local youth, including gang members, often participate in mural projects. Even for street murals done by a single artist, a muralist normally takes the elementary precaution of seeking out local club leadership, consulting with them, requesting their cooperation. In general, local graffiti writers have identified with murals and possessively defended them. The following account about Arnold Belkin's mural in New York City's Hell's Kitchen area is typical:

> The community centered around the playground has developed a fierce identification with the mural and, to everyone's amazement, not one extraneous spot, line, or number has defaced the painting. When a gang from 51st Street arrived one day recently, armed with cans of green spray paint, and threatened to attack the wall, the local stalwarts gathered in front of it and warned the invaders that they were risking their lives if they put one spot on the mural![5]

Occasional murals, however, have been defaced or obliterated by graffiti. In some of these cases, the murals had been painted over previously existing gang rosters and emblems without "permission" or participation from the owners of the names. Their response to this lack of etiquette was simply to restore their names as soon as the mural was completed. People distinguish easily those projects done *to* them from those done *with* them: often graffiti are a sort of direct-action criticism of top-down improvements. One must, how-

[5] From a letter to the editor by E. S. Heller in *The New York Times*, September 10, 1972.

ever, make a sharp distinction between the purposeful incorporation of graffiti in a mural by an artist like Willie Herrón (an ex-gang member close to street youth) and those *placas* and embellishments added without the artist's consent in an effort to reappropriate a mural that in itself is found to be unsatisfactory and alien.

Community defense of a mural can extend over several years, as happened in the Green Homes (public housing just north of Cabrini Homes) in Chicago. Bill Walker began to work in the former Saint Marcellus Church (now Stranger Home Missionary Baptist Church) in the fall of 1971 at the invitation of the pastor, Dennis Kendricks. Along with its small congregation, the church housed the welfare-rights office and a high-school-equivalency diploma program of evening classes. "Kendricks left Walker free to invent images within the black context without any dogmatic or supernatural content."[6] The pastor also took full responsibility for obtaining a grant to support the work and for obtaining supplies and scaffolding, leaving Walker free to paint.

Over the next two years, Walker transformed the little church with images of family and community togetherness (figs. 87 and 88). Before he was able to complete this masterwork, however, the chapel was closed down by the archdiocese. Pastor Kendricks was suspended and banished by his superiors. Walker attempted to continue, but first the heating was cut off and then the lights. Walker turned to the core group of supporters he had developed during his three years in the area. Most of them were employed as paraprofessionals in the projects (tenant representatives, clerks, maintenance and recreation supervisors) whose community activism gave them an extensive network of contacts. People like Marion Stamps, Mary Ann Jordan, and Alex Johnson were determined to fight. On a cold night in November 1973, hundreds of residents met in the church to demand that the building be turned over to the community. Over $500 was collected that night and placed in an account to ensure the completion of the murals. This represented a tremendous commitment and financial sacrifice from public-housing residents in order

[6] Harold Haydon, "Showcase," *Chicago Sun-Times*, March 3, 1974.

27. Hank Prussing: *The Spirit of East Harlem.* 1974. New York.

to have monumental art. Soon afterward, however, the sale of the church to a conservative black congregation was announced. Under pressure from the community, the new pastor promised not to paint out the murals, although, to the date of this writing, the Rev. D. T. Thomas has refused permission for their completion.

Identification

People identify with the murals because murals tell the story of the people themselves. They see their lives reflected in the murals on a heroic scale. Those muralists who set themselves the goal of bringing pride to the people have often consciously encouraged this tendency to identify. Walker's inclusion of portraits of local personalities is a characteristic example. Another is the mural that Hank Prussing painted in 1974, on a tenement at 104th Street and Lexington Avenue in New York City. It is entirely made up of giant portraits of the people who live on that block, painted from snapshots. The process of identification is not limited to actual portraits. Other figures have a way of becoming portraits, and people read themselves into any human figure that displays some related characteristic.

The basis for identification is not primarily figure resemblances but theme and its expression in a vocabulary of "vernacular" images, which are embedded in the common visual culture of an area—images that are immediately recognizable and charged with evocative power. This is particularly clear in the many Chicano murals, where we find a heady mixture of contemporary (fist, syringe) and national symbols (flag, eagle, snake) along with elements drawn from Mexican folk arts and pre-Columbian gods and hieroglyphs. The color itself, always vivid and simplified, whether lushly chromatic or stark with red and black contrasts, carries symbolic meaning for the Mexican community. Chicano artists use this symbolic vocabulary to transmit hidden meanings: In a mural painted by the Lil' Valley Youth Association in East Los Angeles (fig. 20), "the apparently harmless little Mexican pottery pig depicts the corruption and indiscriminate brutality of the police."[7]

The Artist Identifies with Community

In the story of *Fuertes Somos Ya,* the role of the artist is somewhat different from that described in *Peace and Salvation.* Here, the artist might be compared to a medium, there to a prophet. Walker, conscious of his roots in his people, could speak in his own voice, confident of his identification with the sentiments of the mass of black working people. An Anglo artist working in a Latin American neighborhood confronted a different situation. The story is told by the artist, John Weber.

[7] David Kahn, "Chicano Street Murals: People's Art in the East Los Angeles Barrio," *Aztlán* 6, no. 1 (Spring 1975): 6.

28. John Weber: *Fuerte Somos Ya* (detail). 1971. Chicago.

In the Fall of 1970, when we were invited to paint in the Museum of Contemporary Art basement, I decided to dedicate a panel mural to one of the free people's health centers. LADO, the Latin American Defense Organization, includes a storefront community-run clinic and a Sunday Liberation school. LADO is the only multi-national Latin American organization in the city, and its leadership is very conscious of the role of visual images in helping people make the connection between religious or folk traditions and social action. LADO members provided for my education in Latin American culture in a very concrete and sympathetic way. I was brought to Pentecostal churches and Spiritistas Santeras, and taught the history of Puerto Rican nationalism. I spent several evenings each week for the next few months immersing myself in the life of the organization and the neighborhood, attending meetings, listening, rapping, searching the LADO files for photos.

The mural, "Fuertes Somos Ya," was dedicated a few weeks ago. The murals on the masonite panel, covering most of the wall, completely transformed and lit up the former storefront.

> Over a hundred adults and children crowded in to hear songs and speeches. Already, a few weeks later, the murals have been completely adopted into LADO's life, each figure nicknamed for a member of the organization, each image identified with well-known events: Mel's son in Vietnam, Francis dressed as Santa Barbara, Pedro and Vicki at the Wicker Park Welfare office, etc. At the beginning, LADO members and I had discussed people seeing themselves as part of the larger picture—that this could happen literally in a mural. I was delighted. Now LADO uses the murals in explaining their ideas to other residents who come to the clinic.[8]

The LADO mural illustrates how murals become a vehicle for a process of self-definition by the people, even when the mural is painted by one person and that person is an outsider.

Murals as Symbols of Place

A mural becomes a symbol of a neighborhood, defining its character in the eyes of both its residents and outsiders. The power of public art to define place is clearly shown in the acceptance of murals by street gangs as a replacement for the graffiti gang rosters that serve as territorial claims. Murals become landmarks, part of the oral geography of an area. Settlement houses and other community centers in a number of cities have used their murals in publicity material as a logo. In Chicago, for example, the Forty-fourth Ward has used its murals as illustrations for its directory of services.

One of the clearest cases of murals defining place is found on Chicago's South Side where, since 1970, Mitchell Caton, assisted by the local regulars, has decorated the walls of an alley on Fiftieth Street between Champlain and St. Lawrence streets (pl. 4). The alley, in the middle of a depressed area, has a life of its own. For years it has been a gathering place, especially on Sunday after-

[8] Adapted from John Weber, "Murals as People's Art," *Liberation* 16, no. 4 (September 1971): 42–46.

29. Mitchell Caton: *Rip Off* (*Universal Alley*) (detail). 1974 version. Chicago.

noons, when, in warm weather, there is always music. Pop Simpson and Little Chuck spin the records; Sonny Stit, Jimmy Ellis, and other musicians may come to play a set. Aside from the many children, for whom the alley is a main thoroughfare, the regulars are semiemployed craftsmen, poets, musicians, and artists, many of whom grew up together in the area years ago. Poetry and jazz are the common language, to which the imagery and style of the murals correspond. The murals and the place are both called *Universal Alley*. The role of the murals in creating an enclosing environment of color for a very specific audience is most unusual outdoors, but resembles the role of many indoor murals in club rooms, clinics, drop-in centers, and labor halls.

The Demystification of Art

As people observe the day-to-day process of painting, they are surprised at the many changes that occur. Those who have watched three or four projects are educated to murals; the inner connections of composition are revealed. This strange thing "art" becomes not only accessible, but a necessary, desirable thing.

During the beginning phases of a project, people ask, "Why are you messing up that nice wall? How much are you being paid? Who is paying you? How long will it take?" The tenor of the question about pay changes during the painting. At first it is cynical: the work is seen as a "good-paying gig" if the artist is on stipend. Some residents may assume that the "community" rap is a cover for another rip-off, that, like the "War on Poverty," the professional is being paid to do things for and to the poor, allowing the opportunist to collect a check in their name. On the other hand, if the artist is unpaid, he is often regarded as a sucker. As work proceeds, this attitude changes. People put the stipend, if there is one, in perspective, admitting that it is a modest wage. Or, if there is no stipend, they now insist that the artist should be paid and that this type of work should be provided for by the government. They calculate how much the mural would be worth at union rates and compare with the actual cost. They see the artists at work in the morning and still at work when they return. In short, they realize that mural painting is work, not a trick, and that the artist is a worker.

The story of Caryl Yasko's experience painting the first mural in the Logan Square area of Chicago provides a revealing account of this gradual change of attitude.

> Many laborers came up to the scaffold to meet the first woman tuck pointer they had ever met and brought their co-workers the following day to prove that I really did exist. If hard physical labor proves anything, it certainly gains respect. Power-brushing the wall was proof to the Action Sales Company that their

30. Caryl Yasko: priming the Logan Square wall. 1974. Chicago.

31. *I Am the People* (drawing).

32. Caryl Yasko with Celia Radek and James Yanagisawa: *I Am the People* (finished mural). 1974. Chicago.

wall was in good hands. To the public, anyone who could submit to such hard labor must either be crazy or getting grand union wages.

The clean look of a newly primed surface always stimulates some reaction from women. "You really improved that wall." But just when their expectations have been satisfied with a freshly painted wall, a new process begins.

People who happened by one week and chanced to come another were astounded with the changes that took place. Around the second week of painting, Chagall's mural downtown was dedicated. All of the Belorussians from Logan Square went to the dedication, but came back to say that Chagall presented no new ideas and lacked the impact and color that "their" mural has. They thought their mural was better and were proud of it.

One Polish woman, who called the artists her "darlings," would always bring something to eat—warm root beer, kapousta, fried bananas, honey—and would ask if she could do anything to help (she eventually assisted in fund-raising). The merchants showed their appreciation of the project by cooperating with our requests and putting up with our antics and errors. One day, Action Sales and the B.V.L. heating company treated the artists to lunch. We were asked to descend the scaffolding, whisked away into the back of a truck with paint rags and all, fed, and brought back to the scaffold, each with a good cigar and a full stomach.

A new type of mass education occurs. The local public learns to pronounce the word *mural* (from "murial" to "mural"), and the vocabulary used in questions changes from "What does it mean?" to "What does this mural represent?" The public also experiences the meaning of murals through an eyewitness opportunity to watch the painting develop. The result of this experience is best summed up in the frequent Logan Square boast: "We have the best mural in Chicago!"[9]

People Need Art: We Want a Mural

The most universal result of a successful mural project is the public's desire for another mural. The first wall in an area is often very difficult to organize: obtaining permission to paint a wall and local backing may take months, but often before the first mural is finished people are already thinking of another. Other walls are offered; other groups ask if the next mural can be done for them; young artists and school art teachers ask for advice on starting their own murals. By the time a neighborhood has a few murals, many residents begin to consider themselves art lovers and refer to their neighborhood as an artistic center.

A fresh appetite for public art was likewise a notable result of the 1930s post-office murals. On June 6, 1939, Edward Bruce, czar of the Treasury Art Section, received the following letter from Basil B. Jones, postmaster of Pleasant Hill, Missouri: "In behalf of many

[9] Chicago Mural Group Report to National Endowment for the Arts, 1974. The Logan Square residents' aesthetic comparisons between "their" mural and Chagall's were partially confirmed by Chicago art critics, who unfavorably reviewed Chagall's *Four Seasons* mosaic.

smaller cities, wholly without objects of art, as ours was, may I beseech you and the Treasury to give them some art, more of it, whenever you find it possible to do so. How can a finished citizen be made in an artless town?"[10] The difference is that today it is not postmasters begging for ennobling objects of art as a federal handout, but ordinary community residents planning and organizing support for their own public art.

This important difference, the replacement of a sense of dependence by one of affirmation, corresponds to a historical era that has consigned the "melting pot" to the realm of myth, as well as to a fundamentally different conception of "art for the people" and a different structure of patronage and control, which we discuss in chapters 10 and 11. The desire for another mural constitutes not only the most universal result but also the most essential baseline of the mural movement's existence.

Demanding a Mural—Washington High School, San Francisco

> The high school houses white-oriented murals executed in 1939 by WPA artist Victor Arnatov. The Arnatov murals depict the life of George Washington, including scenes of Washington as plantation owner and slave-master. From 1965 on, student members of the Black Panther Party and Black Student Union raised objections to the mural's content. . . . Serious negotiations over the students' protests didn't occur until 1968, and then only after frustrated students began defacing Arnatov's scenes.
>
> A near riot finally commanded serious attention from the Board of Education, which commissioned a mural to coexist with Arnatov's. . . . The Board promised students that they could select the artist and the mural's content, with the proviso that the Board and the Art Commission would retain ultimate power to approve the themes and design. These terms led to lengthy delays.

[10] Quoted in Richard D. McKinzie, *The New Deal for Artists* (Princeton, N.J.: Princeton University Press, 1972), p. 72.

33. Dewey Crumpler: *Black History Panel.* 1970–73. George Washington High School (interior), San Francisco.

Six years and a mere $1,700 later, Dewey Crumpler completed the murals, now sited in the hall adjacent to Arnatov's "Life of Washington." When he began, Dewey was a high-school student, when he finished, a college graduate. His years of work resulted in three panels portraying the historical struggles of Blacks, Asians and Latins, Native Americans.

Working closely with the students, Dewey created themes and images appropriate to the specific histories of each group. But although diverse in imagery and cultural symbols, a common theme pervades the three: "We dealt with the people who were most important historically in breaking those chains of oppression, the chains which have kept these people down."

These murals would never have been painted without unrelenting demands from the students. By pressing their cause, the students successfully asserted their right to influence the shape and content of their surroundings.[11]

[11] Ceci Brunazzi, "Portrait of a Muralist," *Common Sense* (June 1975): 12.

The story of the Washington High School murals underlines the enormous difference between the WPA and the context of today's murals. (Ironically, Arnatov's murals at Coit Tower were the subject of controversy and attempted censorship in the early 1930s because of their offensively radical tone.)

Controversy and Conflict: At the Cutting Edge

> Public art differs from other art media in that the large scale and public visibility automatically elicit public response. The art work thus created becomes part of community life, and therefore the creators are necessarily in a more vulnerable and responsible position than if they were creating "gallery" art.[12]

The reader should not be left with the impression that community response to murals is an unending series of celebrations. Many murals spark controversy and become the focus of sharp struggle. The aim of most muralists is not to create a safe, pleasant, or comfortable art. Beautification is placed second to meaning, and subject matter is not decided by a Gallup poll. Although designs are often publicly posted for comment or submitted to community meetings, prior censorship, to the extent that there has been any, has been exercised only by that constituency generally sympathetic, or those active and concerned enough to attend meetings.

The occurrence of conflict around a mural does not usually indicate a failure of the artists or inappropriateness of design. On the contrary, the tensions are already present; the mural only brings them to the surface. Murals neither create nor increase these tensions, but they may provide a vehicle for a symbolic resolution of tension, or compromise, which may have real consequences of enhanced communication, mutual respect, and unity.

In the complex multiethnic Lower East Side of New York City, where blacks and Latins have moved in among the remnants of the old Jewish and Italian immigrant communities, Cityarts Workshop

[12] Cityarts Workshop Proposal, 1972.

34. Susan Caruso-Green and Jewish youths. *Jewish Ethnic Mural.* 1973. New York.

has shown great resourcefulness in helping each group create its own murals, in spite of inevitable misunderstandings. For example, residents of Bialystoker House, a Jewish old people's home, objected to having to look out their windows at the Henry Street Playhouse mural, with its greater-than-life-size figures of blacks and Latins breaking the chains of oppression (pl. 11). Particularly galling to Jewish sensibilities was the religious symbol of the cross in the very center of the mural. In a meeting between Jewish community spokesmen and the teen-age artists, a compromise was reached in which the top of the cross was replaced with a loop, thus converting it into an ankh, an ancient Egyptian symbol of life. Jewish teen-agers, with the assistance of Cityarts' Susan Caruso-Green, spent the following summer creating at Bialystoker House an elegant historical-cultural mural on the struggle of the Jewish immigrant masses.

In changing neighborhoods, racial tensions may be reflected in the conflict over whose values and stories are to be represented. Various ethnic groups demand equal representation. In the uptown area of Chicago, Native Americans demanded to be included in a mural that already included various color figures representing whites, Asians, Latins, and blacks. Even more frequently, however, individual whites have imagined themselves excluded simply because nonwhites are included.

In recent years there has been increasing pressure on male muralists to avoid stereotyped images of women. (Why are they all shown with children? Why are they wearing tight dresses? Why are all the heroes men?) No group, however, has been more sensitive to their public image in murals than the "guardians of order," the police. In one Chicago mural, a cop was shown strolling east with a billy club on his shoulder amid a crowd of other figures walking west with their sundry burdens and cares. The artists were questioned repeatedly by the police: Were they trying "to bad-rap the cops"? One day, the police figure was covered with paint. The artists repainted the figure, adding a container of Mace in the officer's belt. Next day, the figure was again defaced, this time with spray paint. When the artists decided to compromise and turned the police figure around, there was no further incident. The story shows how each detail is interpreted and given symbolic meaning, even if none is consciously intended, and how sensitive particular groups in a community are to their inclusion or omission from a mural. "You have to be prepared to take criticism," Caryl Yasko says. "Everyone who comes by has some comment, either complimentary or critical. People grumble about no dogs or cats or the color of someone's dress. That's okay. They're not indifferent, and they feel they have a right to have a say because it's their street and their wall."[13]

An outdoor mural visible to the heavy traffic of intersections or main streets elicits response from a socially diverse audience, with

[13] *Chicago Tribune,* Lifestyle section, August 20, 1972.

an equally varied notion of what is appropriate to public expression. In a sense, murals serve as a litmus test for class attitudes. In general, working-class and street youth delight in the dramatization of problems, conflicts, and hopes—a dramatization that is itself both an exorcism and a celebration—the more dramatic and powerful, the better. The middle class, however, with its eternal concern for respectability, may feel implicated or embarrassed by the public expression of discrimination, drug abuse, etc., as part of their community. A chamber-of-commerce consciousness of public image would dictate themes that are reassuring and pleasant rather than truthful. Often "respectable" citizens have attempted to censor the designs proposed by artists.

One underpass mural in Chicago's Hyde Park area, for example, drew fire from a local critic because of its honest portrayal of recent local history. John Forwalter wrote: "One wonders if this is a true picture of Hyde Park? Even more one wonders if we need to be reminded of violence daily, even if it were true? As for me, I resent having anger and conflict thrown in my face daily. . . . Is this the image we want to project to the city?"[14] Forwalter's appeal for censorship of "propaganda" art found few echoes, but his article stirred discussion and interest as no favorable notice could have and served to rally support for the mural. Artist Astrid Fuller's vision of Hyde Park as an involved neighborhood appealed to the many residents who are "concerned people, prepared to act on their ideals . . . with a high degree of tolerance for differences." Fuller recalls that her group of young helpers "banded tightly together around me, wrote letters, got petitions signed."[15] Supporters of the wall easily won the debate, both on the street and in the media. Fuller's optimistic vision seemed fully vindicated when at the dedication on November 17, 1973, the Chicago Children's Choir sang, standing in front of the panel filled with their painted counterparts. Nonethe-

14 *Hyde Park Herald*, July 25, 1973.

15 Chicago Mural Group South Side Report to National Endowment for the Arts, 1973.

less, those critical of the Hyde Park underpass murals represent a certain minority and a certain class viewpoint in the neighborhood, an integrated one dominated by the University of Chicago.

John Weber, like a number of other muralists, has consciously sought to work at "the cutting edge"—at these points of tension—and to address the question of unity and disunity among the people. The stories of two controversial murals he has worked on illuminate what art can do in such situations.

The *Wall of Choices*

Part of the nature of being public is to struggle for communication to the majority. In oppressed communities, this is pretty straightforward. In a predominantly white neighborhood, one is faced with the more complex task of fighting racism and winning a majority. This means actually dividing the community on the question of the wall, but placing racism in a minority position. This was brought out clearly around the mural at Christopher House Settlement, called the *Wall of Choices*. It poses the alternative in contrasting symbols of either all peoples uniting to struggle for a better world, or destroying each other through repression, racism, and war.

> To put forward this question—race war or class struggle—in a community where almost everyone is uptight over impending "integration" and in the absence of any active community organizing might seem to preclude winning majority support. In 1968 during the riots, whites had stood on rooftops on the north side of Fullerton armed with shotguns. We decided the mural should be controversial and should put forward the theme of black-brown-white unity forcefully. Thus we began from a minority position, with the intention of challenging people's anxieties. We believed that most working people could not reject images which appealed to their desire for peace, health, and education for all children as well as their own. We wagered the mural on this belief and events proved it to be correct.
>
> Malcolm X, the universally recognized symbol of radicalism

of that time, was eliminated from the design at the request of the board of directors. But as images of John Brown and Frederick Douglass appeared, a few people shouted, "Why are you putting niggers on the wall?" or "Who's that nigger with white hair?" The image of bound hands, with the inscription "Free all Political Prisoners, Free Bobby Seale" (Black Panther Party leader, then on trial with the Chicago Eight), brought a stormier reaction. Three elderly women threatened the director with umbrellas. There were anonymous phone calls, a bottle was thrown, and the director asked me to change the image. I promised to check it out with the community and found that "Free Bobby" was the objectionable part. Its removal satisfied our critics. If they thought of "political prisoners" in their native Eastern Europe, the neighborhood youth certainly applied the slogan closer to home. As the work went on, more and more people praised the wall or said it was all right.

The wall was the subject of widespread spontaneous debate. In the meantime, more people volunteered to help. Members of the Satan Angels Motor Cycle Club helped scrape windows.

35. John Weber: *Wall of Choices*. 1970. Chicago.

> At the dedication and afterwards, "shares" were sold in the mural at $1.00 per brick. Several hundred dollars were raised in this way to buy paints for the next mural and to buy materials to rebuild the playground. People in the neighborhood were proud of their mural and proud of themselves for accepting it. It has become a fixture. The neighborhood, still mostly white, has integrated slowly, without any block-busting and relatively little friction. I like to think that the mural helped in some way to prepare people for change, allowing them to come to terms with their fears in a symbolic way.[16]

Realistically, it must be said that the mural was not accepted because of its message alone. The bright colors and crisp design overcame some reservations. The wall was partly protected by the prestige of Christopher House. There was no racist leadership in the community, and the mural's supporters were better organized than its critics. The artist and his community supporters won a majority, successfully using art as a human force rather than as a cosmetic decoration.

Unidos para Triunfar ("Together We Overcome")

An even more intense struggle took place around a mural project in Chicago's Westtown area the following year. Our account is taken from work reports written in 1971 and 1974. Designed by a racially mixed group of teen-agers led by John Weber, and paid for by a coalition of Association House, Division Street YMCA, Barretto Boys Club, and El Centro, the mural *Unidos para Triunfar* (pl. 10) evoked prolonged controversy about its theme, which contrasts gang fighting with a "march" of unity.

> Westtown has become largely Puerto Rican over the last ten years. However, many older Poles remain, as well as a scattering of other whites, Chicanos, and a few pockets of longtime black settlement. Throughout, the project was controlled by an open community meeting held about once a week, usually at

[16] Adapted from John Weber, "Murals as People's Art," *Liberation* 16, no. 4 (September 1971): 42–46, and Chicago Mural Group Report to National Endowment for the Arts, 1970.

Association House. Attendance ranged from 10 to 50, virtually all Puerto Rican youth. Debate was very specific and often stormy. Community meetings selected themes for three walls: one on history, celebrating Puerto Rican heroes; a second on unity among youth and such problems as drugs; and a third on housing, welfare, or the religious-cultural heritage. The first wall was postponed when an absentee landlord, a certain M. F., demanded various legal papers. We decided to go ahead with the second wall at Hoyne and Division "in the meanwhile."

The street had been the scene of shoot-outs in June between the Vice Lords (recent black "intruders"), the PVP's (Pulaski-Venturers-Playboys—"retreating" whites), and the Latin Kings (defenders of the "home turf"). The shoot-outs had left at least one dead and several jailed or hospitalized. We felt that if we were serious about art being meaningful and speaking to crucial problems this was precisely the spot for a mural on unity (certainly it was NOT the spot for a mural on Puerto Rican heroes). We knew we were testing the limits of "What can art do?" and putting ourselves on the firing line. We took warnings about the situation seriously enough to drop Jimmy Smith, a black member of the Latin Kings, from the work group, since he risked being a target of resentment from both sides.

During the project, a constant stream of cars turned into Hoyne to stop and watch; swarms of children asked for chalk; there were endless explanations, debates, and friendly raps. People's reactions to the two hands, black and brown, clasped in the center, proved to be a regular inkblot test for the contradictions of the area. At first, the dope pushers opposed us because they had heard the mural would be anti-drugs. Detectives from the notorious GIU (Gang Intelligence Unit) questioned us and tried to intimidate Sra. Negron, the owner of the wall. Street-club leadership checked us out. We won their support, especially after we agreed to paint in the "colors" (the club tams) on the unity side of the mural. Club leaders gave orders to protect the mural. The idea of unity and a respected role in the community had great appeal to the older members of the clubs, who had had their fill of gang war. From the last week in June until well into September, there was not one incident of gang fighting in the Westtown area. Was it the usual lull after heavy casualties, or did the project draw tension to itself like a lightning rod, tensions which found a verbal and visual outlet there?

From the beginning we enjoyed the support of a large number of plain family people, Puerto Rican, black, and white. Later, we had testimonials from several young people who came to us individually, saying the wall "really made me think, it made me see some things."

On July 21, a poorly attended meeting at Association House voted that the black-brown hands violated the general will that the wall be only Puerto Rican and that both hands should be "brown." We spent the next days going door to door to get people's opinions of the wall. With support expressed by almost everyone we visited (some 50 people), we called another meeting for Friday, where the decision was tabled. Out of this meeting came two petitions: one addressed to M. F. requesting permission for his wall in support of a mural on Puerto Rican history, the other in support of our unity wall, "Unidos para Triunfar." During the next two weeks, we gathered several hundred signatures on each petition. With this convincing support, we finished the wall.

It had also been decided that the Puerto Rican Art Association, a group of young nationalistic painters, should go ahead with their own wall, honoring Puerto Rican heroes. They took two months to paint their mural, which was dedicated on September 23rd, anniversary of the Grito de Lares. Suspicions remained, however, and a slanderous leaflet was circulated against my presence in the community. The leaflet had little effect, but coincidentally a bucket of paint was later splashed on "Together We Overcome."

The third week in August we started on a wall at the corner of Rockwell and LeMoyne, with permission from the residents of the building who helped develop the design. Here, only a mile away, the street scene was relaxed, even festive, during the three weeks of frantic painting. Jimmy Smith now rejoined the Neighborhood Youth Corp team helping us. Dedication of this mural, "Rompiendo las Cadenas" (Breaking the Chains"), October 3rd, was attended by hundreds.[17]

Sequel, 1974

I agreed to restore "Unidos para Triunfar" when two community leaders asked me to do so during the wake for Orlando Quintana, a widely respected youth worker and a personal

[17] Adapted from Chicago Mural Group Report to National Endowment for the Arts, 1971.

friend, shot by an off-duty policeman in July, 1973. Orlando, a staff member of Association House, had actively supported the murals in 1971.

The block by now was a fourth demolished and majority black. Gang fighting had all but disappeared. Most of the merchants are commuters and the landlords absentees. The Negrons, owners of the building on which the mural is painted, are outstanding among the working families remaining. The street scene during the day consists mainly of junkies and ex-junkies, many of them petty dealers, and a few older winos. It is a block with a bad reputation, even among its regulars.

My return there was greeted with a chorus of skepticism. I was repeatedly told the mural would only be defaced again. One junkie said, "no sense painting about people being together, because no one is together here and nobody is going to get together."

For a few weeks there was frequent discussion of the earlier defacement. Everyone seemed to condemn it. Some Latins were convinced that blacks had defaced the wall, despite clear graffiti evidence that the predominantly Polish PVP's from several blocks away were responsible. This was confirmed when two white youths warned me not to include any club berets,

36. John Weber and team: dedication for *Unidos para Triunfar.* 1974. Chicago.

> insignia, or colors, explaining that their presence had motivated the defacement. (In our concentration on Latin-black unity, we had forgotten about the PVP's and only the colors of Latin clubs were included.) New figures were added, including a coffin—a reference to Orlando.
>
> I was assisted by several young people, including students from the Centro Educacion Creadora Ruiz Belvis, a dropout school run by former LADO activists. As the work progressed, the regulars on the street guarded the materials and offered us coffee and wine. Toward the end, approval seemed universal. Several landlords invited me to paint their buildings, offering to pay. In 1971, absentee landlords had been afraid murals would lower resale value. Now they thought art work would help them sell! A few young Latins, however, still insisted that all the figures in the murals were "niggers," despite the light coloring of many of them. I asked a black who passed who he thought the figures were. He said they were all Puerto Ricans.[18]

Because this mural was defaced and because it did not solve the problem of racism or national divisions in the neighborhood, some have questioned whether it accomplished anything at all. Such criticism reflects unfair and unrealistic expectations. On the contrary, the story of this mural is an account of art playing a real role in ideological struggle and change, despite errors made in the original project. Most notably, these errors were the misestimation of the importance of Puerto Rican nationalism, on the one hand, and identifying the mural too explicitly with the Latin street clubs, on the other. These mistakes were not, however, made by the artist alone, but by the work team and the Latin supporters of the project as well.

Public art can only live if public artists are willing to be on the scene, to work at points of tension, to be relevant to the most difficult and violent problems of our time and our neighborhoods. Defacements do not occur because of lack of respect for "art." A bucket of paint is not the same as the hundreds of carved initials on

[18] Adapted from Chicago Mural Group Report to National Endowment for the Arts, 1974.

public property that has lost its meaning. It is the price of being in the public arena, which is one of conflict.

Relevance is a question of a given situation, time, and place. The relevance of some murals fades before the paint is faded, like posters for a rally. They serve a purpose only in a limited time frame. But certain issues are woven into the fabric of American society, and as one community leader said, *Unidos para Triunfar* will be relevant for many years to come.

5

Mural Painting as a Human Process: Those Who Paint

Community mural painting is something quite different from the lonely "aesthetic experience" that we are taught to cultivate in school. Many artists testify to the impact that mural painting as a social activity has on them.

> Never have I had the total sense of being an artist relevant to society, until working on a public wall. Finally, by visual means alone, I can express my concern for humankind without a conflict of interest.
>
> —Caryl Yasko, Chicago Mural Group.[1]

The artists often speak of an inner change, a "turning over" experienced during a first outdoor mural. Identifying with the audience entails for the artist a *taking of sides,* which is no less real, although perhaps a little easier, for those who paint in the neighborhoods where they grew up. Many of the muralists are the sons or daugh-

[1] From text of "On Chicago Walls," Exhibit at Chicago's South Side Community Art Center, November 12–December 6, 1972.

ters of workers, and more than a few have become artists without benefit of degrees or art schooling. Whereas for some the mural experience is a way of returning, for others it is a transformation.

> Painting the mural was an extraordinary experience, a conversion. I found that I was able to create an imagery which spoke directly to ordinary people, which was accepted as their own.
>
> —John Weber, Chicago Mural Group.[2]

The artists' vision is altered. Everywhere they see walls in a new way, measuring them in the mind for a possible design.

> Our interest as artists is to put art close to where it needs to be. Close to the children; close to the old people; close to everyone who has to walk or ride the buses to get places. We want our art either out in the streets or in places where a lot of people go each day, the hospitals, health centers, clinics, restaurants, and other public places. . . . We offer you colors we make.
>
> —Mujeres Muralistas, San Francisco.[3]

Of all the visual arts, mural painting is preeminently social not only because of its direct relation to audience, but because most mural painting is to one degree or another a collective act in which community residents are the creators as well as the audience. There is a long tradition of collective execution of murals by teams of artists, but today the design is often collectively created as well. There is also an important difference in the composition of many of the mural teams: Few of the participants consider themselves artists. They are community residents selected solely on the basis of interest and willingness to work. Usually, most are high school age, but older residents sometimes join in. Children also participate, and there are murals done entirely by teams of children.

The artists quoted above do not speak for themselves alone but also for the dozens of local residents and young people who have

[2] From *The Artists' Statement,* Chicago Museum of Contemporary Art, 1971.
[3] From Victoria Quintero, "A Mural Is a Painting on a Wall Done by Human Hands," *El Tecolote* 5, no. 1 (September 13, 1974): 6, 7, 12.

painted with them. For many, doing a mural is a vital formative experience, and a few go on to become professional artists. The influence of a mural expands outward from those most involved—the painting team and support committee—to their friends and relatives, the members of sponsoring organizations, the immediate neighborhood, and beyond that, with diminishing effect, to a vastly larger casual audience and those who hear about it secondhand.

In this chapter we examine the dynamics of collective mural work in terms of those who paint. For purposes of organization, we distinguish between directed team murals, collective youth murals, and children's murals. In fact, there is no way to draw a hard-and-fast line. The common denominator is collective execution led by a "director" or artist-organizer-in-charge. In every case, regardless of how collectively ideas and images are developed, the role of the leader is pivotal in facilitating the mural process.

Directed Team Murals

By directed team murals, we mean those murals that are executed (and often also planned) by a group, but in which the design itself bears the stamp of one or two artists in charge of the project. This style of work is particularly identified with the Midwest, where it was used early on by the Chicago Mural Group and the Public Art Workshop. Often, the theme is planned and approved by adult members of the community, the actual painting team being assembled later.

Directed team murals continue a central tradition of mural painting. It was exceptionally rare for a fresco to be executed entirely by one artist. During the Renaissance, painters often began their careers grinding colors and plastering for a "master." Many muralists worked with entire teams of assistants and apprentices, usually referred to as their "workshop" in art-history texts. The "hand of the master" was responsible only for the basic composition, correction of final sketches, a few important figures, and final retouches. Virtually all of Giotto's murals were produced in this way, to the dismay of later art historians trained to look for personal brushwork, something quite irrelevant to Giotto's purposes. Even in the nineteenth century, Delacroix had assistants prepare his walls, paint the backgrounds, and lay in the basic tones of the figures. In the twentieth century, Siqueiros, beginning with his murals in Los Angeles in 1932, always worked with a group of disciples. Usually young artists, they were considered collaborators rather than mere assistants, although the "maestro's" concept is clearly dominant in the result. Siqueiros considered this apprenticeship-collaboration as the most effective method of teaching mural painting and for experimentation with new materials. All but a few of the muralists in Chicago have begun as volunteer assistants under the direction of another artist, not in a workshop, but out on the street.

The mural team was also "rediscovered" in the 1930s by the Public Works of Art Project (PWAP) artists for the same reasons it has always been used: to allow "new" muralists to gain experience and skill in a supervised situation.

> Grant Wood, working at the University of Iowa, supervised what was probably the most successful project. Wood became an assistant professor and his artists received university credit for their work. When the 22 artists first descended to their workshop, a revamped swimming pool, Wood discovered equal numbers of artistic conservatives and radicals. The original polite tolerance between factions, Wood reported, grew into such strong community feeling that eventually each man was willing to subordinate his own personal mannerisms to make a harmonious whole. They were proud that their panels looked as if one man had done all the work. When the PWAP reduced regional quotas, Wood's artists decided to pool and reallocate their checks rather than have the group broken up. Later, to finish the work, the group made plans to live in tents, have the wives cook army style, and pay group expenses by sending a few members elsewhere to work. An additional grant made this unnecessary, but Wood believed they would have carried on. The result of Wood's teamwork, while frustrating to critics accustomed to praising or blaming individuals, won considerable renown.[4]

[4] Richard D. McKinzie, *The New Deal for Artists* (Princeton, N.J.: Princeton University Press, 1972), pp. 27–28, referring to a PWAP report, Wood to E. A. Jewell, quoted in *The New York Times,* May 27, 1934.

Today the same community spirit and passionate solidarity usually develop among members of a mural team. The formation of a team, however, is no longer viewed as simply a practical expedient. The involvement of local youth is a positive value and is often the pretext for a mural in the first place.

Teams are assembled in many different ways. Often a core group all come from one program, sponsoring organization, or school, but others may volunteer on the spot. For example, Caryl Yasko writes of her Forty-seventh Street mural *The Health of the People:*

> The painting team came from the Dr. Martin Luther King Jr. Urban Progress Center Art Workshop. Mr. Douglass Williams is the workshop instructor and helped recruit the team by moving the workshop into the street for the duration of the mural. Besides Williams and myself, there were six teenage "students" from the workshop and Don Claybourne, a young man who lives next to the wall site. Claybourne came up to me on the first day and said, "If anyone is going to come into my community and do anything to make it a better place to live, I want to know what I can do to help." Don got up at 5 A.M. each morning to help set up the scaffold.[5]

John Weber, writing of the Central Lakeview mural (fig. 61) in 1971, reports:

> Our team was made up of young adults, both students and unemployed. We were joined in painting by a dozen children ages 6 to 13. The children who lived in the building were most regular, and two of the oldest became quite accomplished at mixing and shading. Decisions on basic design problems were limited to the regular team, but whoever was working with us that day sat in on the discussion. We were also joined occasionally by a few older adults. One, an engineer who had studied in Mexico years before, came to paint with us before work and during lunch hour. He would strip off his suit and paint in his underwear.[6]

[5] Chicago Mural Group Report to National Endowment for the Arts, 1973.
[6] Chicago Mural Group Report to National Endowment for the Arts, 1972.

37. Ray Patlán and youth team. *La Causa*. 1972. Chicago.

38. Lower East Side Community artists team: Rivington Street mural. 1973. New York.

39. Esther Charbit and Barry Bruner, directors: youth team at work on *City Sounds*. 1973. Chicago.

In contrast to the preplanning and deliberate recruitment involved in most team murals is Caryl Yasko's *Under City Stone* (fig. 94), painted by a team entirely assembled from passersby ("walk-ons"). When Yasko began, she had a flexible scale drawing, modest funding (up to $500) from the Hyde Park Merchants Association, but no community base. The way she assembled a team from the predominantly middle-class neighborhood seems like a feat of prestidigitation.

> The paint was picked up on Tuesday, and painting began the following day. Some standard or policy on volunteers had to be established to discourage a stampede of 30-minute-one-time-never-come-again volunteers. I decided to establish a quota of fifteen workers, out of which maybe there would emerge four steady people. All citizens wishing to participate had only one restriction: to write their name and what hours they could offer from the beginning to the completion of the project. That

40. Alan Okada, director, with team working: scaffolding for *Chi Lai—Arriba—Rise Up!* 1974. New York.

> discouraged half the populace. By Wednesday, there were already fifteen people: four newspaper boys who came at 5 A.M. (I started early), one middle-aged professor's wife and her daughter, a lawyer's wife, a waitress, a young boxcar loader from the *Tribune,* a bartender, four elementary school children, and two artists. . . . By the beginning of August, my log had tallied forty-four people who had actually participated in painting. Out of forty-four were twelve faithful workers. Five of the twelve had carried through to the end.[7]

This type of team formation was facilitated by the heavy pedestrian traffic, which provided a very large pool of potential volunteers. The long horizontal space permitted a large group to work at ground level, and the design, composed of numerous walking figures representing various social types, allowed a variety of personalities to identify with and to contribute personally to the result.

Teen-age participants sometimes receive pay from the Neighborhood Youth Corps or other federal Manpower work-training programs. Usually, these programs offer pay for only twenty to twenty-five hours per week, but many of the "NYCs" volunteer to paint extra hours in order to complete the mural on schedule. Occasionally, high school students have been able to earn class credit for their work, but many teams are entirely made up of volunteers. In some cases, college students on "work-study" have been assigned to mural-painting programs.

Whether paid or unpaid, a core group is formed, ranging from three to fifteen of those who are willing and able to work regularly. This is the team. In the course of the project, they receive training in color mixing and shading, care of brushes and equipment, etc. They participate in discussions of every aspect of the mural, from drawing changes to color composition. They usually meet several times a day to discuss the progress of the mural, make suggestions for changes, and assign tasks. Although team members work within a design framework established by the director, who also has the final decision on all changes, the most successful teams are also the

[7] Chicago Mural Group Report to National Endowment for the Arts, 1972.

most democratic. (Perhaps this was also more true of murals in the past than we know of.) The leader must, without being dictatorial, set a pattern and method of work, insist on maintaining the unity of design and theme, instill a sense of responsibility to the group and to the community, and revive flagging spirits with tireless enthusiasm.

Leading groups is obviously not every artist's cup of tea. Some artists feel it is a burden and compromises the quality of their work. Answering endless queries and greetings on a busy street can also be distracting and debilitating and has led more than one artist to choose working at night! Many feel that the necessity to teach and to maintain a common style with a group of inexperienced nonprofessionals sometimes holds them back from experimentation, forcing them to stick to tested methods.

Other muralists are addicted to group work, finding it challenges their inventiveness. They enjoy the interaction and cannot imagine community mural work without a team. Many of them have chosen to concentrate on working with those young people whose need for self-expression, self-definition, and for a responsible role in the community is greatest.

Collective Youth Murals

A collective youth mural is not only executed but also conceived and designed by a group of nonprofessional young people. The role of the artist in charge is that of a facilitator, whose skills and knowledge enable the group to carry out their own ideas. This type of mural, as Cityarts Workshop puts it, "is based on the belief that latent creative talent exists in abundance among many people who have just not had the opportunity to express and refine it."[8] Many muralists around the country believe that the creation of an authentic popular culture, a people's art, demands the activation of the people's own creative powers. This commitment to facilitate the birth of a people's art has nothing to do with an anachronistic and

[8] Cityarts Proposal, 1972.

nostalgic appreciation for folk art or for eccentric naïve art, since today's murals are done by urban youths, collectively, in an essentially contemporary idiom. Although facilitated collective murals have reached a very high level of achievement on the Lower East Side of New York City, numerous examples of this type of work, some of them excellent, can be found in Chicago, Milwaukee, Philadelphia, Los Angeles, and other cities.

Cityarts writes that a collective mural "provides a permanent testimony to achievement, which is . . . an important aesthetic experience with equally important educational byproducts."[9] In analyzing collective youth murals, one cannot separate the aesthetic and social significance of public art from the teaching and learning experience. The nature of this learning process is especially rich and complex because it occurs in a *group*. The leaders try to ensure that the active creativity of each group member is elicited and valued so that it contributes to the give-and-take from which emerges a shared vision.

The public nature of this process is equally important. Often the youths involved have already abandoned the classroom to make the streets their stage, although their self-dramatization may be antisocial. A mural project, in offering them an infinitely more effective platform, also places them in a role of responsibility to the community, a role daily reinforced by public reaction to their work. Individualistic expression gives way to expression of community, and the young painters are able to identify personal liberation with community struggles. The participants are thus enabled to redefine themselves in a larger context. To allow this to happen, the authorities involved, whether school or city, funding agency or landlord, must be willing to take the calculated risk of an authentic learning experience made public.

Drawing attention to the internal community formation that goes on in group projects, to their consciousness raising and effect on personal growth, does not imply that the work of art itself is merely a gimmick to accomplish therapeutic ends. Participation in such proj-

[9] *Ibid.*

ects is effective only to the extent that the mural is accepted by the public as embodying genuine community purposes (beautification, as well as recovery of ethnic heritages, support of real struggles, etc.) and that the result is actually qualitatively bigger, more significant, and more accomplished than any of the individuals could have done separately.

Work-Report Examples

Community Participation in Team Murals

The following work report illustrates the close relationship and interplay between a mural team and the community. Jim Yanagisawa reports that the mural he and Santi Isrowuthakul directed in 1973 eventually involved a team of some forty high school and college students, of which twelve constituted a core group. Many were members of the Sansei Project, a program for third-generation Japanese Americans sponsored by the Japanese American Service Committee (JASC). After showing the Sanseis a slide show of Chicago murals and discussing the time, manpower, and money that had gone into each wall, Isrowuthakul asked the Sanseis if they still wanted to go ahead. Yanagisawa recalls: "They said yes, but were doubtful that they could carry out such a project without supervision. Santi and I replied that we would plot out everything except the choosing of the theme. They would have to do that, and all of us together would then decide how their theme would be given form. They agreed to this and to our feeling that we would share the credit and responsibility for the mural equally." After some planning meetings, which led to community funding, including $200 from the Sansei Project, and selection of a wall on the north side of the JASC building, the artists and young people addressed the question of theme:

> Many images were discussed and sketched out, but the ones commonly agreed to were these: (1) a picture that would portray the identity crisis of the Sansei's who were feeling the

41. James Yanagisawa, Santi Isrowuthakul, and team: *Nikkeijin No Rekishi* (partial view). 1973. Chicago.

> pressures and stress of being hyphenated-Americans; (2) the concentration camps where all Japanese Americans were incarcerated during World War II; (3) that these "heavy" images be offset by a third more hopeful vision of the future, an image combining symbols of all the races in America joined in fellowship. This last image gave birth to our theme: a pictorial survey of Japanese Americans—past, present, future; a movement from hardship and sacrifice, to a questioning present, towards a free and fruitful future for all people.

A number of community leaders shared in these preliminary matters: Diane Kayano and Reverend Nambu of JASC, Colin Hara of the Japanese American Citizens League, Rex Takahashi of the Asian American Studies Program at Roosevelt University, Rev. Ron Miyamura of the Midwest Buddhist Temple. The JASC board approved the final sketch design. The mural team received the support of many neighborhood people who stopped by on their way to and from work to encourage them.

The mothers in the neighborhood stopped by often to chat and to cheer us on. They thanked us over and over for helping to beautify their block. Many sent their children over to help us.

This is one reason why on the list of artists on the wall you will find, beside the names of the Sansei's, the names of young people, including children, from all races and ethnic groups. One of our consistent helpers was a Greek boy, Peter Maroutsos, whose mother and father supported us from the very beginning. There were also many young Appalachian and Southern whites, new to the city, who came to help. For many it was the first time they had painted—this may sound incredible, but there are NO ART PROGRAMS in their public schools!

As we were finishing, we began thinking about an official title for the mural. I suggested we let the Isei's [first-generation Japanese Americans] who work in the small JASC factory decide. The name they chose was: NIKKEIJIN NO REKISHI, which means literally the History of the Japanese American people.

I came back several days later to paint the official title on the wall. I finished about the time the Isei's were punching out to go home. One Isei after another stopped by to shake my hand and tell me how much they like the picture. Several women nearly wept as they recounted to me their memories of that first boat ride to America. Others told me of all the forgotten feelings inside them brought to life again by our painting. I was moved beyond words.[10]

Doing a First Collective Youth Mural

Motivating adolescents and organizing a group are often far from easy, especially when a mural has never been done before. The proposed project has little credibility until it actually begins. Eva Cockcroft's narrative of *Which River,* a mural painted by rural white youth in 1974, illustrates some of the early problems. Warrensburg, the site of the mural, is in the Adirondack Mountains, several miles from Lake George, New York.

I tried to interest some of the youth in painting a mural (the idea was wholly new to them). The newspaper articles, posters,

10 Chicago Mural Group Report to National Endowment for the Arts, 1973.

42. Area youth with Eva Cockcroft: children working on *Which River* (process shot). 1974. Warrensburg, New York.

newsletter notices, etc., produced no results whatsoever. Negotiations with the owners of the building were also stalled. . . .

When it was clear that the mural really could proceed, I solved the problem of getting workshop participants by holding the first planning session at a time when there were usually a number of teenagers hanging around the [Warrensburg] art center—I personally invited each one to watch the slide show. In this way, four teenagers, two boys and two girls, became involved. They chose the theme of ecology (pollution of the rivers).

From photos and drawings they brought and others I provided, we selected images, traced them, and arranged them into a design. One of the team, who was involved in psychedelic drawings, provided the overall pattern of the river area; another designed the debris in the polluted section of the river. As our meetings continued, interest increased, but there was still not the intense involvement that I knew would be necessary to carry out the project. There were many times when I felt discouraged

43. Area youth with Eva Cockcroft: *Which River* (team shot). 1974. Warrensburg, New York.

44. Area youth with Eva Cockcroft: *Which River* (finished mural). 1974. Warrensburg, New York.

and ready to give up the whole thing. No sooner did we set the date to begin the wall preparation than one of the two really committed teenagers left for a week to visit a girlfriend. My discouragement was complete, and I decided to postpone the mural idea for a year while we worked to build more support locally for the project.

To a meeting set for cleaning up the wall I arrived late, expecting to find none of the teenagers there. But Randy, who tended both to show off and goof off yet had come faithfully to the design sessions, was there. I informed him that without serious commitment to work every day from some of the group there was no sense in going ahead. He swore that he was ready to work. I realized that after all the preliminary work the kids had done, if even one of them would be hurt by my backing out, it would be an irresponsible act on my part. We got some buckets of soapy water and started scrubbing the wall to remove the grime and charcoaled graffiti. For a break, we went to the local paint and hardware company to ask for a donation. The manager agreed to donate half the paint (later, he donated all the paint).

These events marked the turning point. We rented scaffolding inexpensively in a neighboring city. As we set it up, more of the local kids joined in to help, among them some of the toughest boys in town. This gave the project a certain prestige. We squared off the wall and began to transfer the design with the same charcoal briquets other kids had used to write their names. Younger kids began to ask if they could help. Through my insistence, the design had been kept very simple, in entirely flat areas. As more and more children showed up, we divided the painting process according to age and height. At the top of the wall, perched on the two-level scaffold, were the teenagers. In the middle, on the single-level scaffold, were ten-to-twelve-year-olds. Smaller children down to six years of age painted on the ground level. On some days as many as twenty children and teenagers were working all three levels of the wall at the same time.

Once the color began to go on we got a lot of people stopping to tell us how, while they had thought at first that we were just making a mess, now they could see that it was a good thing for the town. The Historical Society and the town board began talking about another mural, on a "Bi-Centennial" theme [work on this project began in 1975]. Photographs and news stories about the Warrensburg mural appeared in the local and regional press. A number of nearby towns and organizations, including schools which had never before heard of murals, began to consider how they might undertake such community-oriented art projects.[11]

Every group leader has gone through moments of discouragement such as those described in this narrative, but the young people are much more subject to discouragement and disbelief in their own abilities. The role of the leader is to see it through these low points by hook or by crook. Starting on the wall itself is always a turning point, as it is in this narrative. In fact, muralists often say that when you start on the wall, you are already half done.

Hay Cultura en Nuestra Comunidad: An Unplanned Mural

In the Pilsen neighborhood southwest of Chicago's Loop, there is a neighborhood house, Casa Aztlán, covered with pre-Columbian designs. This mural series, begun by forty local Neighborhood Youth Corps (NYC) workers under the direction of Ray Patlán, is titled *Hay Cultura en Nuestra Comunidad* ("There Is Culture in Our Community"), a title that sums up much of the accomplishment of the community arts effort. According to Patlán, "The idea for the first wall at Aztlán was to negate all planning and attack the wall directly with the medium."[12] In preparation, Patlán had the NYCs spend about two weeks studying Mexican history and design. *Design Motifs of Ancient Mexico* by Jorge Enciso[13] was a basic source. After the wall was primed, one of the NYCs asked Patlán if he had brought the design. "There is no design," Patlán answered. "It's your wall to paint."

At first they all sat down, angry and discouraged. Then one girl

[11] North Country Arts Center Funding Proposal to New York State Council on the Arts, 1974.

[12] Chicago Mural Group Report to National Endowment for the Arts, 1971.

[13] (New York: Dover Publications, Inc., 1953).

got up and started to draw on the wall. Others joined in, choosing images and enlarging them freehand on the wall. In some cases, size had to be adjusted several times: a quetzal bird that is two inches high in the book eventually was painted fifteen feet high. The wall, which is broken up by several windows, two doors, and various brick moldings, lent itself to this type of space-by-space improvisation. The young artists exploited its possibilities, entering into the decorative spirit of pre-Columbian art as easily as if five hundred years of colonialism had not existed. Decorative borders were invented to tie elements together and to fill narrow spaces. A lamp over the door became a flaming sun, a buttress became a plumed serpent. Pre-Columbian design was both a source and an equalizer, allowing those who would not invent to choose their contribution instead. Patlán allowed for a loose compositional structure and added large doses of encouragement. One of the young artists recalled: "When we started ours, nobody knew what to do and nobody wanted to touch it, because we were afraid we might mess it up. And then Ray told everybody to do it—even if you mess it up, it'll turn out all right."

There is an ebb and flow to participation in any project, and of the twenty-four who began this wall and the dozen or more children who also painted, only ten were still working at the finish. A member of this core group commented: "I didn't ever think it would come out that nice, but everyone did his share. . . . In the beginning, your painting might not look so good, but after you're through, if everybody sticks together, it works out."

It is the core group that experiences "everybody sticking together." They will often put in a forty-hour week or more, remaining late in the afternoon despite the lure of the beach or pressures of part-time jobs. They shoulder much of the responsibility for the dedication, making posters, soliciting local merchants for refreshments, and getting their musician friends to play. The group often celebrates its own existence as well as the mural with its own party along with the dedication. Success is a heady new feeling. "Everyone was proud of it," said one of the young painters, "be-

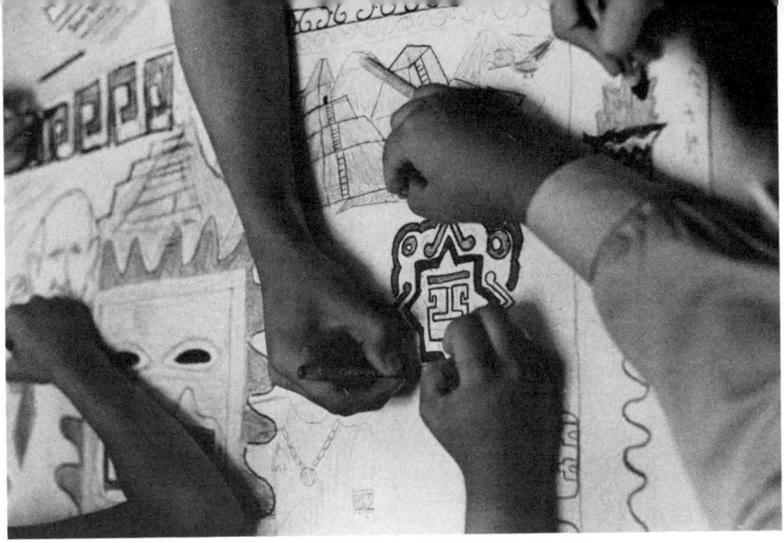

45. Ray Patlán, director: working on the design for *Reforma y Libertad.* 1971. Chicago.

cause it brings out the Mexican and Puerto Rican background and everything—and a lot of newspaper reporters, like the *Sun-Times,* came out and took pictures of it. It was in the *Tribune,* too, and my mother bought a lot of copies and she was showing them to everybody she met."

Although the lack of planning of the first Aztlán wall dictated the limitation of theme to the evocation of the Indian past, using readily available flat patterns, a second wall, *Reforma y Libertad,* painted that same summer, dealt with a wider horizon of Mexican history from Moctezuma to Benito Juárez. In the course of painting, older residents came forward to share their knowledge with the young artists. Many older residents not only remember the ancient monuments and living folk art of Mexico, but have personal knowledge of Mexican revolutionary history, in which they or their relatives were participants. Some days, impromptu seminars were held on the sidewalk; one neighbor held the group spellbound for an entire day recounting lessons from Mexican history.[14]

[14] Details of the story of *Hay Cultura en Nuestra Comunidad* from *Youth* 23, no. 9 (September 1972): 58–66.

46. Ray Patlán, director: *Hay Cultura en Nuestra Comunidad* (process shot). 1971. Chicago.

47. Ray Patlán, director: *Hay Cultura en Nuestra Comunidad* (detail of finished mural). 1971. Chicago.

Planning Process and Design Methods

Hay Cultura is not the only Chicano unplanned mural that has turned out well. In other settings, however, in which the resources of traditional design might be unavailable or inappropriate, such an approach could lead to a disaster of superficiality. Without a context of struggle or stimulus to focus more concretely on their own experience, the first image-ideas participants come up with are invariably those visual clichés borrowed from advertising, record covers, and the always ready-at-hand repertoire of adolescent and preadolescent airplanes, horses, flowers, hearts, mountains and pine trees, sun and moon, the eagle and flag, peace signs and smile buttons, etc. This cliché repertoire is a distant echo of the sentimentalized "American Scene" painting of the past, reduced to a catalogue of mere emblems, and it holds so little credibility, even for those who suggest it, that it is impossible to interest teen-agers in such drivel for more than a few days. Consequently, these emblems are found in raw form only in those "murals" sponsored by middle-class white suburbs that want a safe and quick teen-age project to brighten an underpass or construction fence.

To unlock people's creative energy, it helps to focus early discussions on "who we are, what is our history, what is our experience," rather than on imagery. The leader must listen carefully to identify meaningful themes and to help the participants unfold them. It would be shortsighted not to see that days upon days of informal raps were the prologue and theme preparation for *Hay Cultura.* That the study was about Mexican history was conditioned simply by the setting being a Mexican American neighborhood.

The story of the 1974 mural *Wall of Respect for Women,* directed by Asian artist Tomie Arai of Cityarts Workshop, confirms the importance of the planning process. In conversations with Eva Cockcroft, Arai recalled the many meetings preceding the actual painting of this, her first mural as a director. The mural team consisted of nine working-class women from the Lower East Side, most of them

48. Tomie Arai and Lower East Side women: design session for *Wall of Respect for Women.* 1974. New York.

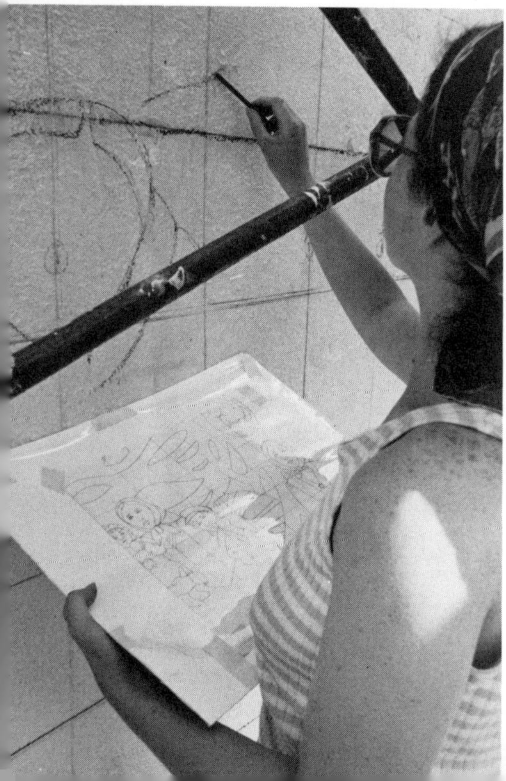

49. Tomie Arai and Lower East Side women: transferring squares, *Wall of Respect for Women.* 1974. New York.

50. Tomie Arai and Lower East Side women: *Wall of Respect for Women* (finished mural). 1974. New York.

under twenty-one and not really sure that women alone could actually do murals. Reflecting the multinational character of the community, the group included Chinese, Italian, Jewish, WASP, Puerto Rican, and black women, most of whom had worked on Cityarts murals before, hung out at the Workshop, or attended the local high school. The underlying motif was that of women's liberation, and the early concept meetings resembled consciousness-raising sessions. The team's first question was: How do we liberate ourselves? No one was very familiar with feminist ideas, but all had a firsthand understanding of women's oppression—in fact, of oppression in general.

Someone suggested better jobs; they could paint women as doctors, lawyers, etc. This idea was rejected; after all, how many girls like them realistically had a chance of ever becoming doctors? Instead, women should be portrayed in the roles they actually lived, historically and today, in the Lower East Side. Unlike some feminists, who sometimes tend to see men as the enemy, these women emphasized the need for unity: of class and of races. They selected images of women in characteristic roles, traced them, and arranged them in the tree design provided by Arai, concluding with the multinational unity configuration at the top of the mural.

The mural was painted on the side of a Manpower office near a busy corner location where groups of unemployed men hang out. The mural team was initially greeted with laughter and derision, including comments like "That's a man's job." But as work progressed, things changed. One of the men who had been making comments earlier, a mason by trade, gave the team advice and helped them cement the wall. Others helped them move the scaffolding each morning and night.

The neighborhood, a mixture of Puerto Rican, Jewish, and Catholic people, identified strongly with the mural down to the smallest detail. One figure was depicted with a Jewish star around her neck. The girl painting the star had problems with the drawing, so the group decided to paint it out. Next day, Jewish women from the neighborhood, who had quietly been watching the mural, came around to ask what had happened to the star and to request that it be put back. It was. Another figure, that of a Puerto Rican, had a cross around her neck, which angered one of the Puerto Rican girls in the team, who pointed out that the Pentecostal church was very popular among Puerto Ricans in the area. Out came the cross. The priest from the Catholic Church around the corner then objected to the removal of the cross, but it was not put back.

The mural was a major event in the block, and all kinds of people sought to have their say. Two very tough black women from the area demanded that the muralists put a gold ring in the nose of the black woman at the top of the mural. When the team refused, the two women threatened them. There followed lengthy discussion within the group about whether they would let themselves be intimidated. The team's black members took a strong stand against this attempt to intimidate them and eventually cooled out the threats.

Low-key politically, the mural succeeded in relating to the women workers who live in the area and in showing women's contributions to the community. Later, the muralists discovered that the location of their *Wall of Respect for Women* had been a historical rallying place for women strikers in the early days of the labor-union movement. It has become such a site again. In 1975, the Lower East Side Women's Coalition of Gouverneur Hospital used the mural as the location for a rally to kick off the International Women's Day march.

Marie Burton is one of today's muralist-teachers whose methods of theme development are applicable in many situations, whether with children, adolescents, or adults. Coauthor of the *Mural Manual,*[15] Burton has painted such excellent murals as *Bored of Education* at Saint Mary's Center for Learning in Chicago and *Celebration of Cultures* at Saint Rose Catholic School in Milwaukee. The following narrative is from her report on *The Wall of Life* at the Child and Family Development Center on Milwaukee's north side:

15 Mark Rogovin, Marie Burton, and Holly Highfill, *Mural Manual,* ed. Tim Drescher (Boston: Beacon Press, 1975).

The implementation of art exercises each morning. The stress was on the positive aspect in the kids' work. Many of the kids felt that their art was "no good."

In order to reinforce this ego-building, we found examples of artists' work that went well with the kind of style a kid already had. We worked hard at introducing them to black artists through slides and books.

In order to give the group more concrete images to work from, they brought their cameras and we blitzed the area with cameras. We got excellent pictures of community life, and these pictures were the best help in the bringing of the group's concept of a children's mural to more maturity.

To follow up on the photographic images, we devised an exercise that proved to be excellent. Using the theme "The Walls Have Tongues," we put the word "communication" on the board. We talked about the significance of the concept of "Word" in the abstract. Word as word is very meaningful. This was difficult but intriguing to the group. We then listed as many "genre" words as we could that related to the camera's eye, the walks and the talks with people in the community. We also continually stressed that the students think about their own feelings—feelings that came to them in any part of the project so far. After this introduction, we then listed the words that were agreed upon:

Brutality	Work	Hopelessness
Mind (spirit)	History	Feeling
Happiness	Understanding	Religion
Love	Family	Education
Greed	Respect	Prejudice
Recreation	Community	Heritage
Suppression	Justice	Pride
Death	Dignity	Security

Really, not much was left out! We asked the group to find images to fit the words for the next session. I then followed this session with a slide presentation showing murals that enhanced every word on the list. This helped all of us to focus

51. Marie Burton, director: dedication for *Celebration of Cultures*. 1975. Milwaukee, Wisconsin.

> concrete images with each word. We then had the group list concrete images from their community to fit the words. This word exercise not only deepened everyone's visual image of their community, but it also gave me an opportunity to give them some history of the great mural artists that have been talking through walls for centuries.[16]

Even without cameras, a walk around the neighborhood helps participants see the reality of their surroundings in a fresh way. Connecting related concept words together in groups and dividing them into contrasting lists of positive and negative can also sharpen the group's focus.

Further steps are the teaching of a sense of mural scale, through large drawings and study of the wall and the combination of ideas

[16] Log for Northside Mural, 2822 North Fifth Street, July 1–August 24, 1974, submitted to Milwaukee Youth Foundation by Marie Burton, unpaged.

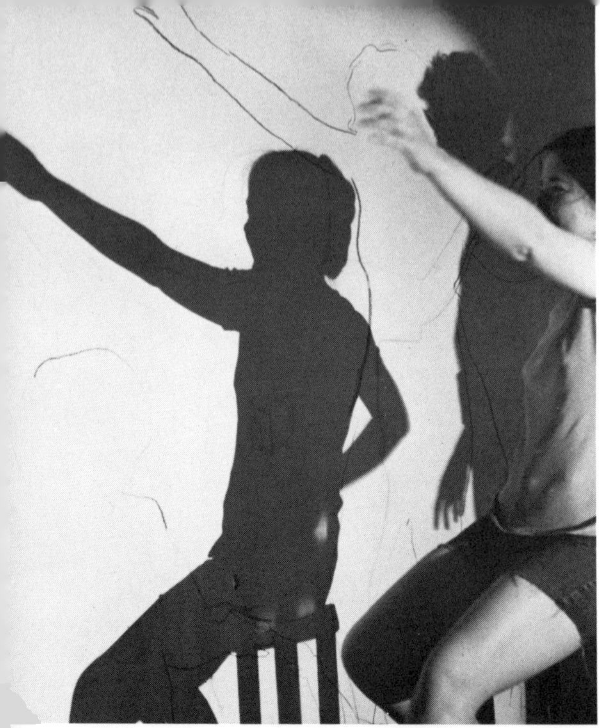

52. Direct-projection technique: posing for a silhouette. 1975. University of North Dakota Center for teaching and learning workshop, led by John Weber. Grand Forks, North Dakota.

53. Direct-projection technique: painting in the silhouettes. 1974. Elmhurst College Union building murals, led by John Weber. Elmhurst, Illinois.

54. John Weber, Oscar Martinez, and team: rhythmic-line technique from design sessions for *Defend the Bill of Rights.* 1973. Chicago.

into a single design. The montage of individual idea drawings is undoubtedly the most widely used group-composition method. It assumes, however, that the participants are able to draw to their own satisfaction. Adolescents are often inhibited by self-critical and self-conscious attitudes.

A number of methods have been developed that permit maximum participation and produce a professional-looking result that gives artistic form to group experience. Obviously, flat styles (including abstract designs) that avoid problems of modeling and perspectives are easier for beginning groups. Cityarts Workshop has pioneered a very flexible and effective method using an opaque projector to abstract and combine photo material and drawings. It allows a free manipulation of scale and placement, leading to very accurate mock-ups (figs. 48 and 49). Mark Rogovin introduced the use of direct silhouette projection, a rapid and simple technique for indoor murals, which allows direct dramatization to replace freehand drawing. Members of the group mime poses in front of a focused light, while other members draw the outlines of the shadow on the wall (or on a large sheet of paper). Shadow silhouettes can also be used as an aid in composing dramatic groups of figures on paper that can later be used as part of the design for an outdoor mural. John Weber helped develop a method using "danced" free rhythmic line as a matrix for imagery. Members of the group take turns drawing sweeping lines on the wall or on wall-size paper. After a network of rhythmic lines has been created, the participants begin to pick out forms, emphasizing certain lines and eliminating others, until a coherent composition begins to emerge (fig. 8). Unless it is possible to spend a number of months in designing, however, much of the design has to be worked out directly on the wall.

These design methods, which are generally effective with adolescents and adults, may be inappropriate for younger children. All children pass through quite distinct style stages in their aesthetic development. Respect for the child demands adapting method to age level. For example, whereas adolescents are attracted by the naturalistic contours that are readily achieved with shadow silhouettes, younger children are unlikely to understand or be satisfied with the irrational qualities of shadows. Most children up to puberty draw what they know rather than what they see.

Children's Murals

Children have participated in many community murals, but real children's murals have also been an integral part of the current upsurge in public art. By "real" children's murals, we mean permanent murals in which a group of children collectively master a theme and a wall, creating a single more or less unified composition. The difference between children's art and that of adults is the type of themes expressed and the mode of representation. For children,

55. David Garlovsky and William Walker, directors: children painting on *Walls of Unity and Truth*. 1971. Phillip Murray School, Chicago.

these are necessarily dependent on the children's stage of growth as developing persons, whereas adult murals more directly reflect the current styles, historical consciousness, and social concerns of the adult culture.

The history of murals by children goes back to the 1930s and the placement of artists in New York City settlement houses by the Public Works of Art Project (PWAP). Thereafter, something called murals never wholly disappeared from the schools, but it usually consisted in highly stereotyped temporary hallway decorations, e.g. a large sheet of paper covered with stenciled turkeys and pumpkins for Thanksgiving. Backdrops for school plays occasionally allowed more meaningful involvement. Real mural work by children was revived as early as the middle 1960s (before the *Wall of Respect*) by Lilli Anne Killen Rosenberg[17] at Henry Street Settlement. Susan Shapiro-Kiok, later founder of Cityarts, and sculptor Pedro Silva participated in the large tile mural at Henry Street Settlement. By the late 1960s, children's murals were being done in a few Philadelphia and New York City public schools, and in San Francisco the Alvarado School–Community Art Program was founded by parents led by Ruth Asawa and Sally Woodbridge. Boston's Summerthing, New York's Summer in the City (Susan Shapiro-Kiok had a hand in that, too), and Harlem Youth Opportunities Unlimited (HARYOU—Pedro Silva, again) gave children a chance to paint outdoors and to help create their own play areas in vest-pocket parks.

The most common form of children's "murals," however, continues to be short-term fence painting (a few days or one weekend). Each child expands a personal image to arm's-reach size, perhaps overflowing into the next child's space. The whole usually lacks any compositional awareness of the wall or collective planning of theme that might properly raise the result to the level of public expression. This sort of activity is appropriate only as a warm-up exercise or for very young children (three to seven years roughly) who have not yet established a compositional-form concept (preschematic stage in art) and whose social sense is not yet developed enough to participate in an extended group experience. It is better done on large sheets or rolls of paper than directly on a wall, since children at this age are engrossed by the process but have little interest in the permanence of the product.

Just as the fence-, trash-can-, and fireplug-painting contests sponsored by various businesses impose competitive values on teenagers, children's quickie fence-painting-type murals reflect a highly distorted view of children's art. Within the regimented school day, the art period has been regarded as a sort of mental recess. Here the embattled self, bombarded by "objective" demands for "performance" the rest of the day, might escape into individual nonsocial "fantasy." This point of view has nothing to do with the real role of

[17] See her book *Children Make Murals and Sculpture* (New York: Reinhold Book Corp., 1968).

imagination in children's learning and in their mastering of reality, but has everything to do with the alienating routines of our schools. From it comes the commonplace distinction of "cognitive" versus "emotive" learning, and the equally commonplace anarchoromantic view of children's art. Although other teachers are called on to browbeat their pupils into conformity, the art teacher supposedly functions as passive appreciator. And since art is thought to be a frill, a purely emotive release, the art teachers have been eliminated in many city elementary school systems. Instead, the classroom teacher teaches what art he or she can shoehorn into the curriculum. In many places, only a vestige survives in formula take-home crafts projects commemorating Columbus's discovery of America or Mother's Day as a way of helping the bankrupt educational system front-off to the parents.

In contrast to art as "recess," creating a collective mural is a process of self-expansion and conquest. The child's image expands not only to arm's-reach size, but to the size of the whole wall. For once, the child is acting on his own environment rather than being acted upon. The social nature of the process, if carefully supported, allows each child to grow, to be valued, and to define himself or herself as a member of the school community or larger community, rather than as an isolated dreamer. The children gain self-respect as they learn to respect the wall, the materials, and each other.

Ruth Felton's narrative about the Miller School mural in Evanston, Illinois, an integrated Chicago suburb, shows the imaginative activity of the children being enriched rather than suppressed by the group.

> A community mural experience is in progress. The site is a 30 by 8 foot wall in the basement lunchroom. Participants are 100 children ages 8 to 10 drawn from among volunteers from five different classrooms. Children paint eight at a time, and about 15 of them spend recess painting as well—they are the regulars.
>
> First, there was talking together, endless conversations, meetings, huddles. . . . Possible themes were developed over 3 to 4 weeks. It takes time to speak and listen. One doesn't dive into a mural.

56. Children and Ruth Felton: Miller School mural. 1975. Evanston, Illinois.

Then began sketches of the verbal ideas that were discussed. Someone suggested a rainbow—they sketch a rainbow; someone wants to sketch mountains; many sketches are developed by all of the participants.

Third, a compromise must be reached on the theme. Sketches are presented and discussed. Certain ideas are brought out as being central, and a theme is reached. Ideas are drawn and redrawn on the wall now, working directly. The steampipes will be part of the rainbow; a door and alcove lead us to extend the mural: a ship with children in it, the racial rainbow.

The acceptance of compromise has to be developed. Realizing that you have more to give than the wall can visually handle is a happy-and-sad awareness for the students. Speaking, listening, and thinking together is a process that reveals to us our depth and wide range of choices. "We-us": I level with the children about our problems at each step of the way, we are feeling our way to this mural together. We must let go of good ideas and use them on other walls in the future.

Teachers have said it is "fantastic" how the project has affected the behavior of the children. The participants care about their wall. Very often a student may direct comments to the wall: "How beautiful you are, how you have changed since last week!" Each day one sees parents, friends from the community, coming in to see the wall. "Did the children do this? is it finished? No, not yet." A critical time is ahead in terms of completion. One has to work toward firming up and developing total color balance.

The mural is jobs for many people: one can do something alone or one can help others. There is a role for the small children and for the older children, as well as teachers, staff, parents: (1) development of ideas in small groups; (2) painting a base coat (color mixing, cleaning brushes); (3) blocking in big shapes; (4) developing inventive or repetitive patterns; (5) reflecting on many things ("problem solving")—how does it look close, far away? should one tie in a column or extend it to another part of the wall? how does the waterfountain tie in? (become a cloud). People play these different roles by turns.

Students initially not interested watch the wall change and others working, and then they too want to become involved. Some start slow and end up spending as much time as they

> can on the wall. More and more people join in. The wall needs everyone, that is why it is a rewarding community experience. It is both for the brash and the shy. There are no drop-outs.[18]

One mural, *The Wall of Influences, As Seen through the Eyes of Children,* executed by more than one hundred students at Florence B. Price Elementary School (Forty-third and Drexel, Chicago) with the assistance of Bill Walker, includes graphic scenes of school life, urban renewal, a liquor store, police harassment, and a protest march. This spillover into related studies—poetry, math (measuring), social studies—is typical of an integrative activity that allows children to cope imaginatively with their world. Another children's mural done with Walker's assistance at Phillip Murray Elementary School (Fifty-fourth and Kimbark, Chicago) dealt with ecology, peace, love, and brotherhood. The mural, Walker says, gave them "the opportunity to express their ideas on social matters in a positive way."[19] David Garlovsky, an environmental-education teacher in District 14, helped the children organize the mural and later create a book about it.

This type of investment by the children cannot be motivated without a purpose beyond decoration or cleanup. In our experience, we find that, regardless of social or cultural circumstances, children choose themes that fall into a small number of categories or combinations. Quite young children will paint about "our neighborhood" (the people in school, on the block) or nature (animals, a jungle, a forest). Children from seven to twelve years of age add the themes of the world (races of mankind, earth in the cosmos) and history (people of another time or place, e.g. colonists and "Indians," a village of ancient Mexico). Each of these types of themes can stimulate group and individual learning. If there is a child who feels a need to paint a dog or a flower, there is room for that in any one of these basic themes. As children approach puberty (and with the influence of television, sometimes much earlier), these themes are

[18] Ruth Felton, Report for ESAA [Emergency School Assistance Act], 1975.

[19] Quoted in Harold Haydon, "The Walls Have Tongues," *PTA Magazine* (March 1973): 16.

transformed by growing social awareness. The neighborhood theme shifts to commentary on social issues and problems (drugs, gangs, housing, etc.). The world theme turns into the theme of peace and brotherhood; the nature theme shifts to emphasize the problem of ecology; and the history theme becomes more focused on national heroes, social justice, and the cultural heritage of the group involved.

These themes are not imposed; they are in the children already. The adult's role is to help the children develop, not to censor or manipulate them. The integrity of the children, the adults, and the learning process is at stake. Harold Haydon recalls that "for Walker . . . this was not a political or social issue, but simply a matter of integrity, of respecting the wishes of the children. At the start of the [Phillip Murray School] project, when a parent said to him, 'I hope there will be no clenched fists' (there are), Walker replied, 'Please do not tell the children what to do.' "[20]

The most interesting children's murals usually grow out of other studies, as a natural extension of them. The story of *Beginnings, A Children's Creation Myth in Clay* shows this organic development. The children, from a racially mixed area of Chicago's Hyde Park, ranged in age from eight to thirteen years. Some had worked on a painted mural the previous year and were now ready for an even deeper involvement.

> The project was conceived last winter, 1972, as part of the in-kind service given by the Art Tillers, a community arts workshop, to the First Unitarian Church, in exchange for space and maintenance services. It grew out of a study of creation myths from many cultures, including the study of the Babylonian myth *Gilgamesh.* The elementary school children of the church, working with Kathie Judge, wrote their own stories of the beginning of the world. This collective story became the basis for the imagery of the ceramic mural. The children made mural-size drawings, combining them around a basic scheme of trees and sun. The next step was preparing the clay panels—over a ton

[20] *Ibid.*

57. Children with Kathie Judge: *Beginnings, A Children's Creation Myth in Clay* (detail). 1973. Chicago.

of clay was used, divided into five great slabs on wooden frames.

The designs were created by pounding, squeezing, modeling, cutting, pressing textures, etc.—an eight-foot crocodile and tiny bugs. Technical as well as design inventions were made. The children carved figures into plaster cylinders (reminiscent of Babylonian cylinder seals) to press raised figures and animals into the Aztec-calendar-like great disc of the Sun, in the center of the mural. The slabs were cut into small sections to avoid warping and cracking in the long drying and firing process. The 528 pieces were fired twice for bisque and glaze. Again

> great inventiveness was shown in the glazing—broken colored glass, marbles, etc. were used to create vitreous pools. The project took almost 9 months to complete, but the young artists never lost interest. When one section exploded in firing, the children matter-of-factly set about redoing it. The mural was finally mounted piece by piece on the wall of a sunken garden courtyard, using a special epoxy cement and angle iron support. It was dedicated in June 1973.[21]

Murals such as *Beginnings* need no apology for being "children's art." They hold their own quite well next to the best. A ceramic mural is an ambitious undertaking, but it is a fact that quite a few children's murals, including several of the best, have been done in ceramic, cast cement, tile, mixed mosaic or even Venetian-glass mosaic, whereas very few adult community murals have been undertaken in such permanent media. Media like mosaic and ceramic call for a certain stylization that lends itself to a child's sense of design and texture. They allow children to work directly with their hands. Difficulties of execution seem to inspire rather than discourage children, once they are well started. The dignity of the medium, combined with the children's sense of craft, elevates the result beyond the casual aspect of most children's painting.

Permanence is of great importance to the intermediate age group—third through eighth grades. The permanence of the result proves to both children and adults that the work is fully, not conditionally, accepted. The children respond to the implied responsibility of permanent work by surpassing themselves. In Rosenberg's words, "Children value themselves as they experience, in turn, our value of them."[22] They extend this respect to the work of their contemporaries as well. In 1973, Harold Haydon was able to report of the Price School mural: "The mural itself remains unmarked, although other walls of the school have been written on and painted over repeatedly since 1971.[23] The beautiful Gaudiesque mosaic

[21] Chicago Mural Group Report to National Endowment for the Arts, 1973.
[22] Rosenberg, *Children Make Murals and Sculpture*, p. 131.
[23] Haydon, "The Walls Have Tongues," p. 15.

benches surrounding Grant's Tomb in New York City were, in fact, commissioned by the National Parks Service in order to combat defacement of the monument. Directed by Pedro Silva of Cityarts Workshop, the benches were executed by 2,500 children, teen-agers, and adults over a three-year period (pl. 13).[24] Indoors, of course, paint can (with luck) last as long as the plaster does; and if a school mural lasts past the graduation of all its participants, it is permanent for all intents and purposes.

Mural painting has attracted an increasing number of teachers, but it is easy to see why such time-consuming projects have often met with resistance from school administrations. Permission must be obtained from the board, the district superintendent, the principal, and the engineer, all of whom are apprehensive about a process of unknown result that breaks down their accustomed categories of self-enclosed classrooms, of teachers versus students, of school versus community. It is easy to see why most children's murals have been done outside the public school situation. In Chicago, Barry Bruner's students at Calumet High School did four successful murals outside (for the YMCA and a local church) before they were permitted to paint inside. Esther Charbit, chairperson of Lakeview High School art department, directed two portable murals and two murals on community walls, before she was given permission to use class time for a mural in honor of the school's centennial.

Since in elementary schools there is little budgeted to support even scheduled art activities, a mural project must almost always be initiated and led by an outside specialist or parent volunteers. Parent involvement is the critical factor in solving the problem of obtaining materials and in breaking through the immobility of cautious administrators. Although occasionally a specialist may be supported by a grant, or made available through a federally funded artist-in-the-schools program, the activity will have no sequel unless parents organize to support it and carry it forward.

San Francisco's Alvarado School–Community Art Program is an

[24] Also participating were artists Phillip Danzig, Nelson Mercado, Alan Okada, and Moshe Shaw.

outstanding example of how parents can enrich the public school curriculum and environment with community-based arts and crafts. Initiated and sustained by parents, the program won the support of teachers and staff (and eventually the board of education). It has spread from two schools in 1968, to fourteen in 1973, and to many more since then. In addition to murals, it has provided experiences in ethnic cooking, gardening, puppets, Tai Chi Chuan, and a long list of other activities adapted to the parent resources, ethnic makeup, or special requests of each school. The murals, however, have been a focal point, and are currently being used as catalysts for the development of similar school-community art programs elsewhere.

58. Alvarado School–Community Art Program: ceramic art project. James Lick Junior High School, San Francisco.

6

The Chicago Mural Group by John Weber

There is no way to explain in words why we in the Chicago Mural Group paint murals. But meeting people outdoors on the street to talk about the richness of human experience and history is ONE very important part of it. To be complimented by hard working and righteous people, rather than gallery owners and the hoi polloi, is for me another crucial part of why I paint murals—murals about the lives and experiences of real people.

—Jim Yanagisawa.

Founded in 1970 by William Walker and myself, the Chicago Mural Group (CMG) is a cooperative with a dozen members—black, Latin, Asian, and white; both men and women—dedicated to meaningful public art in Chicago's neighborhoods. Its programs function under the auspices of the Community Arts Foundation (CAF), a nonprofit organization that also accommodates various community and experimental theatre groups. CMG gives equal weight to professionalism and community involvement. Each of CMG's more than fifty outdoor murals and two dozen indoor murals has been locally sponsored. CMG receives funding from the National En-

59. CMG artists (Caryl Yasko, Mitchell Caton, Justine DeVan, Celia Radek, Lucyna Radycki, Joseph Pajkos): *Prescription for Good Health Care*. 1975. Chicago.

dowment for the Arts (NEA) Visual Arts Program and various local foundations. Members of neighborhood organizations and other local residents and youths contribute to the development of themes and often participate in painting. The group has organized photo-documentary exhibits on mural art and has given seminars, workshop courses, and innumerable slide shows for community audiences. It maintains a workshop–information center in CAF's "Body Politic" building.

In the late fall 1974, William Walker left the group to form his own program. At the time of this writing (1975), members of the group include myself, Mitchell Caton, Ray Patlán, Caryl Yasko, Barry Bruner, Jim Yanagisawa, Santi Isrowuthakul, Astrid Fuller, Esther Charbit, Oscar Martinez, José Guerrero, Amit Ray, and Justine DeVan.[1] The following account reflects on the reasons for the group's vitality and longevity, as well as its chronic internal problems.

[1] Other artists who have worked with the group include Lucyna Radycki, Don Pellett, Eugene Eda, Albert Zeno, John Robinson, Kathie Judge, Louis Boyd, John Allen, Doug Williams, Ron Blackburn, Ruth Felton, George Lee, Anne Sevaglio; young artists Steve Stahl, Celia Radek, Beth Shadur, Vanita Green, Dalton Brown, Turtle Onli, Yolanda Galvan, Carlos Barrera, Patti Hesse, Renée Majeune; and numerous nonprofessional neighborhood artists.

Early History

It was the *Wall of Respect,* which I first saw in 1968, that made me think of walls. I had participated in artists' contingents at demonstrations and in antiwar art shows with a mounting sense of frustration. The following summer, 1969, with the encouragement of Brother Joachim of Saint Dominic's Church in Cabrini-Green, I painted a mural in the church courtyard together with a group of teen-agers. It was a simple declarative statement on a low retaining wall: *All Power to the People.* I was excited about the possibilities of large-scale mural work.

Characteristically for someone practiced in completing scholarship forms, a veteran of social programs such as More Encouragement and Push-Up, I wrote articles and proposals. I drafted a proposal for a community-based mural project in three low-income North Side neighborhoods, which called for "collective mural painting to be done by teen-age youth from economically deprived and culturally excluded communities with the direction, encouragement, and participation of young professional artists."

In late spring 1970, Margaret Burroughs, founder of the DuSable Museum of African-American History, put me in touch with Bill Walker, and Walker asked Eugene Eda to come from Washington, D.C., to join us. Financial problems limited what we could do. With less than one fourth of the funds originally requested in our proposal, only Walker, Eda, and myself could be paid. We received no monies until late July—a pattern to be repeated every summer, causing us anxiety and delays. Consequently, there were no paid assistants as foreseen in the proposal and no true collective murals, although we did provide paint for a number of satellite murals, and community involvement was active and real. Our experience led to the conclusion that large-scale projects involving the commitment of scaffolding could only be done on a full-time basis, implying the continued necessity of outside funding.

Nonetheless, we concluded our season in high spirits, with feelings of mutual solidarity, commitment, and confidence. We were inspired by a larger vision of mural art and a high sense of our responsibility as public artists. Before us opened the vista of an independent "people's art," challenging the gallery art world and challenging us to equal and surpass the Mexicans. In November, Joseph Shapiro of the Museum of Contemporary Art, Chicago, approached us with a proposal for an exhibit in the museum's lower gallery during which the public could watch us paint on panels. Mark Rogovin joined us, playing an important role in the negotiations and relations with the press. Mitchell Caton also participated. Much to Shapiro's surprise, the artists were more concerned about their standing with the community audience than with the "unparalleled opportunity" he was offering. We were equally concerned that the middle-class art public not be merely entertained by a novelty without ever seeking out the murals in the neighborhoods. We obtained the publication of a manifesto (*The Artists' Statement*) and a directory of murals, two thousand free tickets for distribution by community organizations, permission to hold a forum on public art in evening hours, as well as all supplies and the right to donate our panel murals to community organizations of our choice.

At the end of the show, which had run during February and March 1971, Rogovin went his own way, already deeply involved in efforts to create the Public Arts Workshop (PAW). Walker, Eda, Caton, and I continued meetings concerning a proposal Walker originated for giant murals in the Robert Taylor housing project. Eda gradually drifted away. The museum panels he had done for Olivet Church went unmounted, and he later withdrew from the group to pursue his personal development.

All of this winter activity, including Walker's two murals with children that spring, was considered separate from the CAF Community Mural Project summer program. Not yet a cooperative group, we were a fragile, seasonal *ad hoc* coalition. During July 1971, while I was deeply involved painting murals in Westtown and in despair of long-delayed funding, I lost touch with the other artists. When Caton and Walker called us together in the second week of August, it was the first meeting of the Community Mural Project as such.

Much was accomplished that second summer: Nine murals were painted, some of them team murals; a pattern of materials and equipment being paid for locally was established; Ray Patlán joined the staff; the first seminars and tours for residents of mural neighborhoods were held. But we also encountered fundamental problems with which the group would struggle periodically from then on. These were the contradictions between three tendencies: the self-reliant local autonomy of each artist in his area; centralized administrative decisions concerning funding, at that time basically in my hands; and our cooperative ideals. With five artists scattered on the North and South sides, the difficulties of communication and planning had outgrown the possibilities of informal visiting and consulting. The administrative work—proposals, reports, photography, publicity—was an intolerable burden for one person. At the same time, it created an irritating situation of dependence for the other artists, isolating us from one another and holding back our development. We had to become a group. In a series of meetings that followed from September into the winter of 1971/72, we hammered out a basic program. Bit by bit, in response to specific problems, we clarified our aims and program, preparing for a leap forward the following summer.

During the summer of 1972, the group expanded to its maximum limits, including women and Asian artists. Walker brought Caryl Yasko into the group. Astrid Fuller was one of Caryl's volunteer assistants. Jim Yanagisawa worked with George Lee on the first Chinatown mural. Ray Patlán introduced us to his 1971 assistant, Santi Isrowuthakul. Isrowuthakul, a Thai national studying at the Art Institute, worked as my assistant in Central Lakeview along with Barry Bruner. He then directed two murals with Steve Stahl. With his extraordinary adaptability, which enabled him to work with every different ethnic group and age level, and his delight in the

60. Santi Isrowuthakul at work, 1972.

social activity of murals, Isrowuthakul brought several other student artists into mural painting.

Throughout the summer of 1972 and into the fall we had regular business meetings in this expanded group—"veterans" and "beginners," volunteer apprentices, and student artists. We examined what we had been doing in a scattered, spontaneous way and realized that in effect we were involved in year-round activity—in the communities, in the schools, in planning and preparation for the summer, in educating the public, as well as in actual painting. We made some modest attempts to share administrative work. For the first time, we took a name, the Chicago Mural Movement Group (later shortened), which was distinct from our federally funded summer program (the Community Mural Project). We held our first retrospective exhibit at the South Side Community Art Center in November.

The summer of 1972, our third season, ends the early history of the group. Since then, although other artists have joined and a few have left, the size of the group has remained roughly constant. Its organization and programs have developed along the lines already suggested. We have built up our workshop center (which opened in June 1973), experimented with various approaches to training young artists, and worked in the schools. Kathie Judge was our first workshop coordinator, succeeded by Caryl Yasko, who also took over coordinating administration in 1974. For funding purposes, summer activity was divided into South Side and North Side projects in 1973. Since 1972 we have been consolidating and stabilizing, learning from one another and raising our level of work.

A Neighborhood-based, Community-sponsored Group

Local sponsorship means local control. The artist is accountable to the local sponsors in a far more direct way than to any outside funding, because it is the local sponsors who supply the absolute essentials: the walls, the paint, and the equipment. The necessity of raising funds locally makes the muralist an organizer, with a certain margin of initiative and possibilities for choosing one's own situation. We have made it a policy to refuse commercial work, "pizza-parlor murals," and contests. The only purpose of a competition is to place the choice of design safely in the hands of a select few: owners or bureaucrats. We insist on a relationship of mutual trust and respect. Control of the theme must rest with grass-roots people, whether the membership of a sponsoring organization or a designated group (teen-agers, etc.), and control of design must rest with the artists (to be worked out in dialogue between the artists and the community).

Consequently, our themes have dealt with aspirations of the oppressed; with unity (in multinational areas especially); with community concerns about housing, health, drug abuse; and with ethnic and labor history. We have rarely been able to deal with international themes directly and explicitly, whether the Vietnam war or

61. John Weber and team: dedication for *People of Lakeview Unite*. 1972. Chicago.

62. Caryl Yasko, Celia Radek, Lucyna Radycki, Justine DeVan, Jon Kokot, and community helpers: dedication for *Razem* ("Together"). 1975. Chicago.

African liberation. On the other hand, local sponsorship has been a bulwark against outside forms of censorship, since the community sponsor assumes public responsibility for a mural's content. We have been very aware of this as a strength when confronted by local police, cranks, or racists. In practice, the artists and their teams have great latitude in interpreting chosen community themes, while the accountability to local sponsors has made it possible to work in almost every type of urban area (pl. 18).

Local sponsorship has necessarily put limitations on large-scale work and work in permanent media. It is rarely possible to raise more than a few hundred dollars in cash in any one working-class area; the rest is made up in donated materials and volunteer help. Corresponding to the spread and scale of Chicago neighborhoods, we have done numerous medium-size walls, but only a few two thousand square feet or more. Much of our winter activity—slide shows, exhibits, maintaining our center—is directed toward broadening our public base. Our training seminars and workshops for student artists and teachers are also part of this base-building activity.

Autonomy of the Artist

Winter activities, largely unfunded and carried on part time, have never engaged the energies of the whole group. The relationship of these winter activities to our basic summer program has been fairly loose, and sometimes questioned by nonparticipating members. Such autonomy of initiative and allowance for individual variance has allowed a large, multiethnic group to continue together with only seasonal funding, but it has also made our existence as a group extremely precarious.

Reflecting our recognition of the need for artist autonomy, our approaches have ranged from individually designed and executed "signature" murals, to directed team murals, to collective children's murals. Walker and I brought complementary conceptions to the group—I that of the artist as organizer and facilitator, he that of the artist as prophet and professional muralist. Over the years, a certain interchange and mutual learning between these conceptions has taken place. Walker made it a practice of working alone during the summer. Nonetheless, in 1972–73 he proposed collective projects following the pattern of the first Chicago and Detroit walls: large horizontal walls divided up into sections, each artist doing one or more sections, the whole to be united by a common theme and perhaps a common color scheme. In 1975, he worked with Mitchell Caton and Santi Isrowuthakul on an antidrug mural of this type. From time to time, Walker devoted himself to assisting and advising other group members. Caton and Astrid Fuller have also emphasized individual work, although Caton has occasionally done joint projects, has allowed children to contribute to his work, and has regularly included poems by Siddha and photographs by Bobby Sengestacke in his murals.

At the other extreme, Ray Patlán, Barry Bruner, Esther Charbit, and Justine DeVan (the last three are art teachers) have tended to see themselves as facilitators of the collective expression of young people. Patlán has designed his individual murals only indoors, leading collective projects outdoors. The Asian and Latin members of the group have been the most active in collaborative murals. In their Asian-Latin mural, Jim Yanagisawa and Oscar Martinez, instead of relying on visual clichés, researched the parallels of the labor history and immigrant experience of both peoples, working together on the drawing and painting for both sides of the two-piece mural. Caryl Yasko and I, also advocating collective and collaborative work, usually work with teams of local residents or mixed student-resident teams and give very strong direction to the design of team murals, ensuring a highly unified look to the result. The presence of this diversity of approaches has allowed the artists of our group to vary their methods from one project to another, according to circumstances and personal needs, without any feelings of guilt about violating a set program.

63. James Yanagisawa and Oscar Martinez: Asian-Latin mural (detail). 1974. Chicago.

Learning

Another major concern of CMG, again a concern shared with other muralists in Chicago, has been with *becoming* muralists. This interest in mastering the lessons of the great tradition and in developing a contemporary aesthetic that reflects a specifically mural character is perhaps nowhere stronger than in Chicago, and is in particularly marked contrast to the attitudes of urban decorators working on a commission basis.[2] Direct work on the wall has been the most important source of learning for us, and is almost a cult among Chicago muralists.

[2] Interesting precedents for our attitudes may be found in the anthology by Francis V. O'Connor, *Art for the Millions* (Greenwich, Conn.: New York Graphic Society, 1973). See, for example, the pieces by Mitchel Siporin, "Mural Art and the Midwestern Myth" (p. 64), and Edgar Britton, "A Muralist Speaks His Mind" (p. 67).

Awareness of the mural tradition entered the Chicago movement from several sources. Bill Walker's affinity to Diego Rivera is both profound and conscious. Eugene Eda's early work shows a certain influence of José Clemente Orozco, together with African influences. I first saw Antonio Rodriguez's *A History of Mexican Mural Painting*[3] at a meeting in Eda's room upstairs in the old DuSable Museum in the fall of 1970. CMG members have had regular contact with Mexico. Patlán visits Mexico every year, and met the "maestro" in 1971. I visited Siqueiros the following year. In 1974, Patlán met with Chávez Morado. In 1975, through the exchange program of Movimiento Artistico Chicano (MARCH), Gilberto Ramírez of the younger generation of Mexican figurative muralists visited Chicago. It must be said that, despite the great fund of technical knowledge in Mexico, the movement of ideas is now primarily from the United States, where mural painting is much more active.

Mexico has not been the only source of design approaches in Chicago. I brought an interest in Fernand Léger to my early murals. Jim Yanagisawa's work reflects his interest in caricature and photomontage. Mitchell Caton's work is a unique combination of surrealism, decorative cubism, and African design elements. Popular "movement" posters have also been source material for many of the artists.

Concern for aesthetic development has led to an increasing emphasis on *realization* among all of us. Increasing mastery has been seen in successful use of wall shapes, incorporation of architectural accident, and more painterly execution. The process of learning from and with each other has been continuous, not primarily through slide-critique sessions held occasionally in the winter, but through informal visits to each other's murals in progress, on-the-site discussions, and many collaborative projects. We have placed increasing emphasis on collaboration since 1972 and are now again discussing the possibilities of whole-group collaborative murals and mural brigades.

Much learning has been exchanged between muralists within the

3 (New York: G. P. Putnam's Sons, 1969).

64. Mitchell Caton. *Philosophy of the Spiritual.* 1972. Chicago.

United States. Muralists and other artists in Chicago, New York City, and Boston periodically meet or correspond. In 1971, I met Susan Shapiro-Kiok of Cityarts Workshop. Since then, artists from CMG and Cityarts have engaged in a fairly regular dialogue and have learned new techniques from one another. Despite moments of tension, we have had a fairly regular interchange with Mark Rogovin's Public Art Workshop as well, exchanging slides, information, and Mexican contacts. In April 1975, we joined with PAW in a mural festival honoring the new edition of the *Mural Manual.* In certain murals, I have adapted both Rogovin's projected-silhouette method and the graphic style brought back from Chile by Eva Cockcroft. We have had sporadic contacts with the West Coast and various other cities. All these exchanges have been part of an expanding network of contacts between muralists and mural groups around the country.

Policy

The structure of CMG corresponds to a clearly understood need for mutual support and a united front in the face of various pressures, a need to minimize competition and individual careerism and to develop common strategies. The central funding of the summer program has allowed the artists to control their own projects, determining commitments and priorities subject only to the limits of ingenuity and energy in raising matching funds. Artist control has always been an essential: We have never had any nonartist administrators.

The prerequisite for membership has been prior mural experience. Walker, Eda, Caton, Patlán, and myself had all painted murals independently before 1970. Virtually all other members have been brought into the group under the sponsorship of one or more members after having worked on at least one mural without stipend. The intention of this requirement is to avoid placing the group in the position of a funding agency open to outside proposals and to eliminate those merely seeking a job. Since 1972, this requirement of at least one mural done on a volunteer basis has generally been understood to mean working with the CMG as an unpaid assistant. This apprenticeship has given new artists a chance to become familiar with both community organizing and mural scale, materials, and equipment without bearing the burden of full responsibility. In the few cases where we have waived this apprenticeship, bowing to the inflated egos of young artists, near disasters or poor-quality work have resulted. Our apprenticeship policy has allowed a wide variety of artists to enter mural painting without regard to degrees or gallery recognition, including self-taught artists, art teachers, art students, graphic artists, and ceramists. However, the demand that the apprenticeship be unpaid puts an unequal burden on unemployed artists and may discourage certain others—in particular, nonwhite or working-class artists. For this reason, CMG has, when resources allowed, provided small stipends.

Our group could be described as a task-oriented cooperative. There has been little discussion of general politics in meetings but a great deal of discussion about practical problems (including political ones) arising in our work. Issues have been struggled through as they arose in the life of the group. From the beginning, the group has had a fairly clear "serve the people" philosophy. The general tone of the group and its multiracial character have placed certain demands on all members. From the outset, we committed ourselves to being based in oppressed and working-class neighborhoods. We emphasized working with the people and winning their support, rather than doing art for them in a missionary spirit. The group demanded that its members do murals with readable themes, create an art that brings consciousness to the people, oppose all oppression, and champion the necessity of all people uniting. In a few cases, artists have left the group in part because of what they felt was pressure from the "heavy" political atmosphere and the emphasis on "struggle" and "relating to community problems."

Problems and Contradictions

Contradictions and problems were built into our group from the outset. Being multinational, we had to deal with differences of language, expectations, and cultural context. The geographic spread of our work created further problems of communication. Lack of transportation reduced visiting. For example, on the South Side, the Chinatown and Pilsen (Chicano) projects tended to remain isolated from the rest of the South Side artists, both black and white. Despite these problems, the multinational character of the group has been a point of pride for all of us and one of the main reasons artists have joined and stayed with the group. The strength of our feeling about being multinational has been reflected in the frequency of multiethnic themes in our work.

There is little doubt that our size, multiracial character, and geographic spread have been severe handicaps in obtaining funding.

Certain foundations have rejected our proposals because they involved more than one neighborhood. We do not fit their guidelines. Remaining together has also put a limit on the federal funds available to us. One result has been our inability to pay assistants or to maintain a core group on stipend more than a few months each year. Each artist in the group has also paid a price in criticism received from other artists of their own community or nationality. Nonetheless, the group has rejected all suggestions that we split up in order to develop single-neighborhood or single-nationality groups.

The recurrent tensions between de facto centralization of administrative decisions, the local autonomy of the artists, and our collective decision making on policy are not unrelated to our heterogeneous character. In practice, the group has been neither a paid-staff program nor a purely voluntary coalition, but both simultaneously, displaying the strengths and weaknesses of each. Until the summer of 1975, the group never designated any official leadership or spokespersons. Moral leadership was exercised by senior members, who initiated and led most of the major internal struggles for unity. Without an elected leadership with clear authority, however, the pressures of day-to-day business and survival continually tended to erode unity. We alternated between attempting to deal with day-to-day administration in whole-group meetings or leaving it in the hands of one or two people—again without any official mandate or provision of salary for administrative work.

Our lack of structure and emphasis on local autonomy encouraged tendencies to regard CMG as a source of funding rather than as a membership group. Certain artists attended meetings sporadically and only during our summer grant period. Artists neglected to mention membership in the group in their community work in order to avoid explanations. Since our policy was to put emphasis on the local community, promoting each mural as the accomplishment of the artist and local sponsor only, we maintained such a low profile that until our first retrospective show few outside of our immediate circles even knew the group existed or who its members were.

Beginning early in 1972, Bill Walker led an extended struggle for unity and greater definition that proved crucial to our later growth and survival. We decided that all artists were to credit the group, CAF, and the sponsors on each wall and were always to identify themselves as CMG members. Newspaper stories had precipitated this struggle, which also taught us important lessons about the media: to exercise care, but also to take it with a pinch of salt. The media's orientation to events and personalities builds in a tendency to promote "stars," to seek invidious comparisons. A failure to discount for this can easily destroy any group.

At the same time, the limits of our unity were defined by another decision concerning relations with the media. We affirmed, on the one hand, that rights in the murals belong to each artist individually and to the community sponsors and, on the other hand, that permissions for publication of photos should be sought. To enforce this, we began copyrighting our murals in 1972. The purpose of copyright is to check potential abuses, not to hinder the working press. Copyright gives us legal protection to ensure that correct credits are given, and enables us to negotiate with publishers for either contributions toward future murals or for numbers of complimentary copies for distribution in the community. In practice, however, the necessity of contacting each artist separately makes this system difficult to maintain.

Inequalities in Funding

Our stipends have been low compared to "professional" standards—less than half the union rate for house painters—but nonetheless high compared to the flat fees prevalent on the West Coast (excluding the commissioned work such as that of the Los Angeles Fine Arts Squad). Before 1970, Bill Walker and Eugene Eda had worked on a basis of equal shares. However, as soon as the artists were involved in separate projects of varying size, this could no

1. Twenty-one black artists: *Wall of Respect* (partial view). 1967; destroyed 1971. Originally at 43rd and Langley, Chicago.

2. Sharon Dunn: *Black Women.* 1970. Yarmouth and Columbus Avenue, Boston.

3. Dana C. Chandler, Jr. (Akin Duro): *Education Is Power.* 1972. Dudley Station, Boston.

4. Mitchell Caton: *Rip Off (Universal Alley).* 1970; renovated 1974. Fiftieth between Champlain and St. Lawrence, Chicago.

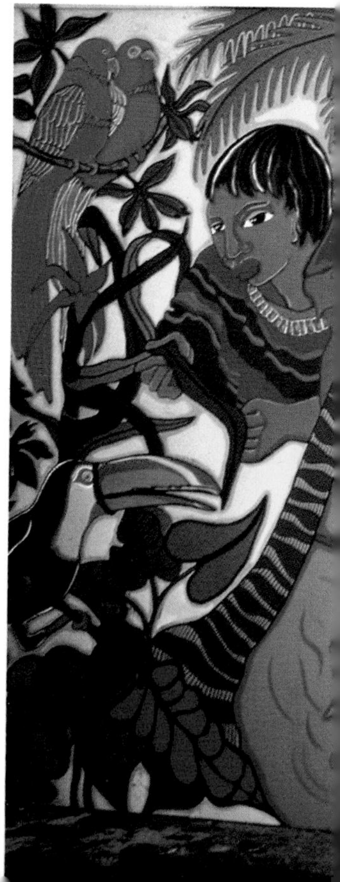

5. Ray Patlán: *Salón de la Raza* (detail). 1970. 1831 South Racine, Chicago.

6. Mujeres Muralistas: (Consuelo Méndez and others): *Para el Mercado* (detail). 1974. Twenty-fourth and Van Ness, San Francisco.

7. William F. Herrón, Jr.: *My Life in the Projects* (detail). 1973. Ramona Gardens Recreation Room, Los Angeles.

8. Hoyo-Mara gang: *Unity Among Young Chicanos* (detail). 1974. Los Angeles.

9. William Walker: *Peace and Salvation, Wall of Understanding*. 1970. Locust and Orleans, Chicago.

10. John Weber, director: *Unidos para Triunfar*. 1971, 1974. Division and Hoyne streets, Chicago.

11. James Jannuzzi and Susan Caruso-Green, directors: *Arise from Oppression*. 1972. Corner Grand and Pitt streets, New York.

12. Alan Okada, director: *Chi Lai—Arriba—Rise Up!* 1974. Madison Street between Pike and Rutgers, New York.

13. Pedro Silva, director: *Grant's Tomb Centennial Bench*. 1972–74. Riverside Drive and 123rd Street, New York.

14. People's Painters: *Imperialism* (detail). 1973. Livingston College, Piscataway, New Jersey.

15. Artes Guadalupanos de Aztlán: Las Vegas High School mural (detail). 1973. Las Vegas, New Mexico.

16. Artes Guadalupanos de Aztlán: *Huitzitlopochtli.* 1973. New Clínica de la Gente, Santa Fe, New Mexico.

17. Mujeres Muralistas (Patricia Rodríguez, Consuelo Méndez, Irene Pérez, and others): *Latinoamérica*. 1974. Mission between 25th and 26th, San Francisco.

18. Caryl Yasko with Celia Radek, Lucyna Radycki, Justine DeVan, Jon Kokot, and community helpers: *Razem* ("Together"). 1975. 4040 West Belmont, Chicago.

19. John Weber and Celia Radek: *The Builders.* 1975. 2834 North Ashland Avenue, Chicago.

20. Ray Patlán, Vicente Mendoza, and José Nario: *History of Mexican American Workers* (detail). 1974–75. Blue Island, Illinois.

longer be maintained. Our solution was to provide a per-month or per-week stipend spread over the time necessary to complete each mural. This, of course, raised other problems, since some artists work faster than others and some walls and designs are inherently more difficult. Our solution, under austere conditions, was to try to set a very high standard of productivity (two hundred square feet per week), to demand total commitment (sixty-hour weeks), and to provide stipends only during actual work time and not during preparation time.

Expanding our group in 1972 led to various attempts to stretch funds. As new artists joined, a further inequality was introduced. New members received only half stipend in their first or second years with the group. Since our federal funding had to be matched, this practice of keeping pay low on certain murals made up for the inability to match funds spent on full stipends elsewhere. Thus, the funds to provide full pay for some depended on others getting half pay. At meetings in late spring 1975, these problems were fully aired for the first time. Our new policy will be an equal rate for equal work time for all members, with a pool left over to pay assistants or extend time in special cases. The new policy of equal pay has the support of all of us, but it will demand that all of us work faster, collaborate more, and work much harder at local and group fund raising.

Perspectives

Our early concept of the group as uniting all the active mural forces had to be abandoned as the movement continued to expand and as we reached the practical limits of our own expansion. Nonetheless, there has been a recurrent tendency to overestimate our forces, to spread ourselves thin in attempting to meet the demand for mural-art education from the schools and the general public.

Some members opposed this overextension, putting forward the concept of the group as exemplary rather than comprehensive. They demanded that we concentrate on raising the technical and aesthetic level of the group to eliminate the internal division between "old hands" and the beginners. Overall, the last two years have accomplished some of this needed consolidation. Part of this process has been a shift away from spontaneous immediacy and toward muralism as a fine art, an evolution that has mirrored changes in the character of community struggles, especially in the black community. This necessary process of maturation raises new questions concerning the future.

As the gap between veterans and beginners has been closed, the consciousness of the group has evolved, leading some members to call for the writing of a new manifesto. Latin, Asian, and women members have played an important role in these changes. Within our group, men had often dominated discussion. The difficulty of changing traditional male attitudes was probably an element in Kathie Judge's decision to leave the group. Women are now playing leading roles and are actively promoting murals on women's history. Asian and Latin artists have helped broaden the group's perspective on struggles against national oppression, educating the group to see the links between democratic struggles here and anticolonial struggles in Asia and Latin America. An internationalist perspective has begun to replace narrow localisms or the idea of a coalition of nationalisms.

An additional key point emerged in early 1974. At the time, Bill Walker was studying labor history in preparation for his Packinghouse mural (for the Amalgamated Meatcutters Union). José Guerrero and I had been painting at the United Electrical, Radio and Machine Workers of America Hall for almost a year (figs. 89 and 92). In a dramatic meeting, we discussed the central importance of the labor struggle and resolved to orient our work more clearly to the working people. Despite most of our activity being in working-class areas, we had conceptualized the unity of the people under the vague term *poor and oppressed.* Now we began to examine the common experience of a *class* (pl. 19).

Walker's leaving the group was a severe blow. At first, it seemed as if he had left a gap that would never be filled. In retrospect, I can see that it was perhaps a natural progression for him. Since 1972, he had secured his own funding for a series of long-term projects beyond the scope of our summer program. Increasingly, he felt a need to work many months on each mural and to concentrate on his own work. Although he continued his teaching role in the group, he was, I believe, reluctant to immerse himself once again in the emotional internal struggles that would be necessary for our group to survive into the new period.

His departure left many questions unresolved. Walker's moral prestige had seemed to ensure our link to the beginnings of the movement, and to strengthen the CMG commitment to multinational work. In a series of discussions, as well as in our practice, we have strongly reaffirmed our multinational character. To maintain our commitment to the inner city in the face of cutbacks and economic crisis, and, on the other hand, the growing popularity of murals in middle-class areas, we shall have to swim against the tide

65. John Weber and Celia Radek: design for *The Builders*. 1975. Chicago.

and maintain the greatest clarity of purpose. We have had to rethink the problems of collective leadership. Certainly the establishment of equal pay is a step forward, but it does not by itself guarantee unity. The sharing of administration and the relationship between summer and winter programs, between professional mural painting and facilitative-educational work, will have to be worked out in practice. Hopefully, the new steering committee will play an important role in resolving these problems, but it will only be possible if a higher level of commitment inspires our practical work.

The life of the Chicago Mural Group has progressed through continuous struggle for definition and unity. It is essential that we understand that even leading members may, for whatever combination of reasons, decide that participation in a group—with its intense demands, chronic centrifugal tendencies, and recurrent need to reaffirm basic orientations—no longer meets their own needs for development. A greater danger, I believe, is the possibility that CMG will stabilize itself by becoming a closed guild, unable to elicit and absorb new energies and unable to respond with immediacy to unforeseen events and changing social and political conditions. Art groups are notoriously fragile—few groups last as long as one or two years—but entering its sixth year, CMG is getting a second wind.

7

Cityarts Workshop: Out of the Gallery and into the Streets by Susan Shapiro-Kiok

In 1968 I was given the opportunity to develop a creative-arts workshop in a low-income community on New York's Lower East Side. I accepted this offer with apprehension, because I knew from experience how difficult it would be to make art relevant for this community.

I had first come to the Lower East Side in 1962 as a pottery instructor at the Henry Street Settlement and as coordinator for a community arts project known as "Summer in the City." During this period I made numerous home visits to the families of my art students, which destroyed many of my middle-class concepts about the relevance of art to our lives. I came to see that the primary concern of these people was to provide food, clothing, and shelter for their

66. Cityarts Workshop staff, 1972.

often large families. They did not have the time or energy to affirm, or even notice, their children's artistic achievements. Art was a superfluous and extravagant activity in a world where the rudiments of everyday life were barely being met.

Furthermore, the vast supermarket of cultural activities housed in museums, galleries, and theatres was even more remote to them, as they could neither afford the entry fee nor would they relate to the imagery that had been conceived largely for middle- and upper-class America. How could art, with all of its promise of enrichment and rewards, find its way into the lives of low-income America?

During this period I was also privileged to witness the innovations of numerous artists who were meeting this problem head on. The most outstanding was Peter Schumann, the sculptor-puppeteer who created enormous rod puppets of papier-mâché and cloth. His unique Bread and Puppet Theatre was comprised of an awesome cast of characters with which he depicted the oppressed and their oppressors in a great variety of controversial theatre pieces. He reached a wide audience by traveling his troupe to churches, college campuses, theatres, and peace marches throughout the country. Peter Schumann had found a unique way to share his creativity as sculptor and dramatist with the community at large.

Urged by my own conscience and inspired by the work of innovative artists like Peter Schumann, I too began to carve a new role for myself as a community artist on the Lower East Side. The question of relevance was still unanswered when I began the groundwork for Cityarts Workshop. The program was based in a recreation center located in a housing development known as the Alfred E. Smith, or more popularly referred to by its residents as "the Smith."

Although the Smith was populated by Asians, Hispanics, blacks, and poor whites (largely of Jewish and Italian origins), the normal everyday traffic at the recreation center was practically all black, with a sprinkling of Puerto Ricans who were tolerated by the blacks. During the late 1960s I observed the mobilization of many Lower East Side residents into exclusive ethnic groups who were discovering their unique ethnic identity and power. Against this background, I felt challenged to develop a creative-arts program that was community-responsive; the question in my mind was never why, but how, to implement this objective.

I started by finding two young community residents to assist me. They were Susan Caruso-Green and James Jannuzzi, both lifelong residents of the area. Caruso-Green was eighteen years of age at the time (1968) and a college student with an interest in art. Jannuzzi was only fourteen and a student at the High School of Music and Art who showed a good deal of talent and commitment toward art even at this early age. Their youth was an asset to me since we were to develop a program primarily directed to teen-agers with whom they could easily identify.

Initially I looked to Caruso-Green and Jannuzzi as knowledgeable guides to this neighborhood, though eventually they developed into very fine workshop assistants, and subsequently, directors. We spent a great deal of time together in those early days discussing the conceptual framework of community arts. I impressed these young art students with the fact that our cultural institutions, despite all their riches, had failed to reach low-income America. We spent many long hours discussing why this condition existed and how we could attempt to change it, at least on the Lower East Side, where they had both grown up.

They in turn brought me in touch with intimate details of their everyday life, making me aware of the neighborhood ethics, its past as well as its present. They informed me of a ten-year cold war between the Italian and Afro-Latin communities; of tensions between the Asian and black communities; and many other examples of key ethnic interactions. All this knowledge enabled me to assimilate to the community much more quickly than would otherwise have been possible.

The relationships between Caruso-Green, Jannuzzi, and myself, based on mutual respect and responsiveness, developed into a process that is ongoing and that became a model to each of us as we worked with community groups and individuals in creative endeavors. Open and frank discussions about community arts with artists and residents helped us develop a rich program. Although our concepts changed and expanded with each new mural, most of the original tenets are still sound and respected by us.

As artists, we have seen our role evolving as a catalyst to people's art. We have shaken the presumptions of the elitist view of art by challenging minorities to develop an art form that is public and reflects their own cultural heritage and class consciousness. Blacks, Asians, Puerto Ricans, Jews, and Italians have all rallied to our call, some with stunning results, and all with murals that have integrity for their respective communities. These murals were each the result of a collaboration between an artist from Cityarts Workshop and a particular group of community people from the Lower East Side. Each mural pays homage not only to class difference and cultural heritage, but also to an egalitarian concept of art that celebrates and integrates the images and ideas of not one, but a group, of community artists. The group process, which has become the hallmark of Cityarts Workshop murals, has undergone significant changes over the years, as have the murals. For a better understanding of our growth and development, let us take a hard look at how some of these murals were actually carried out.

In our first mural project, we agreed upon a simple objective: We wanted to involve a large number of people of all ages in a collective experience that would result in a permanent and public work of art, in order to demonstrate both their power as creators and also the power of art itself.

We carried out this plan through the creation of a mural sand casting in cement. It seemed to have all the elements that we were seeking. Planned in a modular format, it allowed for wide participation; and mounted on a prominent wall in the entrance hall of the recreation center, it boasted a permanent home. Over a hundred community people of all ages created designs for this wall mural. We would move the workshops from one place to another in hopes of attracting greater numbers of people. Armed with wheelbarrows, cement, sand and casting forms, plus clay, mosaic tiles, and found objects, we set up shop wherever they would have us—in the halls of the recreation center, in the parks, playgrounds, and streets. After two months of workshops we had collected over a hundred designs and had met many more people who lived in the Smith.

By summer's end, each casting had been bolted to the wall of the recreation center to complete the grand design of this mural. The result far exceeded our expectations. Although the castings were beautiful unto themselves, when viewed together as a collective work, they gained even more power and generated tidal waves of pride among those who had created them, as well as among their friends and families. This mural became a symbol to the community of its creative power and went a long way in reinforcing our role as artist-catalysts.

We had been privileged during this entire process to come in touch with the spirit of many people, to taste their joy, despair, and dreams. We found the most challenging group to be the black teen-

67. Sandcast technique (mass-participation cement mosaic). 1971. Washington Square Park Plaza, New York.

age boys who lived in the Smith. We saw the daily drama of drugs and street life beckon them, and we felt compelled to offer them equally dramatic alternatives. We had gained a toehold with this group during the creation of the sand-cast mural, and now we hoped to build a relationship with them.

We spent weeks with them in the hall of the recreation center and in the gymnasium where they hung out, familiarizing ourselves with their life-style and their concerns. Before long we began to sense their fears about life in the community. They had personally witnessed violence and addiction. Some member of their own or of a friend's family was almost bound to be implicated in the heavy use of drugs or even to have died from an overdose, others were implicated in street crime of various sorts, and many were already saddled with prison records. Needless to say these burdens did not

68. Susan Shapiro-Kiok, director: *Anti–Drug Abuse Mural.* 1970. New York.

inspire these young people with self-confidence or optimism for the future.

It seemed to us that a mural would provide a good arena for an expression of these concerns if the boys could trust us enough to work with us. However, these teen-agers had no frame of reference for themselves as artists, and murals particularly were completely out of their ken. We had heard of an ethnic-murals program in Roxbury, Boston's black ghetto. In an effort to inspire these boys, we organized a weekend trip to Roxbury to view these murals created by black artists. The trip strengthened the boys' relationships to us and to one another and showed them the significance of the mural form to the black community. While there, we met with the artists and had a good interchange with them about their concepts of a mural as a tool for social change. The mural form finally had enough power and excitement to challenge this group of youths; and once they had decided to create a mural, they concurred quickly on the theme of drug abuse.

Now Cityarts was faced with a second challenge: the need to develop skills and techniques that would enable inexperienced teenagers to create a mural with artistic integrity. Using a Polaroid camera, the boys photographed each other in assumed dramatizations of street life: drug abuse, fistfights, gang assaults, police arrests, etc. The photographs were then placed in an opaque projector, which enlarges the image as it projects it onto a wall where it can be traced. After the photographs were simplified to silhouette form, images were selected by the group, organized into a cohesive mock-up, and then painted onto four- by eight-foot plywood panels to comprise an overall wall mural measuring twenty-six by fifty-five feet. With this method a stunning mural was designed and created within six months. Larger-than-life red and blue figures were painted on contrasting red and blue backgrounds, depicting various aspects of violence, narcotics, and corruption. As the mural develops its theme from left to right, a twenty-six-foot male figure is shown turning his back on these negative forces, his black-power salute suggesting a better life through black power and pride. The mural received accolades in the media as well as in the community, but it also generated opposition in some sectors. Threatened by its images, various community groups attempted unsuccessfully, through petitions and other means, to remove the mural from the recreation center, where it had been installed.

Many of us believed opposition to this mural was a direct result of its power as a creative tool for communication, and this belief was borne out by subsequent developments. The mural form, with its high visibility, sparked the interest of ethnic groups throughout the Lower East Side. In the early 1970s, heightened ethnic consciousness sought new forms of expression. It was therefore entirely fitting for community groups to seize the opportunity offered by Cityarts to create collaborative murals celebrating their cultural heritage.

In order to become more responsive to an ever-widening community, it was necessary for Cityarts to regroup. In the fall of 1970, our staff still consisted of my two part-time assistants, Jannuzzi and Caruso-Green, and myself as director. The three of us had worked jointly on all projects, which enhanced our spirit of camaraderie but limited us sharply in the number of projects that could actually be carried out. Caruso-Green and Jannuzzi, now well trained after assisting with two major mural projects, were ready to accept more autonomous roles as mural-workshop directors, and my role changed from artistic director to include the responsibility of administration and fund raising. Until now we had depended entirely on the New York City Department of Cultural Affairs for support, but in order to increase mural activities, we needed to widen our base of financial support and to become tax-exempt through incorporation.

This grass-roots workshop, whose beginnings were fraught with cautious definitions of community arts, had, after two years of hard work and self-scrutiny, developed into a community arts program that, we felt confident, was becoming increasingly relevant for the residents of the Lower East Side. At this time (1971), Cityarts did two additional murals with the black community: one with a group of young black women portraying a march back to Africa, symbolizing their search for identity and pride; and the other, symbolizing black liberation, with a group of black teen-age boys, some of whom had worked on the *Anti–Drug Abuse Mural.* All of the murals executed by Cityarts from 1968 through the summer of 1971 were painted on exterior plywood panels and later installed on the walls for which they were designed.

After the completion of these murals, we geared up for numerous other program developments at Cityarts. We discovered muralists in other large cities and were impressed by their artistic achievements as well as by their technology. It was at this time that we made contact with John Weber in Chicago, who influenced and assisted us to do direct wall paintings by utilizing scaffolding. This method enabled us to abandon the cumbersome plywood panels.

By the fall of 1971, we made a conscious staff decision to respond not only to the black community of the Lower East Side but to other ethnic groups as well. This meant that we must gradually increase Cityarts' staff. Alan Okada, a professional artist with expertise in drafting, joined us at this time to conduct mural workshops in the Asian community. Simultaneously, a new mural was planned with the Puerto Rican community, and shortly thereafter with the Jewish and Italian communities.

As mural activity expanded and as the Cityarts staff grew, we began to develop new creative methods for planning group murals. Okada, in his 1972 mural workshops with the Asian community, introduced a variety of new techniques. He abandoned the use of the Polaroid camera and opaque projector in exchange for 35mm color-slide film. He then projected the images by normal means in a carousel projector. In addition, his workshops drew upon materials from various picture archives, creating drawings freely from them and later integrating them into the overall mural design. These techniques provided the opportunity to work with sharper and more colorful images. Since there were a number of trained artists within Okada's workshop, freehand drawing methods were also employed for the first time and incorporated into the murals.

The first Asian mural depicted Chinese immigration to the United States and was created by approximately a dozen teen-agers and young adults (fig. 93). Its creators viewed identity as the crisis issue at the time and felt that a greater understanding of their culture and heritage was implicit in their chosen theme. As a young activist in the Asian movement, Okada was associated with many activities in Chinatown. A contributor to *Yellow Pearl,* an Asian-movement publication, and to the Chinatown Health Fair, he came in contact with many young Asians. It was a core group of these people who were to form the basis of the Asian mural movement.

This first Asian mural, painted on a prominent wall facing Chinatown, caused a great deal of sentiment in the community. Most Asians whom we polled were glad to have it there as a further declaration of their existence in an often hostile world, but many found its message obscure. The left section of the mural depicts a massacre of Chinese miners in Rock Springs, Wyoming, symbolic of other massacres and general persecution. The four large faces in the middle, those of an old woman, a man, a young girl, and a child, were meant to represent people recognizable to the Asian community. To the right of these central figures are images of the locomotive, indicating the Chinese involvement in the building of the American railroad, mainly in the West. The upper parts of the mural show other aspects of Chinese life in America: a woman at a sewing machine, symbolic of the sweatshops, and the more positive image of a man playing a musical instrument. At any rate, these were the representations intended by the muralists. The public interpreted them somewhat differently. The most controversial interpretation focused upon the central and largest figures in the mural, those meant to portray the men and women in Chinatown today. However, many residents of Chinatown viewed these figures as political portraits of Mao and his followers. This is not surprising since the issue of loyalty to mainland China or to Taiwan was a very hot one in Chinatown at the time.

Cityarts did not overlook criticism of this kind; our growth was really dependent on it. We wanted our murals to communicate as widely as possible. If we failed in this, then we failed ourselves in our primary objective. Each new mural group continues to face the rigors of carrying this out, and each mural project is challenged by unique and often unforeseen circumstances.

The second Asian mural project took place during the summer of 1973, against the ominous background of teen-age gang activity. There was already a history of open warfare among Chinatown teenagers and a number of them were killed that spring and summer by members of opposition gangs. Okada was faced with several dilemmas. In selecting his mural group, he tried to steer clear of gang members since they would pose a potential hazard to the entire group. The group, once formed, must develop a mural concept that did not mix in any gang issues, lest this implicate them in a struggle in which they definitely preferred to remain neutral.

69. Alan Okada, director: *Chinatown Today*. 1973. New York.

Surrounded by these hot issues and working daily during one of the hottest New York summers I can remember (it was ninety degrees in the shade on most days), this group proceeded to create the second Asian mural. Done in striking two-point perspective, it shows us a Chinatown stripped of clichés. At the center of the mural are two teen-agers "trucking" down the street. They are flanked on either side by prostitutes, a caravan of vulgar tourists, a deck of cards loosely falling above the head of a man who lies dead beneath them, and the figure of an old man who is looking back on all of this, his life in Chinatown.

As the mural neared completion, Okada and some of his associates began to feel restless about the limitations of working only with teen-agers. They wanted to deal with broader questions of aesthetics and community development. Simultaneously, Jim Jannuzzi be-

70. James Jannuzzi and Afro-Latin neighborhood artists: *Ghetto Ecstasy*. 1973. New York.

gan to feel similar constraints. By now Cityarts had become acquainted with the National Murals Movement and many of the muralists associated with it. We were dazzled by the beauty and complexity of many of their murals, and felt for the first time that we too would like to begin planning collective murals with professional artists, in addition to our work with teen-age groups.

Jannuzzi was the first to put this idea into practice. He had decided to work in a neighborhood of the Lower East Side that was new to Cityarts—East Fourth Street between avenues B and C. It was a poor neighborhood populated primarily by blacks and Hispanics and laced with gangs, but there was also a generous sprinkling of minority artists. The artists had remained there because the rents were lower than elsewhere in New York City, and because they felt a strong identification with "the People."

In preparation for the mural project, Jannuzzi sought space in this new neighborhood for supply storage and other general workshop tasks. He was directed to the basement of Clyde, a neighborhood artist. As with prior Cityarts murals, street kids were brought in during the early stages to plan the mural mock-up depicting their life on this part of the Lower East Side. There was general agreement that the theme should reflect an Afro-Latin coalition that existed in this neighborhood. In addition, they felt it was important to represent the well-entrenched gangs and cliques who lived there. And since music was such a positive and pervasive force in all of their lives, they felt that this element should become a backdrop to the whole mural.

As these workshops progressed in Clyde's basement, many neighborhood artists would drop in to see how things were progressing and make suggestions on how this or that idea could best be carried out. The street kids and Jannuzzi, impressed by their ability and interest, seized the opportunity to offer the artists an active role in designing and painting this mural, and so it happened that Cityarts did its first mural with community artists. Each artist was assigned a mural section to design and paint in harmony with the theme already chosen by the neighborhood teen-agers and Jannuzzi. The teen-agers who started this mural project continued with enthusiasm, but in somewhat different roles. They now were apprenticed to a group of artists and very actively sought the opportunity to assist them. The responsibility for orchestrating individual sections into a cohesive mural fell largely on Jannuzzi. The mural, which celebrates the roots of Afro-Latin culture, is painted in a spectrum of pastel colors, punctuated with lush green foliage.

The success of this mural project encouraged relationships between Cityarts and the artists from this community, and from the Asian community as well. The artists who worked on the Afro-Latin mural were joined by others who wanted to explore murals as an art form that would serve their communities. In the winter of 1973/74, they began to hold meetings with Cityarts to plan their future projects. They agreed upon some basic ground rules: (1) they would seek feedback on their mural mock-up from the community—in other words, they would plan a community-responsive mural; and (2) the artists involved would receive stipends during the planning and execution phases of the mural project.

The following summer, a group of between seven and ten Lower East Side artists worked again with Jannuzzi to develop a mural for a wall located at the corner of Chrystie and Rivington streets, which focused on the contrasts between primitive and technological societies. The mock-up was circulated throughout the area around the wall and was added to and approved by the local residents.

Meanwhile, during this same summer on yet another wall in another neighborhood of the Lower East Side, a core group of young Asian artists were producing the first Asian artists' mural, *Chi Lai—Arriba—Rise Up!* (pl. 12, fig. 40). This mural project was perhaps more complex in its overall organization and structure than any of the Cityarts murals that preceded it.

The Asian artists accepted a multifaceted challenge. They agreed that a successful community mural must communicate widely. They also believed in working collectively, although with the stringent demand that the mural reflect the ideas of each member of the group. They were involved in a unique learning experience, working closely together for months and sharing their feelings, ideas, and skills, which ultimately led to the development of a cogent mural with images drawn from the history and culture of the Asian American community. They depicted the community as it is today, including the forces that are operating to keep it from changing and growing. Although the context is Asian, the artists aspired to project a celebration of community for all ethnic groups (note the three-language title), in which people are shown working together for fundamental changes in their living conditions. Rather than emphasizing the differences that make each community unique and therefore separate, the artists tried to show those things that all poor people, working people, and minority groups share in common. The mural was a success as a work of art and in its power to communicate.

It is evident from my descriptions of the many murals sponsored by Cityarts Workshop since its beginnings in 1968 that we have developed into an increasingly complex organism. Our original objective of creating in an art form relevant to low-income America led us to the mural. We certainly could not have predicted that our first community Wall, *Anti–Drug Abuse Mural,* would launch a mural movement for the working class of New York's Lower East Side. Murals came to be viewed not only as an opportunity to create but also as an arena for the celebration of cultural heritage, and as the expressions of hope and despair by their creators. Not only has the mural movement taken art out of the gallery and into the streets, but it has also provided an invaluable platform for dialogue between often polarized ethnic groups. The Lower East Side murals graphically communicate the concerns of one ethnic group to another. We feel that the barriers between these groups are lessened by exposure to one another, and by a comparison of their concerns, which are reflected in their murals.

By the end of the summer of 1973, Cityarts Workshop had completed about fifteen murals and was well known throughout New York City. The mural workshops had developed into a bona fide mural movement. Institutions from all over the city clamored with requests for murals. Artists approached us with an eye toward joining the Cityarts staff or painting murals with us. Eager to enrich the mural movement and to provide greater service, we added mural workshops for Lower East Side artists. This has, of course, added new aesthetic and conceptual dimensions to the murals. We have also been responding to the institutions' requests. During the winter 1974/75, Cityarts cosponsored interior murals for the first time with two local institutions—one a hospital, the other a recreation center. Never before had a neighborhood institution made a direct contribution to the cost of a mural.

The trend at Cityarts toward a wider representation continues, and the mural imagery has expanded to include not only ethnic but broader concepts as well. For example, a women's mural, completed in the summer of 1974, depicts a history of women of different nationalities on the Lower East Side (fig. 50).

Because Cityarts Workshop is a dynamic, continually evolving organization, it has responded successfully to the needs of the Lower East Side. The mural movement has enabled me and other artists to integrate our social and political beliefs with our artistic skills and, more importantly, has made art no longer superfluous and extravagant but something that belongs to the people.

8

People's Painters by Eva Cockcroft

Composed of students and based at the Livingston College campus of Rutgers University in Piscataway, New Jersey, our mural collective has emphasized political murals, including semilegal forms of painting. At the same time, we have been a highly self-conscious experiment in collectivity.

Livingston College constitutes a compatible home for a radical mural group. Founded at the time of the urban upheavals that wracked Newark, Paterson, and other cities heavily populated by national minorities, Livingston is the only campus of the State University of New Jersey publicly committed to admitting and serving a large number of minority students. It contains in both its student body and faculty more than thirty percent nonwhites—mainly black, but also Puerto Rican and a smattering of other nationalities. Livingston's white students tend to be poor, working-class, or middle-class, and often radical (culturally or politically). Typical urban problems of racism, drug abuse, etc., have been aggravated

71. People's Painters: *The Livingston Experience* (process shot). 1973. Livingston College, Piscataway, New Jersey.

at Livingston by its physical location—isolated from the urban hub of the region (New Brunswick) on the former Camp Kilmer Army Base, parts of which still function.

Influences from Chicago and Chile affected the beginnings of our group. Ever since I had first discovered the existence of the Chicago murals when I wandered into the basement of Chicago's Museum of Contemporary Art in 1971, I had developed a growing interest in the community mural movement. With those who would become the other members of People's Painters I was able to share slides, anecdotes, and the history of the Chicago murals, thanks to help provided me by various of the Chicago muralists. In addition, we could draw on the *Mural Manual*. In spring 1972, I painted my first mural, *Women's Liberation—People's Liberation*, for a women's center in the heart of downtown New Brunswick. After the inauguration ceremonies for that mural, I ran across photographs of the Chilean murals. That summer, I made a month's trip to Chile, during which I contacted the Brigada Ramona Parra in Santiago.

I talked with brigade members at length, watched them work, photographed their murals, and painted with them. They worked for the most part at ground level along long, relatively low walls, on the streets or in factories. Their images were for the most part positive and affirmative. Their colors were bright, not necessarily naturalistic; the forms in their murals were more closely related to Fernand Léger and European Cubism than to Mexican precedents. They had developed a Chilean style and method of work that had organically grown out of the demands of clandestine painting placed on them during the repressive years of the preceding government. Technically, they executed simple, powerfully drawn symbols over large, flat areas, capable of being quickly filled in with almost any color by any person with a paintbrush. Each mural was designed and painted by a brigade of from eight to fifteen members, composed of young workers or peasants as well as artists, working together with highly synchronized efficiency. One or two members of a brigade would go ahead, drawing in the flowing outlines with black paint, followed by other *brigadistas* who would fill in the colors.

On my return from Chile, I presented some slide shows at area colleges to let people know about what was happening in Chile. At a Chile teach-in at Livingston in October 1972, all the elements came together and our painting brigade was formed. The slide show was preceded by a talk by the Chilean novelist and poet Fernando Alegría, then cultural attaché to the Chilean Embassy in Washington, D.C. When questioned by students anxious to go to Chile on how they could help the Chilean people, Alegría made the telling point that perhaps the students would learn more *from* Chile than whatever little they might be able to teach or share with the Chileans. It was in this spirit that our group was formed. After the slide show, a number of people from the audience gathered to talk about forming a Chilean-style mural collective. We were joined by the

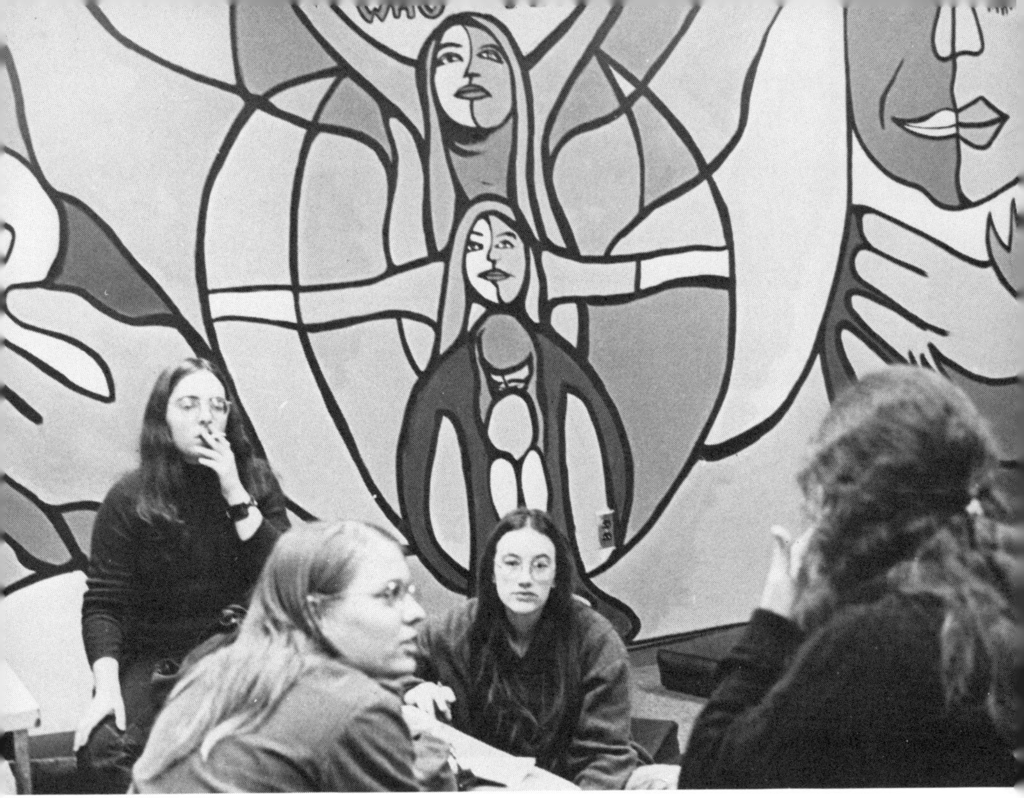

72. People's Painters: *Women's Center Mural* (partial view). 1972. Livingston College, Piscataway, New Jersey.

organizers of the women's center on campus. They explained how they were afraid they might be evicted from the room that they had finally obtained, after months of struggle, from the college authorities, and they proposed that we begin with a mural for the women's center. "Just let them try to kick us out, standing in front of our mural!"

For this first mural, Julie Smith, Kathy Jones, and myself formed the group. Smith had long been active in movement politics, and we had worked together before as part of the local underground-newspaper collective and in the women's movement. Older than most undergraduates, in her mid-twenties, Smith had solid organizing talent and a steadiness of vision. Jones was younger, quiet-voiced and gentle, with a very fine sense for color, pattern, and original design motifs. A member of the women's center studying art and education, she also held a part-time job and taught Tai Chi Chuan.

Although later we felt confident enough to add men to the group, we felt it would be easier to begin without them. All of us had experienced manipulation by men in past cooperative projects, and since we were still uncertain about our direction and methods, we did not want to have to deal with possible problems male egos might pose at this stage. In addition, it seemed appropriate that a women's-center mural be painted by women.

The planning of our first mural involved a determined effort to maintain complete equality and collectivity. Sitting on the floor, surrounded by women's-movement literature, armed with coffee, tea, cigarettes, lots of paper, pencils, markers, tracing paper, we discussed the ideas that we felt needed to be included in the mural and began to sketch out visual equivalents. Very consciously, we worked on refining one another's motifs, simplifying them and putting them into the Chilean style: flat color areas with strong, rhythmic black outlines. By using that style, we felt that the women at the center would be able to participate fully in the actual painting process. Since the project involved three walls, each of us drew the final design for one wall (parts of which had already involved the others at some stage). During the painting process, in which more than half a dozen of the women from the center participated, another conscious effort was made to work on all sections of the mural, rather than to concentrate just on parts one had either designed or conceived. The idea was to fight the tendency toward ownership, toward saying, when the work was finished, "and this part is mine." This kind of deliberate collectivity, necessary because of our previous conditioning and hang-ups, worked better even than we had hoped, although individual differences in the arrangement and meshing of symbols still remained in the finished mural.

With the help of women from the center, the painting took only two days. Our good feelings about the project were matched by those of the women in the center and others who saw the mural in the process of being painted or after it was completed. During the painting process, a video tape was made, and an edited version was played back at the opening so all the people interested in the center could feel themselves a part of the process.

Rather than signing the mural with our names, we decided to give the group a name that would cover all those who worked and would also describe the function we felt the group served: the People's Painters. In this way, we remained unofficial and anonymous, the concept *people's painters* implying that no individual but simply "the people" painted murals. Since most of our murals, like this first one, were to be done without administration permission or approval, anonymity helped protect us from reprisals.

Several other campus groups asked us to paint murals for them; radical organizations on campus and in New Brunswick requested assistance with banners, posters, signs, etc. We agreed to do two further projects: a mural for the sociology department (pl. 14) and a large mural for a proposed student multipurpose room. As we began working on designs for these projects, we enlarged our group to include other students, some of whom participated irregularly and others of whom became core members. Since several students worked part time to support themselves and had innumerable other commitments, time and money always posed a serious problem. While we donated our labor, the groups who asked us to paint murals for them provided paints, supplies, and help with the actual painting. Using leftover paint from our indoor "commissioned" projects, we were able to paint the more political outdoor poster murals on our own.

The day after the take-over of Wounded Knee occurred, for example, we were meeting at the college for one of our regular work sessions. Scattered around the campus were concrete walls, probably used for barracks insignia when Livingston had been Camp Kilmer but now used by students as handball courts or convenient sites for graffiti. We gathered together the paint and brushes left over from the *Women's Center Mural,* found a rickety twelve-foot ladder, walked to the nearest outdoor concrete wall—and three hours later our first "instant" mural was completed: *We Support*

Wounded Knee. This mural drew widespread attention, was reproduced as the cover of the student newspaper the next day, and helped to alert people to the demonstrations in support of Wounded Knee held in downtown New Brunswick and elsewhere in the following days.

The group that worked on this mural now became the core group. It included Mark Reid, a black art student who had previously joined our group, and Pierce Skinner, who had been hanging around watching while we were planning the mural inside the student center. When we went out to paint, we invited Skinner to help. At first he refused. "I'm a psychology student, not an artist," he said, "I don't know how to paint." We explained to him that he didn't need any special skill to help. He soon became involved in the Wounded Knee theme and started to make suggestions, some of which were implemented. In the course of his work with People's Painters, Skinner began to study art and is currently working in the area of art therapy.

In our evolution after the *Women's Center Mural,* we gradually shifted our work method from the strict enforcement of collective discipline and shared designing and painting to a more flexible type of collective work style that made use of particular talents existing within the group. For example, Mark Reid had a remarkable ability to paint portrait faces from photographs directly on a wall without any preliminary drawings or study. In the sociology-department mural, we drew on Reid's talents for the faces of prisoners, which included a portrait of Carlos Feliciano, a Puerto Rican nationalist whose only "crime" had been his having shared a jail cell with Pedro Albizu Campos. In consultation with members of the sociology department, we had chosen the theme of imperialism, which became the title. We completed the painting over a three-day weekend, with the assistance of some of the women who had worked with us on the *Women's Center Mural,* and several students, faculty of the sociology department, and their children. Once the basic outlines were drawn in with black paint, we left the choice of color in most areas to the people painting. We had discovered that with this style

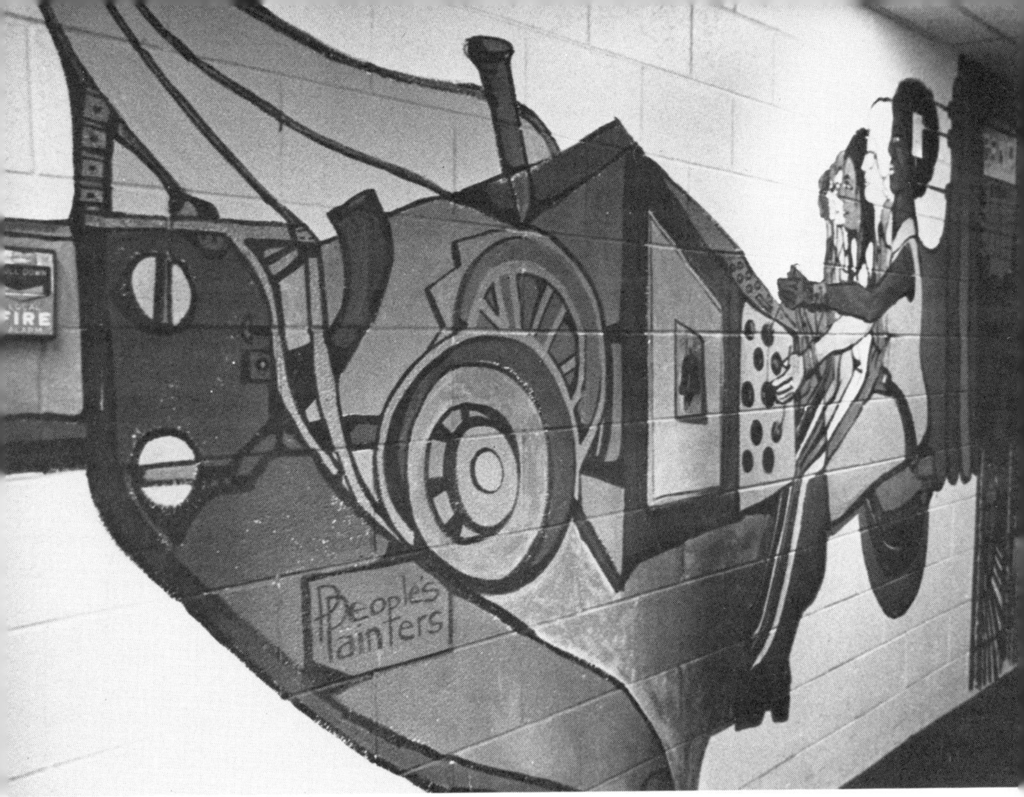

73. People's Painters: *Imperialism* (partial view). 1973. Livingston College, Piscataway, New Jersey.

the exact color within areas was not important—in most cases, any number of choices would work equally well—so we encouraged the volunteer helpers to make their own decisions on color (within a range of bright or dull). The sociologists who helped us paint began timidly, asking for direction at every turn, loudly proclaiming their inability as artists. Soon, however, they tentatively began to make their own decisions. As they did, their involvement and interest increased, and they began to engage more actively in the process. As the mural approached completion, it drew widespread attention and much favorable comment from passersby (including, some time later, the only graffiti addendum: "Right on").

Consequently, when three of us were putting on the finishing touches, we barely looked up to notice yet another passerby pausing to examine our work: a distinguished-looking man dressed in a conservative business suit.

"Who's in charge here?" he asked, with barely suppressed anger. "Who gave you permission to paint on this wall?"

We explained that we had been asked to paint this mural by the sociology department.

"Who do they think they are?" he replied. "They don't own this wall." And he left.

We continued with our finishing touches. About five minutes later, two workers from the buildings and grounds department came strolling down the corridor. They eyed the soldiers with their feet on the globe, the American flag with dollar signs instead of stars, the names of corporations on the colored squares of the businesses that rested on top of the heads of the prisoners, and the women workers tied into their machines. When they were abreast of us, they stopped. "You better have a lot of white paint to paint over this," one of them snapped before walking on.

Threats against this mural by members of the administration and the buildings and grounds department continued through official channels. However, the sociology department came out strongly in defense of "their mural." Letters went back and forth between the deans and the department, and an informal lookout system was established to prevent the painting out of the mural during those times when school was not in session.

Shortly after this wall was completed, an incident of police brutality against two Puerto Rican students, a young man and woman, each of slender build, occurred on the campus. We painted an outdoor mural depicting a policeman beating a handcuffed Puerto Rican girl, with the message "Ya Basta! Unite to End Police Brutality." During the time that we were painting the mural, campus police cars cruised by about every fifteen minutes while we coached one another on escape patterns. At one point, two hulky cops stepped menacingly out of their car—and slipped parking tickets under our cars' windshield wipers.

74. People's Painters: *Unite to End Police Brutality*. 1973. Livingston College, Piscataway, New Jersey.

75. People's Painters: painting Chile mural over the defaced *Unite to End Police Brutality*. 1973. Livingston College, Piscataway, New Jersey.

This mural also was photographed by the student newspaper and used as the cover page for the next issue. It served as a symbol for university-wide protests, which united many black, brown, and white students on all three New Brunswick campuses of Rutgers in protest against racism and the unjust treatment of students by police. After about three days, though, *Unite to End Police Brutality* was defaced by being largely painted over with blue paint, across which were scrawled the words "Fact or Fiction."

The Puerto Rican students were indignant. They asked us to paint the mural over again. Anxious to have people's protest art be taken up by as many people or groups as possible, we refused and instead offered them our paints and brushes to paint a mural themselves. They accepted our offer and repainted the image of police brutality in the hallway of the New Academic Building near the office of the Puerto Rican–Studies department, and then they went on to paint a whole series of images up and down adjacent corridors. Since the Puerto Rican–Studies department is next to the sociology department, this meant that by now a considerable area of an entire wing of a building had become muralized. Administration pressure to remove the murals was intensified, but the aroused Puerto Rican–Studies department as well as the sociology department strongly protested any attempts at removing the murals, and their united defense proved successful.

One of the supporters of the new murals was the then dean of student affairs. We had agreed to paint a mural for the mammoth new student multipurpose room he was having built on the second floor of the Student Union. For the first time, in addition to supplies, we were to be given a token fee. The theme of the mural requested by the dean was violence on the campus. He was concerned that problems relating to drugs, thievery, and rape had appeared on the campus. One solution being advocated by some sectors of the college community was the introduction onto the campus of large numbers of armed police and extensive related security measures. The dean of student affairs opposed this policy, agreeing with our position that alternative solutions needed to be implemented. In the multipurpose-room mural we attempted to show the genesis of Livingston's problems of violence in the larger society of which the college was a part, and alternative solutions based on a philosophy of student initiative and control. The mural covered two walls: a large side wall broken by four doors and one of the end walls of the room, a total area of over one hundred by fifteen feet. In terms of size and complexity of theme, this was the most ambitious project we had attempted.

Our planning was extensive, with much debate focusing on style. Those favoring a realistic figurative style won out, but they discovered when the painting began that they had real difficulties in creating the kinds of effects they wanted to produce. Our tendency toward specialization and division of labor, begun in *Imperialism,* was thus exacerbated. Only two of our group were really comfortable painting realistic figures. Since that time, we have learned methods of systematizing modeling that might have alleviated some of our difficulties and made possible a more unified, cohesive whole in the final product. Whereas the first section, portraying the divisions of society, contained a true collective dynamic in the creation of the design, parts of the larger and longer wall tended to consist of more individualized conceptions. The planning and execution of the multipurpose-room mural took almost a year (including the summer break). Although such a long-range project might work out all right in other settings, it is difficult to maintain an extended involvement with a student group.

During this time, the spirit of group solidarity and enthusiasm held firm in our continued painting of outdoor instant murals. We completed two more of these while still at work on the multipurpose-room mural. One of the outdoor murals called for support of the grape and lettuce boycott sponsored by the farmworkers' union, and the other was painted in memory of Salvador Allende and in support of the armed workers and peasants' struggle in Chile (we painted this over the defaced police brutality mural).

Coincidentally, the opening of the multipurpose-room mural, titled *The Livingston Experience,* occurred when the long-standing

76. People's Painters: *The Livingston Experience* (detail). 1973. Livingston College, Piscataway, New Jersey.

problems on the campus came to a head with a series of demonstrations by black students for better services from the administration. The demonstrations called for many of the same demands that had been painted into the mural: student power, disarming of the police, student patrols of the dormitories, better health care and other services.

Our next project was a corridor mural in the newly built college gymnasium. Since the gym serves as a community resource for youth from Piscataway, New Brunswick, and surrounding communities, we felt that a painting in such a location would reach large numbers of people, including many who were not connected with the university and who had no or little particular political or art consciousness. The directors of the gym, Phil Shinnick and Jim Smith, worked closely with our core group (which then consisted of

Kathy Jones, Pierce Skinner, and myself) in both the planning and the painting. They introduced us to the aims for which the athletes' movement was working: the end of coach domination of sports and the use of athletes as commercial properties; an end to discrimination against women, nonwhites, and noncompetitive athletics; and, on the national scene, acts of political consciousness by famous athletes. These were all depicted in the mural.

In the fall of 1974, a list of procedures for mural painting was published in the *Rutgers Newsletter,* which required prior approval from both the buildings and grounds people and the dean, thus making the kind of murals we had painted officially illegal. The previous June, the sympathetic dean of student affairs had left Livingston, the liberal dean of the college had resigned, and a new dean, who had worked many years for Rand Corporation (one of those assailed in *Imperialism*), took office vowing to eliminate "ideological dissidence" at the college. The following spring, 1975, we painted an outdoor mural supporting the student movement against budget cuts, political firings, and reduction of Economic Opportunity Funds (EOF) for working-class students. With our signature we included the phrase "ideological dissidence lives." Later that spring, forty-six students were arrested while occupying the dean's office in protest about some of the issues depicted in the mural.

In the more than two years that we had been working, many changes had occurred. The experiment in collectivity contained within it certain tensions inherent in collective artistic work. We had to face the conflict between collective work style and pride in individualized conceptions. This problem is relatively easy to deal with in the early stages of a group's existence when collective enthusiasm is at a high peak. However, over the long haul, we found ourselves aspiring more and more to artistic perfection yet running into the obstacle of compromises inherent in collective work. In some cases, personal resentments about this erupted openly and were dealt with through long and intense discussions. We could never wholly resolve within ourselves the traditional tension in political art between artistic perfection and political clarity.

We also were inexperienced in the dynamics of leadership within a collective. There is a thin line between too much leadership, which erodes collective feeling, and a default of leadership. Although I was almost automatically put into a leadership position, I did not want to lead and sometimes refused to accept the responsibilities of leadership. What I was seeking was a totally egalitarian collective. Although Julie Smith and I generally shared leadership, an impasse would usually be reached if she and I disagreed.

On the positive side, our impact as a group was many times what it might have been had we simply painted as individuals. In addition, we were able to advance further in our designing, drawing, and painting abilities than we might otherwise have done by working in isolation.

We also reacted to shifts in the political climate. The number of murals we undertook varied almost directly with the political intensity or issues of the year or month. The murder of Allende and of countless thousands of workers in Chile hit us hard. We were deeply affected by the destruction of Chile's murals, by the torture or murder of artists and workers in Chile, and by the visits of their widows or friends to this country afterwards; a number of us have continued active in Chile Solidarity work. I and others from People's Painters helped the group of fifty New York artists and writers who re-created the "No to Fascism" section of the Río Mapocho mural series in the streets of New York as an act of solidarity with the Chilean resistance. Also participating were Cityarts Workshop, Chilean and South American artists-in-exile, Artists and Writers Protest, and various prominent American artists and critics.

The direction of our thinking in 1974/75 moved away from campus work into more community and urban-school work. I worked in the summer of 1975 with Puerto Rican youth on a mural in northern New Jersey; Mark Reid and I have also gone on to do some individual murals. Kathy Jones, Julie Smith, and Pierce Skinner entered various fields of art education. Most of the student membership of People's Painters has graduated, and it remains to be seen whether other such groups will spring up either at Livingston or nearby urban communities. But the experience of People's Painters has proved instructive and rewarding, and the need for such collective endeavors in mural painting is not likely to disappear.

9

Artes Guadalupanos de Aztlán by Geronimo Garduño

There are several murals in Santa Fe, New Mexico, that predate those of Artes Guadalupanos de Aztlán, but they can't be considered people's art even though they are in such public places as the post office, a theatre, a monastery, and a couple of schools. For one thing, they weren't painted by a number of people in response to anything but were commissioned as decor for the buildings in which they exist. Also, they are obscure in the sense that they have never produced any kind of public reaction, and in fact, I'd go so far as to say that few people are even aware of them. On the other hand, when Artes Guadalupanos de Aztlán hit the streets, there was a flurry of excited reaction (pls. 15 and 16). Reporters created controversy; supporters came around to see what they could do for us; and committees sprang up to see how they could stop the Brown Threat, which, to them, seemed to be the same as the Yellow Peril and the Red Menace. Some people circulated petitions against us and got into heated argument with liberal advocates for our side who were comparing our work to Diego Rivera's.

We began painting in 1971 in Santa Fe and have since painted in Denver, Colorado, and Phoenix, Arizona. It's been hard financially, but we maintain the hope that eventually we can paint all over these United States. And I'm certain that with a little help from our friends, the dream will come true.

Although Samuel Leyba, one of the founders of the group, had been painting the inside walls of what would be La Clínica de La Gente before 1971, these murals were not yet a conscious collective effort toward a people's art. The group was a product of many factors: poor housing, lack of jobs, urban renewal, the degradation of welfare, delinquency, alcoholism, and on and on. But the prime factor, possibly the worst, was heroin addiction and death by overdose. This factor, rampant all over the country, was brought to the foreground of three artists' lives in a very personal way when their brother George died of an overdose. It was in his memory that his brothers Samuel, Albert, and Carlos Leyba painted a children's mural and organized Artes Guadalupanos de Aztlán. Why not, it was reasoned, approach the methadone-maintenance program (then called El Vicio) and recruit addicts to paint several murals as a means of providing jobs and training for addicts as well as demonstrating, publicly, the talents that are submerged in the *barrios* of Santa Fe? After a few meetings with groups and individuals, a contract was entered into with one of the *barrio* organizations in charge of distributing federal appeasement money while local government did its thing with urban renewal. Six weeks, $3,600, nineteen addicts, and four murals later, Artes Guadalupanos de Aztlán held an exhibit of canvases, furniture, leathercrafts, tinwork, needlepoint, clothes, quilts, and sculpture to show what we had uncovered in the *barrios* and, hopefully, to help us find future funding.

This, then, was the first funding received by the mural group, some of which was used for incorporating as nonprofit and to rent a small apartment, which we called the Studio. The addicts, unfortu-

77. Artes Guadalupanos de Aztlán: working on the Clínica de la Gente murals. 1971. Santa Fe, New Mexico.

78. Artes Guadalupanos de Aztlán: former Clínica de la Gente murals (detail). 1971. Santa Fe, New Mexico.

79. Artes Guadalupanos de Aztlán: *Memorial for George Leyba.* 1971. Santa Fe, New Mexico.

nately, went back to doing whatever they did before, and we began floundering around, having daily meetings designed to find ways and means. Now that we were incorporated, it seemed there were endless possibilities for funding—all kinds of private foundations, the Museum of New Mexico, and the state arts commission. Our troubles were over. In short order, we applied—proposal, talk to a few people—man, we're in. Also in short order, we found out we had to wait about six months before any money would come in.

A rude awakening, all right. Largely confined to our small city and our own set of problems, we didn't know we were involved in something of national scope and significance. Hell, we thought we had started something. Something big. It was still a while before we found out that other groups and individuals were painting murals all over the East and West coasts and other places. For years they had been painting. This was brought to our attention in many ways. People that were traveling through had photographs, or else they talked about other murals they had seen. Somehow a *TRA—Towards Revolutionary Art*—publication got to us; a friend sent some newspaper clippings of what Manuel Unzueta was doing in Santa Barbara, California; and so it went.

In the meantime, broke and burning with the fever of the "true artist," we were making all sorts of plans for a school of mural painting where people could come from all over the Southwest, the country, the *world,* to learn and teach, to share the magic of this people's art. Goddamn it, we'd start a movement. Yet, we weren't painting.

It was the middle of winter. We had no money, we were having trouble starting cars, and we were freezing our asses off just getting from our homes to the Studio. And we had never before tried to get a group of painters to work together. Everyone had his own ideas as to just what the murals should say. Gone were the frantic days of getting it together when people painted what seemed right; now we needed a goddamned philosophy.

Those first six weeks had been easy because we were simply looking for painters, trying to bring them together. Now that we were together, we had to define precisely what we wanted to do. One thing was clear: We couldn't go on doing pretty pictures of zoo animals and pastel Aztec gods.

Things were looking fairly dismal, when an independent slate was thrown together to run in the upcoming city elections against Republicans and Democrats. This was the Citizens Coalition for a Responsible Government. Sounded pretty good to us. As it turned out, one of its organizers was helping to organize our clinic, and we were acquainted with some of the candidates, so our next piece of money came from their campaign funds. There was a time when I may not have admitted that, but at this point, what does it matter? We were asked to do some large signs or billboard-type paintings to help promote the C.C.R.G.

Artes Guadalupanos de Aztlán was back in motion. It was so good to have cash in hand after so long that we forgot our differences and began hauling out sketch pads. The word *liberty* from someone got a large pad shuffling around a table, and the cartoon for our first controversial mural was drawn in about ten minutes. The site for this mural was a tool shed. The tool shed was owned by Roman Salazar, who was running for mayor. It was located on Canyon Road.

When Artes Guadalupanos de Aztlán hit Canyon Road, we were vaguely aware that there would be some kind of opposition. After all, Canyon Road is *the* "arts and crafts road" in Santa Fe and is known across the continent as an art colony by patrons of the void called American art. Suddenly, we Chicanos were the intruders. Suddenly *we* were invading the comfortable patterns of life established over the long years. Suddenly *we* had come around and decided to let these devils know we were still alive. And the devils raised hell. From the very first day at the site of the Canyon Road mural, the artists, the *real* Santa Fe artists, provoked a stir of excitement among the people who currently occupy the area. Their ex-

80. Artes Guadalupanos de Aztlán: *Lady of Justice*. 1972. Santa Fe, New Mexico.

citement, however, was not based on respect for art or the fact that nothing comparable had ever been done by themselves, the so-called Santa Fe artists. It was an excitement bordering on panic, fired by indignation, and nurtured by the fear that the natives were opening their mouths and were about to expose them—the residents, or occupants, of Canyon Road—for the frauds that they were, and continue to be to this day.

Now the natives were stirring and, having learned English, were saying: "Look, you phony bastards, our art has no commercial value. It's by the people. Here is the art of Joaquin, alive and vibrating for all to see and enjoy."

Public art is a great threat to people who peddle pictures. The galleries, those great makers of an artist's fame and fortune, are a laugh, a great shuck. And, together with the "artists" who put themselves at their mercy, they have duped the world. Art as a class privilege has not only reduced the artist to a sniveling wretch who goes around sniffing the behinds of gallery owners, it has also created a set of in-between parasites, the gallery owners themselves. But worst of all, it has degraded art by giving it money value, as opposed to social value, educational value, and cultural value. Make no mistake, so-called American art is not cultural unless we see American culture as an insane rip-off of other peoples' cultures. The sum total of this American art is a vacuum; it reflects nothing, stirs no emotion, is flat, and creates no response.

It's been argued that our murals are American art in fact because we're Americans, and that my statements on art in America don't make sense. But then again, we've never been known to call ourselves Americans; that nationality was laid on us by the existence of imaginary borders created by warmongering colonists. We are, as a matter of cultural fact, Mexicans.

The controversy over the Canyon Road mural was settled for good when a lady, whose name, I'm sorry to say, I've forgotten, stated that our work was among the best she had seen anywhere

81. Artes Guadalupanos de Aztlán: *St. Francis Road Mural.* 1972. Santa Fe, New Mexico.

and was, in fact, in the fine tradition of the best Mexican masters. Her qualification to issue such a judgment came from her education, fifteen years or so with the Smithsonian Institution, and extensive travels in Mexico.

It was about this time that the photographers, writers, and others came around talking about magazine articles, art publications, literary journals, and even books. Every few weeks we were approached by enterprising folks about an interview. At first it didn't matter much to us, and a few people scored pictures, answers to perfectly asinine questions, and a great deal of our time.

One of these people, a very enthusiastic young man who followed us around a lot, made up a really extensive portfolio of black-and-whites, large color glossies, detail shots, process shots, portraits of the artists—the whole thing. It still didn't matter much. Then we began hearing that a black-and-white print was going for ten bucks and the color prints for twenty-five. Well, we thought, after all, he's invested a few bucks in film—it's all right. The thing was, we had no idea of our own popularity. As it turns out, people were buying entire collections—that is, prints of every mural, both in black and white and in color.

In short, by the time we found out this nice young man had earned a couple of thousand, he had packed up and gone home to New York. And Artes Guadalupanos de Aztlán? Well, we were still bumming a dollar for gas for our '51 Chevy pickup to get to the wall. And if you find just a trace of humor in this on my part, don't be misled. There isn't even the hint of a smile on my face as I write it. Needless to say, we've since adopted a policy of telling people like that to go straight to hell—or, "Don't call us, we'll call you."

The argument in defense of such people, and there are thousands of them, is that they help us by providing exposure to a larger segment of the public. And, in all fairness, I have to agree with that. What bothers me, and I speak for the group as well, is that they often earn money from a by-product of our work, whereas we, as I said before, have to bum gas money, paint money, and sometimes even food money in order to continue painting.

With the realization that our popularity was spreading to other parts of the state, we decided to test it out by approaching the universities for walls to be painted. Our first and, because of the outcome, our last attempt was at New Mexico Highlands University in Las Vegas. We went through all the channels until we reached the president. In a meeting with him, a couple of the art teachers, and several other faculty members, it was concluded that we could paint there. We would find the necessary funding, housing, and whatever else might be needed, while the university would simply give us the walls.

Next, I had a series of meetings with art students since it was our intention to involve as many of them as were interested in painting some murals. On one of these days when a meeting was to have taken place, there was not a single student to be found in the art building. On my way to the Student Union Building, I was confronted by one of the art teachers and a small mob of art students, and an argument developed concerning who had the right to university walls. This art teacher, it seems, had convinced the students that the walls were theirs because they paid tuition, and, therefore, we "outsiders" had no business trying to come on campus to paint. Somehow, other campus organizations were brought into the issue, and we were barred from painting there. Shortly thereafter, the art students at Highlands painted a mural under the direction of the same teacher who hadn't allowed us expression. During the actual painting, this gentleman never touched a brush. Instead, he directed the work from the ground, complete with beret and smock as if he were a real master.

I mention this incident in our development only to illustrate how open some professionals can be, and to try to demonstrate that even through a negative reaction to our group, the impetus was provided to get at least one professor off his dead ass and to get something going. And so, although we didn't paint the mural, we feel a certain pride in knowing that we were responsible for its being there at all. We had a lot more fun painting our Las Vegas mural at a nearby high school where, it seems, the students were more aware of themselves and the world around them than were those involved in higher education at Highlands (pl. 15).

Our next mural appears in Denver. We didn't go there specifically to paint a mural; it just happened. We were in Denver at the Crusade for Justice offices for the purpose of getting information on how to operate a nonaccredited school, such as Tlatelolco, since we were planning to open a school in Santa Fe. By our third day there, we had gotten some very good ideas and were now just sort of hanging out. Our guide at the school suggested that it would be really good if there were a mural by Artes Guadalupanos in Denver. Some of the art students agreed, they bought us material, and in four days we had painted a ten- by thirty-foot wall in the school's art room.

Our school opened in June 1973 with a full curriculum of history,

Spanish, theatre, dance, and, of course, art. Only three murals were painted during the three months that the school was operational. On September 3, 1973, the school was attacked by more than one hundred law enforcers, a student was wounded, another student was killed, and our school, for all intents and purposes, was closed down.

Two police officers were also wounded in the "battle," and several of us went on trial for assault. As it turned out in the trial the following year (1974), the police had not only injured and killed our students but had wounded each other as well. After the trial, having been acquitted of all criminal charges, the group went into a period of quiet inactivity. I went to California to visit relatives and get some much needed rest.

Two months later, on my way back from California, I stopped in Phoenix to look into a two-year-old invitation to paint some murals there for an organization called Valle del Sol. In a couple of weeks, Samuel Leyba, Leroy Ortega, and Robert "Goose" Salazar joined me in Phoenix, and we painted three murals in as many weeks.

Upon returning to Santa Fe, I found that Albert Leyba had started a mural at the Community Law Center, and Samuel and I went to work on it for a while. At this time (spring 1975), the Law Center mural has yet to be completed; but in a sense, none of our murals is finished, and we plan to return to those that are still around sometime in the summer of 1975.

In all, we've painted some seventeen murals since we started late in 1971, and Samuel Leyba is working on the eighteenth as I write this brief history. At least three of our works have been painted over, and one has been stored away somewhere, a portable mural on masonite. Not much for a three-and-a-half-year period, but then, Artes Guadalupanos de Aztlán has been involved in just a few other things besides mural painting.

10

Funding

> I paint my still lifes, these *natures mortes,* for my coachman who does not want them, I paint them so that children on the knees of their grandfathers may look at them while they eat their soup and chatter. I do not paint them for the pride of the Emperor of Germany or the vanity of the oil merchants of Chicago. I may get ten thousand francs for one of these dirty things, but I'd rather have the wall of a church, a hospital; or a municipal building.
>
> —Paul Cézanne.

> If people like murals they should *demand* them. The only way for there to be murals which people in the communities will see and enjoy and which say something, is for people to get together and demand not just that they get painted, but that the city pay for them. By paying for them, they'll not only allow artists to survive, which is absolutely necessary, but they'll also make it possible for them to become more permanent.
>
> —Dewey Crumpler, *Common Sense,* June 1975.

The structure of patronage for the current mural movement differs from that of all previous mural movements because of the important role played by neighborhood funding and, hence, control. Because as many as half the murals have been done with the donated labor of artists, apprentices, and other volunteers, and with small contributions from community residents, it is impossible to determine exactly the total combined costs of all mural projects completed since the inception of the movement. However, judging from figures that are available from organized mural groups, artists' reports, annual reports of the National Endowment for the Arts (NEA) and various state councils of the arts, among other sources, we can make a rough estimate that probably comes within 5 percent of the truth concerning overall funding of murals.

Leaving aside the donated labor of artists and volunteers (a sizable amount), more than half the funding has been grass roots, coming from local community organizations, merchants, and residents. NEA has accounted for about 25 percent. Federal programs geared toward manpower training—e.g. Supplemental Training and Employment Program (STEP), Neighborhood Youth Corps (NYC), Comprehensive Employment and Training Act of 1973 (CETA)—although not intended to support murals, account for the next largest share, say 15 percent, thanks to the imaginative use of these funds at the local level. The various state councils of the arts come next, followed by private and corporate foundations (which, however, also contribute to some of the arts councils and the NEA) and city governments.

There are three other factors that make neighborhood contributions even more significant: (1) the time and labor put in by community or artist organizers in procuring matching components for outside funding (NEA demands matching funds); (2) the political tangle involved with local, state, and federal officials, including having to deal with political appointments to the state arts councils or municipal offices of cultural affairs; and (3) the general art-world climate and its relationship to patronage, wherein the mural movement gets a mere fraction of funds that go to community arts projects, which in turn receive well under 5 percent of total art patronage. In brief, unlike the Mexican movement or the WPA murals of the 1930s, this mural movement is grossly underpatronized and relies on local community support and the initiative of artists.

Outside funding, however, especially through the federal government, has been important in allowing the mural movement to sustain itself and to expand in most of the large mural centers. The NEA, which was founded in 1965 to "provide encouragement and financial assistance" to the arts, first became involved in inner-city arts programs in 1968. In cooperation with the President's Council on Youth Opportunity, grants of $25,000 each were made to sixteen riot-torn cities (Atlanta, Baltimore, Boston, Buffalo, Chicago, Cleveland, Detroit, Los Angeles, Milwaukee, Minneapolis, Newark, New York City, Philadelphia, San Francisco, Saint Louis, and Washington, D.C.) for summer arts programs in the inner city as part of a nationwide cool-out effort. This program, which, when matched on a two-to-one basis by the cities, poured $1,200,000 into inner-city arts in one summer, was discontinued the following year due to "financial stringency."

The 1968 appropriation by NEA of $403,497 to sixteen cities represented 5.6 percent of its total appropriation for that year of $7,174,291. In 1972, when the Endowment's annual appropriation had grown to $29,750,000, the combined funds allotted to Expansion Arts, Alternative Education, and Inner City Murals was only 4.6 percent of the total expenditure (with murals getting the smallest slice). The amount expended for "ghetto arts" by the Endowment in any year represents (in spite of its importance to the community arts movement) only a fraction of NEA's total expenditure, most of which goes to support establishment arts—opera, symphonies, dance companies, museums, famous artists, etc.—and state arts councils.

In 1971, NEA launched its Expansion Arts Program to aid "professionally directed community arts groups with activities involving ethnic and rural minorities" whose cultures had been inadequately supported in the past. Through this program in 1971 and 1972, funds were given to service and teaching programs with a mural component—e.g. San Francisco's Neighborhood Arts ($60,000), Los Angeles's Mechicano Art Center ($14,653), New York's Cityarts Workshop ($8,000), and Philadelphia's Graffiti Alternatives Workshop ($5,000).

NEA grant amounts normally run from $5,000 to $50,000. There are three NEA visual-arts programs that fund public art, each administered separately on a different financial scale and responding to different needs. Grants over $20,000 are designed for application by municipal governments, while those $10,000 and under can be obtained by nonprofit organizations. It is the $10,000-and-under category that has funded inner-city mural projects. The over-$20,000 category corresponds in a general sense to a modern version of the Treasury Section commissions of the 1930s—that is, large works of art commissioned for official places, involving a more complex process and artists of national reputation.

NEA's Visual Arts Program, though one of its subprograms, Works of Art in Public Places, began directly funding inner-city outdoor murals in 1970 with $5,000 for Boston and $4,000 for Chicago. In the same year, a grant of $45,000 was made to Wichita, Kansas, and grants of $20,000 each were given to Scottsdale, Arizona, and Saint Paul, Minnesota—all for works by prominent sculptors.

Government Patronage in the 1930s

The similarities and contrasts between now and the 1930s are instructive. Federal art patronage in the 1930s, amply documented by Francis V. O'Connor in his books on the WPA era, included a series of mixed programs (e.g. TRAP, TERA, and PWAP) but finally consolidated into two major categories: the Treasury Section, which bought the best available art to decorate public buildings and involved competitions and juries, regulations of subject matter, extensive preliminary designs, etc.; and the WPA/FAP, a relief program for artists aimed at furthering employment that would also yield useful and enduring results. At its peak, WPA/FAP employed five thousand artists who were paid by the hour as skilled workers. Over 2,250 mural and 13,000 sculptural pieces for public buildings were produced by WPA artists.[1] Since, unlike the Treasury Section,

[1] Francis V. O'Connor, *Federal Support for the Visual Arts: The New Deal and Now* (Greenwich, Conn.: New York Graphic Society, 1969), and

WPA was not involved in *buying* art, its administration was not overly concerned with the results of the artists' activity and placed no restrictions on artists in terms of subject matter or style. However, as Edward Laning points out in his description of his WPA experience,[2] the designs of mural projects had to be approved by the persons in charge of the intended location. His Ellis Island mural-series designs, for example, painted on canvas for installation in the Aliens Dining Room, had to be approved by the irascible and arbitrary commissioner of the facility. WPA muralists often ran into problems with the local recipients of their works. Treasury Section commissions, on the other hand, were controlled more at the federal level than at the local level.

The problems of Treasury Section commissions are described by Robert Cronbach, a sculptor who worked with both WPA and the Section. In his memoir, Cronbach criticizes the jury system in two ways. First, like all juries, it "can only recognize and employ already developed artists."[3] Treasury could not, as WPA did, encourage the development of new art and artists. Second, the fact that winning the competition was based on the design or *maquette* meant that too much emphasis was put on this phase of the artistic process. Cronbach writes:

> The artist's highest point of aesthetic tension and energy was reached with this *maquette*. Everything afterwards was a slight letdown. If one studies any example of large-scale monumental art, from Michelangelo to Picasso's *Guernica*, one generally finds that many excellent rough sketches and studies were

O'Connor, ed., *The New Deal Art Projects: An Anthology of Memoirs* (Washington, D.C.: Smithsonian Institution Press, 1972). TRAP: Treasury Relief Art Project, 1935–39. TERA: Temporary Emergency Relief Administration, 1934–35. PWAP: Public Works of Art Project, 1933–34. WPA/FAP: Works Progress Administration/Federal Art Project.

[2] Edward Laning, "The New Deal Mural Projects," in O'Connor, *New Deal Art Projects*, pp. 78–113.

[3] Robert Cronbach, "The New Deal Sculpture Projects," in O'Connor, *New Deal Art Projects*, pp. 147–148.

> made for the work, but no one was followed exactly. It was difficult to use the *maquette* only as a springboard, as one must do if the large work is not to be a mere blow-up. . . . It was easier to maintain a more flexible attitude toward large sculptural projects within the framework of WPA/FAP than in the Section.[4]

Cronbach's problems with his Section commission continued throughout the period of his contract and culminated in his disappointment that the works were never placed in the intended location.

The dissatisfaction of Cronbach and other artists (including Thomas Hart Benton, who resigned his Section commission because he felt the restrictions impaired his creative freedom) indicates why it is generally conceded that WPA/FAP produced more interesting art than the Section, which was buying "quality" art. Although the Section was originally conceived of as a means of initiating a government-sponsored mural movement like that of Mexico; in fact, it was never able to support controversial work. As O'Connor writes:

> the Section kept a strict eye on subject matter and style and was not adverse to demanding prudent changes as a work progressed. Very often these changes were prompted by violent opposition from political and religious leaders. A good example of the latter is Ben Shahn's murals in the Bronx Post Office which he was forced to change when a Jesuit at Fordham University objected to an inscription taken from a poem by Walt Whitman. Such incidents, coupled with the lack of any vital mural tradition in the United States, tended to place interest in the Mexicans on the level of nostalgia rather than inspiration.[5]

Since Section projects spent government money to buy art for public buildings, the administration became vulnerable as well to criticism from Congress and thereby was further restrictive of artistic and ideological freedom.

[4] *Ibid.*
[5] O'Connor, *Federal Support for the Visual Arts,* p. 24.

The Relationship Between Funding and Control Today

The structure of the National Endowment for the Arts attempts to avoid these kinds of problems. Rather than buying art or offering useful employment to artists, NEA supports art *services* through matching grants for locally initiated projects with proven local support. This new path, by moving the political responsibility for the choice of works of public art to the state and local levels, avoids the political and administrative problems common in the past at the federal level. Because NEA does not operate as a direct patron, it is less open to political attacks from congressmen regarding the type of art created through its funds, and it can therefore allow more freedom to the artists. Because the Scottsdale, Arizona, sculpture by Louise Nevelson, for example, was chosen and supported *locally* for at least an equal amount of money as the Endowment's contribution of $45,000, NEA cannot be easily attacked for its choice of particular works, as was the United States Information Agency (USIA) in the 1950s for supporting abstract art.[6] Rather, a pork-barrel approach based on geographic distribution is a more likely congressional reaction.

In addition, since a major portion of NEA funds goes to support state arts-council projects in a day when the national welfare system has become an established institution, NEA, by giving federal money back to the states for locally supported projects, is almost a form of that Republican ideal, revenue sharing. State arts councils, because they are generally rather closely controlled by state legislatures (and therefore generally subject to more conservative political forces than the federal body), provide a censorship element at the local level.

NEA, therefore, need exercise no censorship control; that is done locally. NEA can serve as a liberal force remaining aloof from local political strife. In this sense, NEA differs from the more centralized

[6] Cf. Eva Cockcroft, "Abstract Expressionism and the Cold War," *Artforum* (June 1974): 39–41.

control mechanisms at work in the 1930s. Nor does NEA concern itself with employment for artists, as did WPA (where 90 percent of the artists on payroll had to demonstrate need or be on relief). Employment concerns today have been taken over by the government's poverty and job-training programs, especially NYC and CETA. Except for its emergency sortie into this sphere in the 1968 summer programs, NEA has concentrated on supporting *professional* artist activity. Even when NEA has supported community muralists, it has tended to do so only after some evidence of proven professionalism. NEA funding for Chicago and Boston in 1970 was allocated after the outdoor-mural movement had already been producing notable walls for two years and had begun to receive some recognition in the national press and from local museums and art institutes.

In 1972, NEA set up a special category within its Visual Arts Program, the Inner City Mural Program, with an allocation of $102,700. As the Endowment's annual report states: "Murals on public walls continue to be a significant artistic and social expression in many cities, including Boston, New York, and Chicago."[7] However, the Inner City Mural Program did not limit itself to community-based mural programs. It also strongly supported urban-environmentalist groups. As the Endowment's report explains, NEA's funding of the Cincinnati project was designed to transform ten Cincinnati walls into "a visually attractive environment"—not for slum dwellers, but for commuters! "The sites chosen were located in areas heavily traveled by people entering and leaving the city. A similar grant of $10,000 enabled City Walls, Inc., one of the original inner city mural groups [*sic*], to continue its work in New York City."[8]

By 1973, after one year, the Inner City Mural Program was dropped as a special category and reabsorbed into the parent category of Works of Art in Public Places. Although CMG and Summer-

[7] National Endowment for the Arts, *New Dimensions for the Arts 1971–1972* (Washington, D.C.: Government Printing Office, 1973), p. 64.

[8] *Ibid.*

thing continued to be funded, the pattern toward funding city-sponsored "environmental" murals of the Cincinnati–City Walls type became increasingly important. New grants included Baltimore's and Saint Louis's urban-graphics projects. These programs were aimed not so much at the city's poor but rather at middle-class commuters and shoppers. NEA monies as a whole continued to go to traditional art-world programs and institutions; but the point here is that of the 5 percent or less of NEA's budget that might find its way into community programs, the bulk went to urban-environmentalist rather than to community-based art projects.

The pattern of NEA support for murals thus duplicates that observed with Summerthing in the Boston movement. It would seem that the control of funding and distribution of grants for murals by a central "outside," or city, agency, although one solution to the problem of financial backing and coordination, tends toward the dilution of socially conscious statements and a spreading of funds in the name of fairness, which has the net effect of gradually withdrawing funds from those oppressed communities where murals were initially generated through felt need and where they have served a genuine social function. During the time of most intense urban unrest, a considerable amount of support is thrown into impoverished communities (NEA's $400,000 in 1968 to summer art programs). Then, in succeeding years, only the most active ghetto-oriented mural programs are funded, and these few are in turn offered as evidence of NEA's support for nontraditional and minority art programs. Occasionally (e.g. Boston's Gary Rickson, 1971, and Dana Chandler, 1974), black muralists have even been included among those individual artists receiving grants. With the mural movement achieving genuine new peaks and advances in 1972, particularly in Boston, the NEA established a special Inner City Mural Program. However, as in the case of Summerthing, so with the Endowment, NEA spread its mural monies to sponsor more environmentally oriented programs aimed at white suburban audiences and at meeting businessmen's desires for beautifying and renovating downtown commercial areas. By 1973, as the visible protest of the 1960s became quiescent, the proportion of monies going to urban-environmentalist, city-initiated programs became even more significant, although the *established* neighborhood-oriented mural groups (e.g. in Chicago) are still funded.

In a special issue of *Art in America* (May 1974) devoted to public art, only two and a half paragraphs mention community-based murals. These paragraphs occur in an article by NEA's director of the Visual Arts Program, Brian O'Doherty, who praises the community mural movement while giving it a kiss of death. Acknowledging that the trend is to support professional artists venturing into the city to decorate city walls, O'Doherty concludes that the mural movement has "served its role by introducing the idea of the community as the conscience of a work of public art." That O'Doherty's lengthy article includes only brief discussion of the most significant public-art development of recent years—the community murals—suggests to us a major difference between now and the 1930s. O'Doherty's sentiments also reflect the patronizing attitudes the contemporary mural movement has had to put up with. We offer here the entirety of the passage in question.

> Equally important has been the recognition of the inner city mural phenomenon, which was carried through in an irrefutable sweep of feeling not by a single artist, but by groups of artists, and not just by artists, but by an entire class, one that is usually far removed from privilege. No serious study of the inner city mural movement, primarily generated by minorities from the mid-'60s to the early '70s, exists. Yet its search not for an audience, but for an arena to display the values of its audience, reverses the usual currents in public art. The mural artists declare—and this is above all a declarative art—feelings of brotherhood, celebrate heroes, memorialize, attack injustice, notate historical events in a context of ideas eminently socialist and in a variety of styles derived from the Mexican muralists and socially conscious American art of the '30s. So that urban walls became community newspapers, on which were written symbolic essays and reports on its feelings, concerns, and issues—many of them quickly wiped out by the wrecker's ball.

> While general opinion on the value of all this "as art" (i.e. its relation to the area of privileged taste) has not been enthusiastic, the phenomenon introduced valuable coefficients into the dialogue about the nature of public art, and the relationship between artist and community.
>
> Many of the artists who began on walls proved that the "art world" could expand its borders to allow another mode of entry to artists who had no access to its benefits. This has been one of its lasting values. Although moods are less radical now, and the energies of the wall movement diminished—the Endowment's Inner City Mural program was absorbed back into the parent Works of Art in Public Places program in 1973—the movement served its role by introducing the idea of the community as the conscience of a work of public art. The opposite situation—artists from the art community venturing into the city to decorate city walls—has resulted in some lively occasions, but the merits of this are, to many observers, far less certain, and the rationale subject to sharper debate than any other kind of public art. A major asset, it seems to me, is that this activity was generated not by institutions but by artists seeking practical means to realize their own ends in the public arena.[9]

Thus, so far as practicing muralists are concerned, the current funding situation is not very similar to WPA, since WPA provided thousands upon thousands of artists a living wage and the opportunity to work productively and develop their art, whereas NEA has funded, by comparison, practically none. We point this out because of the characteristic trend of our times to substitute rhetoric for practice. While the rhetoric of community has become mandatory for most mural grant proposals, the practice of funding community art has become optional.

The relationship between funding and control in the current situation is complex, often affected by local conditions and best explained by examples of controversies that have occurred. Nevertheless, certain general patterns are discernible. Federal money for murals comes without overt stipulations on content. City money, because of local political pressures, is much more problematic. For

[9] Brian O'Doherty, "Public Art and the Government: A Progress Report," *Art in America* (May–June 1974): 48–49.

example, even in a liberal city like New York, Cityarts Workshop, during its early years when it was wholly funded by the City Cultural Affairs Department, ran into censorship problems. The Policemen's Benevolent Association (PBA) objected to the figure of a policeman taking a bribe in the *Anti–Drug Abuse Mural,* and the city responded to PBA pressure by telling the artists that without changes the mural could not be mounted. A compromise was reached, the mural was finished and mounted (fig. 68), but the experience caused Cityarts to incorporate as a separate entity and seek diversified funding. Cityarts now has perhaps the broadest funding base in the movement, including federal and city grants, Neighborhood Youth Corps money for local participants, and significant private-corporation funding from a range of companies. This kind of funding spread has permitted Cityarts both the necessary artistic freedom and a relative security that is rare in the movement. City programs in general, with an occasional exception such as Los Angeles' Citywide Mural Project, rely on funds from NEA, state arts councils, and private corporations.

Since Manpower funds, although federal, are administered locally, their use (and abuse) depends on the local situation. Denver, Chicago, and Santa Fe, among other cities, have all experienced tense situations involving censorship and violence surrounding mural activity. The Denver mural movement began in 1970 when Manuel Martinez, then working as a park-department lifeguard, painted a wall of the pool building where he worked with bright Aztec designs. The following year, Manuel was painting murals for the Parks and Recreation Department, although he says, "It wasn't out of their good heart." He was a "recreation director," paid $1.60 an hour. He was joined by El Fego Baca and Roberto Lucero. Two of Lucero's murals in La Raza Park provoked the ire of City Councilman Geno DiManna; one of the recreation buildings involved was demolished. The director of parks asked Martinez to paint out Lucero's remaining mural, but Martinez refused, resigning his park job instead. Councilman DiManna then moved to push through a city ordinance against any murals not having the prior approval of the Parks Committee.[10]

A similar attempt to suppress murals was made in 1974 by the administration of Mayor Richard Withers of Blue Island, Illinois, an industrial suburb of Chicago. Three artists undertook a mural depicting the history of Mexican American workers: Ray Patlán, Vicente Mendoza, José Nario (himself a skilled worker and member of Steelworkers Local 3281). Helped by a grant from the Illinois Arts Council and sponsorship by the Illinois Labor History Society and the Latin American Advisory Council of Blue Island, the artists rented a wall for a nominal fee for ten years and sent a letter to the city council informing them of the project. The council, reportedly a mere rubber stamp for Mayor Withers, voted to deny a permit, alleging that the mural was "advertising" in violation of a zoning ordinance relating to signs. It was announced that anyone painting on the wall would be arrested. The real reasons had more to do with ethnic politics (few registered Chicano voters and a large Italian-Polish-German majority) and the feeling of many city officials that murals are "slum art" and lower the tone of an area.

The local press referred to the mural as "the forbidden mural" (pl. 20). *Steel Labor*, a publication of the United Steelworkers of America, headlined its December 1974 issue: "Is Blue Island, Illinois, so far from Red Square art haters?" And the lead paragraph went on: "George Meany recently asked a Senate committee 'What kind of society is it that has to turn bulldozers loose on paintings?' in recalling the recent disruption of an open-air art show in Moscow. A similar question might also be asked of the City Council here, which has 'forbidden' under threat of arrest the completion of a huge wall painting depicting the struggle of Mexican-American workers."[11]

Despite the ban and the threats, work proceeded with no arrests.

[10] *Straight Creek Journal*, October 12, 1972.
[11] "Is Blue Island, Illinois, so far from Red Square art haters?," *Steel Labor* (December 1974): 2.

José Nario received several threatening phone calls, and his home was vandalized. Nevertheless, according to John Weber, on the day he and ten other Chicago-area artists came to help with the work, there was evidence of widespread support from Anglos as well as from the Chicano community. A middle-aged "Sunday" painter from the area had joined the group, and late in the day an independent white contractor drove up in his truck and lent the painters his scaffold for as long as they needed it. Coffee and supper were also offered the artists.

Taking the case to court, the ACLU pleaded that the Supreme Court in *Papish* v. *Board of Curators of University of Missouri,* 410 U.S. 667 [1973] had extended full First Amendment protection to visual expression as a means of communication equivalent to written or spoken words. Judge Richard Austin ruled in favor of the mural, and the city council did not bother to appeal. Before work on the mural could resume in the summer of 1975, it was badly defaced. Nonetheless, the artists completed the mural, and it was blessed and celebrated on July 19 in a festive ceremony attended by community residents, labor leaders, and local and state politicians. In addition, the court's decision may prove to be a landmark victory for all artists and for public art in particular, although it does not remove the problem posed by politically powerful opponents of public art. The defeat of a patently unconstitutional use of a zoning ordinance does not exhaust the mechanisms they have at their disposal; they have other means, including violence.

In 1973, one of the murals by the Artes Guadalupanos group of Santa Fe, New Mexico, was destroyed when La Escuela Colegio Tonantzin, a Chicano alternate school, was attacked by police. The muralists, active in the school, had decorated the small building with bold murals reminiscent of Siqueiros. Police attacked with heavy-arms fire while fifty men, women, and children were inside celebrating the annual Fiesta de Santa Fe. Nineteen-year-old Linda Montoya was killed and several people were wounded. Seven young Chicanos were indicted for assault with intent to commit murder, although no arms were found. They were acquitted when the jury

82. Ray Patlán, José Nario, and Vicente Mendoza: *History of Mexican American Workers* (Teatro de Barrio performing at dedication). 1974–75. Blue Island, Illinois.

saw video tapes of the police vandalism—the entire building wrecked, every book, tool, picture, and musical instrument destroyed along with the murals. The victims have filed suit for damages, and the muralists have joined others in rebuilding the school.

Obviously, this attack was not specifically aimed at the murals, but rather at the Chicano people's movement. But it does show that the fate of community murals is linked to those people's movements and community organizations that have helped give them birth. In Chile, all the murals were destroyed by the fascist junta within a few weeks of the 1973 coup d'état.

The fate of federal funding of the mural movement in Santa Fe is also revealing. As long as Manpower funds were channeled into twenty-six independent street-based "corporations" through the Model Cities Program in Santa Fe, money was available to the mural program. In spite of the constant battle over control of the appropriations between the street-based programs and the politicians and poverty professionals, for two years (1971–72) the money, which included $100,000 for methadone programs, remained under community control. In late 1972, however, the workshops were shut down as the local politicians established control over the funds.

State-arts-council money is directly subject to pressures from the legislature, although the degree of subordination varies from state to state. The New York State Council on the Arts, which is very powerful and well funded, has far greater autonomy than the Illinois Arts Council, for example, which cut off funds for several years because of pressure from a powerful, conservative legislator.

Local Community Support

Neighborhood funding, the distinctive new component in today's mural movement, comes from a variety of sources: individual contributions, community organizations, settlement houses and churches, local businesses and national companies with local branches, schools and colleges. Although some cash donations usually are made, the larger contributions are generally in services, donated labor, and materials. These "in-kind donations" include the wall, paints, brushes, scaffolding, and other equipment, storage space, secretarial and publicity services, volunteer labor, food and refreshments, printing, etc. Some contributions are made directly to the artist. However, most often the neighborhood contribution is channeled through the sponsoring organization or coalition of community groups who back the mural project. Recently, labor organizations have begun to play a larger role as neighborhood sponsors. Amalgamated Meatcutters and Butcher Workmen of America, AFL-CIO, led the way in organized labor's support for mural activity by the early (1972) publication of an illustrated booklet on the Chicago murals,[12] regular publication of mural lists, and sponsorship or encouragement of murals on labor history.

Some neighborhood organizations, in the same way as banks or any other patrons, think of themselves as "buying" a mural and, through their concern "not to offend anyone," impose innumerable restrictions and demands on the artist, design, and content of the mural. This occurs most often when the mural is on an organization's wall in a well-to-do area. One agency director, who wanted his facility painted in supergraphics in order to create a more welcoming atmosphere for youth, initially agreed to let a muralist in Chicago develop designs with the local teen-agers. However, because the designs, though abstract, seemingly suggested clenched fists or other imagined evils, the agency director announced that approval of the board was necessary. Revision after revision was imposed upon the artist (even though the artist was not being paid by the agency). The teen-age painters went elsewhere, painting cartoons and supergraphics in other less public rooms and leaving the artist alone with the remains of his tarnished integrity. An artist must know how to walk away from such situations. The only response is: Since you know what you want, you don't need me. Hire yourself a decorator or paint it yourself.

It is not unheard of that such efforts to control and precensor results extend even to the murals of elementary school children. In the summer of 1974, children at a highly multinational school close to a fashionable Lakeside area in Chicago designed a mural with the support of the parents. Along with a school bus, crossing guard, etc., images of people carrying posters calling for protection of the environment and of consumers were asked for by the children. "Oh, no!" one well-to-do consumer-parent objected, "we mustn't offend the local merchants." In another case, teachers and parents were harassed by police to force the removal of a slogan from a children's mural.

[12] *Cry for Justice* (Chicago: Amalgamated Meatcutters and Butcher Workmen of America, AFL-CIO, 1972).

These instances, although not typical, are revealing. They point to the question of who wants community art and who defends it; for in the last analysis, it is on these forces that the future of public art depends. Many community muralists contend that establishment support for public art is temporary and conditional. Building and relying upon community support therefore becomes even more crucial. Where the local funds come from a single source (a local school, college, bank office, YMCA, settlement or community house, church), if the artist and sponsor cannot agree, obviously the project cannot proceed. Most often, however, the neighborhood funding comes from a coalition of community groups, a kind of united front of organizations, small businesses, individuals, institutions, etc. The base of community support for the mural and muralist may spread to an even larger group of less organized elements—parents of participants, residents and their families or friends, old-timers, etc. The commitment of at least a few conscientious individuals is the indispensable leaven in developing broad support.

Corporate Patronage

There is much talk about private corporations and foundations funding the public arts, but little money is produced. Typical of the talk, and the results, is a cute glossy publication put out by The Foundation for Full Service Banks and the American Bankers Association, entitled *Special Report: Your Role as Banker to the Arts* (1971). It is a guide for bankers who want to help fund the arts and thereby improve their own corporate image. Thus far, corporations and foundations have not provided much funding for the mural movement. Most active have been a few liberal foundations like J. M. Kaplan Foundation and occasional corporate giants like Exxon. Their funding of local "community development" efforts has given important support—all the more welcome because money has been given to support general programs rather than as strings-attached support for specific items. Such support, however, is always for a limited period.

83. Chuy Campusano, Luis Cortazar, Michael Rios, and others: Bank of America mural (central section). 1974. San Francisco.

Local banks have contributed occasional funding, and one major mural has been commissioned by a bank. The Bank of America commissioned (for $15,000) three Chicano artists in San Francisco's Mission district to design a mural for its new Mission branch. Chuy Campusano, Luis Cortazar, and Michael Rios designed and, with five other Mission artists, executed the powerful ninety- by ten-foot work, a far cry from the usual bland reliefs found in bank lobbies. One surmises that the commission was motivated by the destruction of various branches of the bank in recent years and by the mounting opposition to Bank of America in the Mission district itself. It is well known that the banker for agribusinesses that exploit Chicano, Filipino, Arab, black, and other poor farm workers in California is Bank of America. No doubt the presence of the mural serves as a sort of fire insurance for the branch, but one wonders if the Bank didn't get more than it bargained for. One image in the mural is that of a dark-skinned laborer holding a booklet that proclaims, "Our sweat and our blood have fallen on this land to make other men rich." The muralists, who agreed to submit their designs and themes to the Bank for approval, expressed their overall sentiment in the dedication plaque: "We wanted to create a medley of scenes depicting the heritage, life, and hopes of the Mission community. This mural is for everybody—the bank personnel, the people on the other side of the counter, the people walking outside the windows." The muralists' pamphlet, *Tres Muralistas,* summarizing the history of the mural and incidents of Bank censorship, was summarily confiscated by Bank officials at the June 1974 opening.

Inevitably, one thinks of Diego Rivera's *Man at the Crossroads* mural in Rockefeller Center destroyed on order of Nelson Rockefeller, the great patron of the arts, because Rivera would not remove the face of Lenin. The Bank of America has not removed the mural, but it has removed the words from the booklet in the laborer's hand—not on the wall itself, but in the photographs of the mural the Bank circulates in its propaganda about its "social concern."

In considering the nature and limitations of establishment support for public art, the question arises: To whom does the art belong? To those who own the walls or to the masses, to the general public? And will those who own the official art world and run it as a private club see fit to pay for an art that cannot be owned by them? Rupert Garcia, author of *Raza Murals and Muralists: An Historical View,*[13] has aptly phrased the problem: "trying to make art for the public when the public doesn't own public spaces."[14]

Property Rights versus Culture

This conflict between property rights and the human right to culture was manifested in the controversy surrounding the mural *Imperialism* in the corridor of the sociology department at Livingston College by People's Painters (fig. 73). The business manager of the college told the muralists: "Sociology does not own this wall." An experienced muralist in the Mission district painted over a liquor ad billboard with a bright scene celebrating Mis-

[13] (San Francisco: Galeria de la Raza, 1974).
[14] Cited by Ceci Brunazzi, "Murals in the Mission," *Common Sense* 2, no. 6 (May 1975): 8.

84. *Salsa Ahora.* 1975. San Francisco.

sion life, only to have the billboard company cover the mural with yet another ad. The muralist tore down the ad to reveal the mural beneath, and the battle for public space has raged on since. Mark Rogovin's *Protect the People's Homes* mural was painted out after the building was sold. Murals facing upon empty lots have been blocked from view by new buildings constructed after the sale of the lots—e.g. Mitchell Caton's *Philosophy of the Spiritual* (fig. 64) and the Los Angeles Fine Arts Squad's *Venice in the Snow.* One attempted solution has been the leasing of a wall. Although this raises the moral commitment of the present landlord to a legal status, it cannot protect against such "property rights" in cases of sale or new construction.

The Question of Opportunism

Another question arises, for the muralists and for the community—the question of opportunism. The Mission-district muralists, realizing they were subject to charges of "collaboration with the agents of imperialism" in doing the Bank of America mural, noted Diego Rivera's mural for the Pacific Stock Exchange and carefully explained their Rivera-like position. They felt that the advantages of presenting images to their people as they stood before the tellers' cages were important. Chicanos generally mention the mural with pride. The question of accepting commissions from the "agents of imperialism" is complicated by the general dearth of funding for socially conscious murals, especially when one considers that almost all private and public donors are tainted to one degree or another by imperialism.

In essence, all forms of opportunism in community art come down to the single question: Is the artist using art to serve the people and the people's struggle? Or is the people's struggle being used to serve the artist? One obvious form of opportunism is tailoring proposals according to available funding. The desire for success in proposal writing can also operate subtly, encouraging a form of self-censorship. An example might be when an artist seeking funds for a youth program promises that nothing political or militant will be allowed. The opportunism lies in co-opting the expression of the teen-agers in advance.

Muralists often receive offers to do additional murals that are for essentially commercial purposes. They may be as crass as the request to paint washing machines at a cleaner's or dragons for a Chinese restaurant, or they may be more indirect, such as the music store that wanted (and got) a mural about music or the pharmacy that sponsored a mural about health. Where does one draw the line? In the cases of the music store and pharmacy, the offers were accepted because the themes had genuine broad appeal, there were no other strings attached, and the store owners were willing to back the murals financially and morally. The artists were given freedom to relate to the community. The temptation to cater to local business interests is nonetheless real.

A type of careerism that aims higher than this sort of custom sign painting is that of "fine arts" mural painting. By a "fine arts" mentality, we mean the running after approval from establishment critics, the identification of success with certification by the official art world rather than by the community audience.

Two related errors that border on opportunism we might call *bohemianism* and *tailism*. The artist who insists on being bohemian wants to paint murals without sacrificing the bourgeois image of the artist. He feels impelled to continue to mystify; therefore, he cannot discuss or explain. He insists on personal perception only. One can "dig" him but not understand his work. The work of such personalities may result in excellent art. But their insistence on a privileged position creates difficulties for themselves and for other muralists, since they are too "sensitive" to organize, raise funds, teach, or otherwise help. Among Chicanos, bohemian muralism may assume a number of poses based on the "great man" legends of Rivera, Orozco, or Siqueiros. White and black artists also manage to invent "great man" images without the aid of such good scripts.

Tailism is almost the opposite fault. By tailism we mean the tendency for the artist to abandon the responsibility of personal judgment out of a desire to involve and to please the community audience or the members of a sponsoring organization. If one accepts every suggestion willy-nilly, one is likely to paint a meaningless and superficial mural that often bears no relation to anything, except picture postcards. Murals cannot be ordered like wallpaper out of a pattern book although sometimes, after a slide show, people say, "We'd like *that* one."

Another type of opportunism has to do with claiming "territory," as if a neighborhood were a franchise. This involves making every effort to keep other artists out, rather than encouraging them also to contribute their efforts to public art.

The importance of the question of opportunism is not that it is prevalent in the mural movement. In fact, out-and-out opportunism is quite rare. The hard work and difficulty of the mural process itself tend to discourage and weed out opportunists. The openness of the mural process to community participation and the artist's involvement with the audience reinforce principled behavior and support the artist's developing a fuller consciousness. It is nonetheless important to deal with opportunism, because at each step of the way the artist is faced with choices, with temptations, with a subtle or not so subtle struggle for control. Ultimately, the artist is faced with the question, On whom do you rely?

Struggle for Control of Art

In any society characterized by class divisions and class conflict, there is always a struggle for control of art (not only of visual art, but of all cultural expression). The studio artist is often not conscious of this, because his or her art is produced for an unknown audience, to be distributed as a commodity in the art market. The control of the bourgeois collectors, speculators, and bureaucrats, exercised indirectly, is hidden. Despite this mystification, the history of modern art, we would suggest, is the history of the struggle of the artists to elude this control.

A mural, however, is produced directly for the audience, and the struggle for control of its expression is correspondingly direct and immediate. Although the parties involved rarely *state* their intent openly, the artist cannot help but be aware of the existing pressures. Therefore, those artists who might seek to ignore this reality—and who would like to see murals for everyone and no one in particular, who are tired of "partisan propaganda," and who want murals "just to make people happy"—are sticking their heads in the sand.

The artist is always accountable to someone or to some group. If it is not to the community, then it must be to outside forces, e.g. government or agency funding sources. Often, in different ways, the artist is accountable to both—to outside funding for ways in which the funds are spent and to the audience for content and form. In past ages, the artist was accountable to the aristocratic patron. Today, the community artist is thinking of community residents as the collective patron.

The struggle is real, not only between the local community and government bodies responsive to larger-scale interests, but also *within* the community between bureaucracy and rank-and-file, agency directors and agency clients, organization leaders or ministers and membership, owners and tenants, middle class and working class. The conflicts between these elements, however, are not generally the major aspect of community problems, which are mainly produced and controlled by larger forces and interests outside the community itself. Local leadership often sincerely shares the concerns of membership; small owners, local businesspeople, and tenants all suffer, though not equally, from planned deterioration, disinvestment, and dispossession by urban renewal. Community mural work depends upon uniting these different strata in support of a project.

The murals are not for the working class alone, but are for and by a united front of street people, working people, and middle class (or, in classical terms, lumpen, proletariat, and petite bourgeoisie). It is nonetheless true that the masses—in particular, the working class—must lead. It is they (i.e. the working people, the youth, the membership, the tenants, the rank-and-file) whose interest, support, and involvement are crucial, even though the support of the local leadership, ministers, owners, etc., must also be won in order to obtain permission for walls, street permits, donations for paint and equipment, and the like. But the latter only "need" public art to the extent that public art does speak to and win the respect of the masses.

11

Aesthetics

> The highest, most logical, purest and most powerful type of painting is mural painting. It is also the most disinterested, as it cannot be converted into an object of personal gain nor can it be concealed for the benefit of a few privileged people. It is for the people. It is for everybody.
>
> —José Clemente Orozco.

> A mural painting is far from being an enlarged easel painting. Critics agree that there is a mural style, that it involves a composition, a drawing, a modeling, and a color that may be called specifically mural.
>
> —Jean Charlot, "Public Speaking in Paint."

What distinguishes mural from easel painting is the question of context: architectural, environmental, and social. Mural painting is much older than easel painting, Giotto and Masaccio, Rivera and Orozco, like today's muralists, had to deal with all the various dimensions of context in designing their walls. Yet, the current tendency to study art from slides and photographs, and even to remove murals from their original sites to museums for preservation, tends to negate the role that specific site and audience played in determining the forms of these works of art. This "rendezvous of subject matter and site"[1] has, throughout history, provided the aesthetic base line for the criticism and evaluation of murals.

The Wall

In contrast to the virtual space, or "magic window," created by the format of easel painting, the limits of the picture plane of a mural are the limits of the building itself. Before any other consideration of format or architectonics, there is the physical reality of the wall. It has an architectural function as a support, and although one is rather less conscious of this outdoors than indoors, the supportive quality of the wall is an objective and a psychic fact. Horizontal and vertical lines become first of all structural elements related to the architectural quality of the wall, and only secondarily elements in virtual space. The physical reality of the wall can be disguised or affirmed, but it cannot be ignored.

The mural painter begins by studying the wall, the kind of light it receives, its texture, etc. A north wall that will be in the shade almost all year will make the colors appear cooler; intense sunlight bleaches color and makes it pale. While most murals have been painted on brick, many, especially in the West, have been painted on smooth surfaces like concrete or adobe. A smooth cement wall will allow placement of details and lines freely, while on a brick wall with deep-set mortar, the shadow lines of the coursing must be taken into account in placing the detail lines.

Even as the shape of the wall determines the shape of the painting, so the irregularities of the wall—fire escapes, windows, moldings, ins and outs, as well as the shadows they cast—need to be dealt with in a creative way. Often, these "obstacles" can be transformed into creative elements of the design and become assets. The window that forms the mouth of the rain-god in the Clínica mural by Artes Guadalupanos de Aztlán is one example of a simple and ingenious solution, where the entire effect is intensified by the natural shadow and indentation of the deep window (pl. 16).

[1] Lawrence Alloway, "Art," *The Nation,* August 3, 1974.

85. Jim Dong: incorporating obstacles in the International Hotel mural (detail). 1974. San Francisco.

86. Eva Cockcroft, director: incorporating obstacles in *Education Is the Way to Liberation* (detail). 1975. Jersey City State College, New Jersey.

There are three basic attitudes muralists have taken toward such obstacles, and toward architectonics: to *reinforce* the wall with a painted architectural framework, to *absorb* the geometry of the wall fixtures by mediating forms, or optically to *obliterate* and disguise the features of the wall. These contrasting approaches can be identified with the three great Mexican masters—Rivera, Orozco, and Siqueiros. Contemporary muralists have learned from, reinvented, varied, and extended their methods. The difference can be suggested by the various ways that a rectangular air vent might be treated. It might be reinforced by supporting it within a painted pillar; it might be absorbed by a series of rectangular background forms or mediating organic forms that cause it to blend into the general pattern of the mural and become unnoticeable; or it might

87. Reinforcement: William Walker: Untitled mural. 1971–73. Stranger Home, MBC, Chicago.

be obliterated by turning it into a table or bench on which a figure could be sitting. In practice, most artists use a combination of techniques within a single mural, emphasizing some of the architectural features and absorbing others.

Again, the difference in attitude is shown by the treatment of a corner. The corner can be affirmed by a painted post visually supporting the wall, or by using the corner metaphorically as part of a solid building, machine, etc. Alternatively, the eye can be carried around the corner by related forms that echo one another on either side. The third possibility is visually to eliminate the corner by running optically continuous lines or forms through it. This last approach is derived from Siqueiros's polyangular perspective. A concave corner can be completely eliminated (given even lighting) from all angles, but a convex corner can be eliminated from only a limited number of angles.

88. William Walker: Untitled mural (detail). 1971–73. Stranger Home, MBC, Chicago.

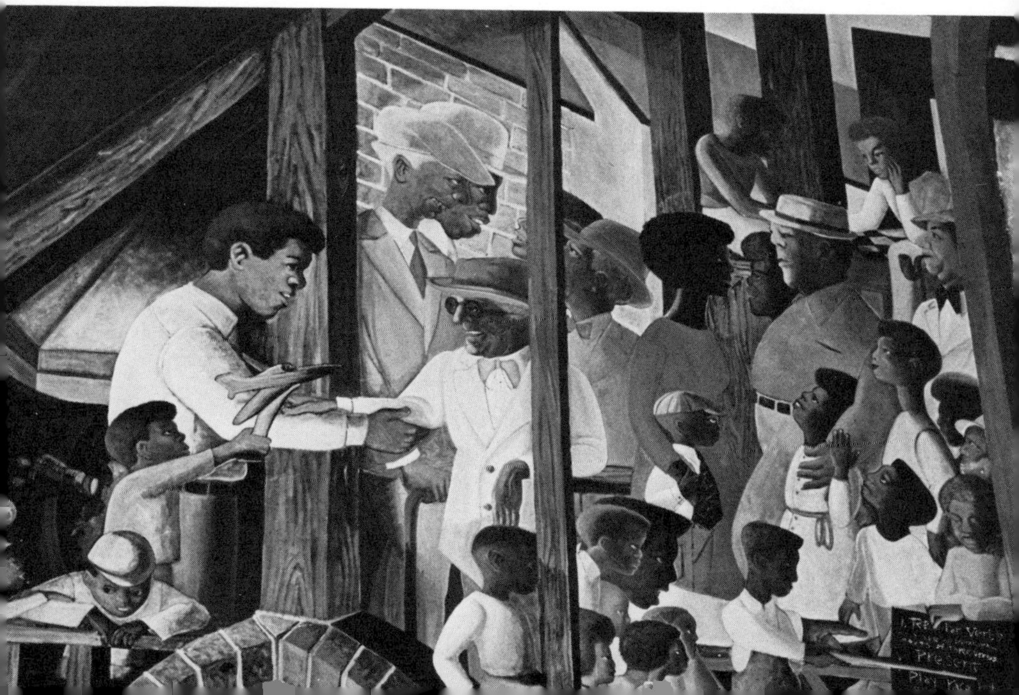

89. Absorption (with reinforcement): John Weber and José Guerrero: *Solidarity Murals* (detail). 1974. United Electrical Workers Hall, Chicago.

90. Opposing approaches to a corner (reinforcement): Astrid Fuller: *Rebirth*. 1974. Chicago.

91. Opposing approaches to a corner (obliteration): Artes Guadalupanos de Aztlán: *St. Francis Road Mural* (detail). 1972. Santa Fe, New Mexico.

92. Opposing approaches to a corner (combination): John Weber and José Guerrero: *Solidarity Murals* (detail). 1974. United Electrical Workers Hall, Chicago.

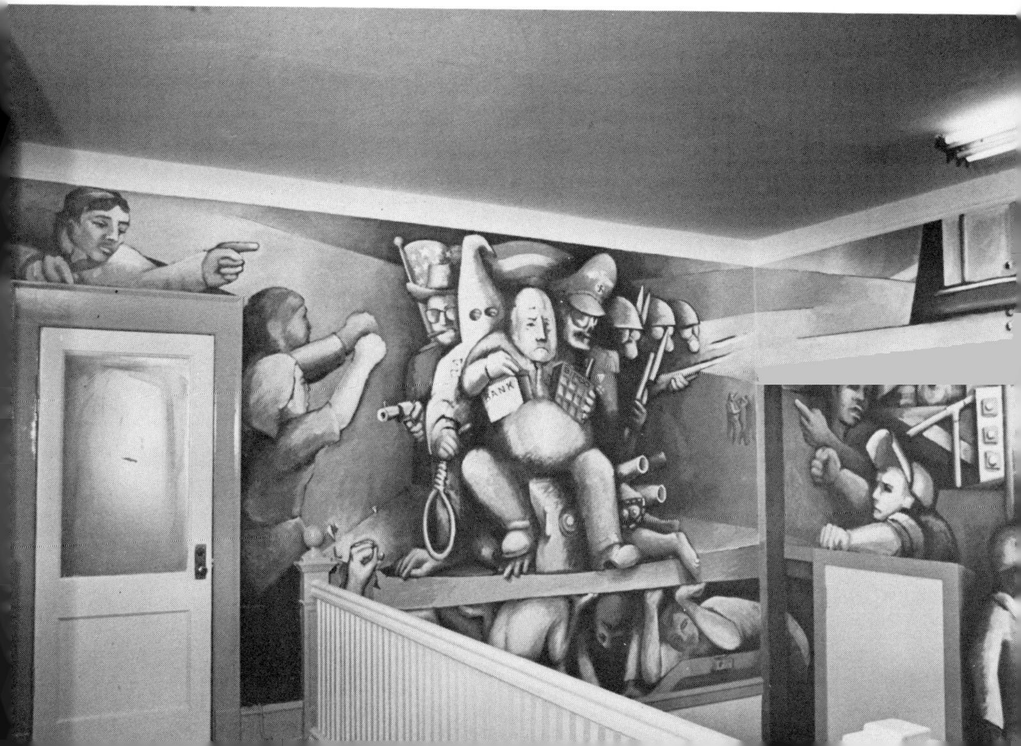

Space

Indoors, a mural is often a painted space extending (and continuous with) the real interior space within which the viewer stands. Such effects are less natural to outdoor murals, where the wall appears as a flat plane in a surrounding open space. However, the photo-realist approach tries optically to eliminate the architectural quality of the wall and present an illusion of continuity with the viewer's space. In this approach, both stage space and the architectural frame of the wall are eliminated; real and illusionary sky blend together (fig. 11).

Although the problems involved in designing within an enclosed space and for an open area differ, certain kinds of adjustments for the angle of vision of the viewer remain constant. If the perspective of the viewer is from below, the muralist must increase the size of the figures as they move higher and higher on the wall, to make them appear the same. If the angle of vision is often from the side, the figures must be widened and made more bulky lest they almost disappear from a lateral view. Rather than a single perspective or viewing point, the muralist has to deal with all the problems of multiple perspectives, of both centered and lateral vision, as well as the distortions of mass created by the angle of vision. All these problems and their solutions tend toward the use of a flatter space and simpler volumes, a solution that happily coincides with the modern preference to respect the integrity of a surface.

Today's muralist must also consider the character of the surrounding buildings, the type of neighborhood, and the kind of traffic. In a location like Chatham Square in New York City's Chinatown, a complex meditative mural like *Peace and Salvation* (pl. 9) would be lost amid the many competing stimuli. On the other hand, the billboard style of the Chinatown mural painted by Cityarts Workshop carries its message and blazons its images above the competing stimuli of other posters, signs, and traffic.

Another sort of problem is presented by underpass and corridor

93. Alan Okada and Asian youths: *History of Chinese Immigration to the United States* (partial view). 1972. Chatham Square, New York.

murals, in which the viewing distance is very limited and the format is exceedingly long and low. In Caryl Yasko's *Under City Stone,* based on the poem "Rapid Transit" by James Agee, the design objective was to brighten the dark underpass. Yasko divided the area into three undulating bands of bright color that repeat the curve of the underpass arches and provide a rhythmic motion. The two upper bands carry the words of the poem and a series of machine forms respectively, while the larger lower area contains a series of 133 life-size figures that are walking along, a mirror of the traffic that passes through the pedestrian walkway toward the lake. Astrid Fuller uses a different approach to the problem in her underpass murals (fig. 90). Using painted architectural elements that repeat the forms of the underpass structure, Fuller divided the area

94. Caryl Yasko, director: *Under City Stone* (detail). 1972. Chicago.

95. Brigada Ramona Parra: *Fabrilana Mural*. 1972. Santiago, Chile.

into a series of scenes, each based on local history and current problems, which unfold for the pedestrian like chapters in a novel.

The narrow corridor murals of the People's Painters, where the problem of short viewing distance becomes extreme, combine the narrative-series technique with a floating rhythmic pattern on the wall to open up space in the corridor (fig. 73). The use of a rhythmic horizontal series of forms that relate to the horizontality of the format manifests the same constructive principles employed by the Chileans in such murals as the *Fabrilana* textile-plant wall, where relation to the elongated format is implied through the movements but not explicitly stated.

Scale

The classical approach to scale was to suggest normal size from average points of view. In the Sistine Chapel, where heroic scale was desired, Michelangelo found, after beginning work, that even the mammoth scale he had adopted was lost when seen from the ground. He was forced to adjust the scale of the figures in the course of painting the ceiling. Scale is also an expressive device used for emphasis; consequently, a number of different-size elements are often combined in a single mural.

The way scale is seen by the viewer is relative to the viewing distance, the size of the wall, its texture, and the scale of the surrounding elements. It is not uncommon for artists to discover (like Michelangelo) that the scale must be adjusted in the course of the painting so that it will read in the same way as it did in their sketches. One of the advantages of direct painting on the wall (as opposed to working on panels or on canvas as was common in the WPA) is that the scale can easily be adjusted to the actual viewing conditions of the site.

Working in very large scale, which reduces the apparent size of the wall, allows a greater viewing distance and permits the mural to compete with large elements in the environment, effects often desired in outdoor work. This technique is often used in those murals

96. Scale: James Brown: Mural at the Third Nail. 1971. Roxbury Crossing, Boston.

97. Scale: Mitchell Caton with Santi Isrowuthakul, William Walker, and poet Siddha: *Day Dreaming, Nightmare*. 1975. Chicago.

intended for motor traffic, to be viewed from great distances or in extremely busy locations. Although sometimes the primary element, as in James Brown's Roxbury antidrug mural, very large-scale figures also lend themselves to combination with other elements of different sizes. Montage-designed murals like those of Cityarts Workshop generally use a series of elements of varying size, with the shifting scale used for both emphasis and design clarity (e.g. fig. 34). Complex scale combinations from the extremely large to the very small are also used by Mitchell Caton and form an important part of his style.

Normal scale, that is, elements that read as life-size, tends to enforce a uniformity of scale in figuration. It is commonly used where the figures are close to the viewer and in indoor work. Smaller-than-life-size forms and extremely small-scale drawings have also been used indoors to expand the wall and the sense of space. On a large high wall like *Chi Lai–Arriba–Rise Up!* (pl. 12), the effect of normal scale is expanded as the figures increase organically in size to the very top, where the unity image grows out of the scenes of oppression below. The scale increase, which is greater than necessary to compensate for perspective distortion, is used here in an expressive manner to emphasize the power of the people in unity and struggle.

The objectively large size of mural elements (even when they may appear scarcely larger than life-size from the ground) affects the way a painter works in a direct physical way. Finger and wrist movements are replaced by a shift to shoulder and whole-body motions. This shift affects mural style, furthering heroic rather than delicate work. The tendency toward broad effects is further conditioned by the fact that fancy brushwork and small subtle changes tend to be lost at the usual viewing distances. Mural painting, therefore, tends to be less dependent on finesse in the actual painting than on the power of the conception and preliminary design considerations.

The broader, more systematic methods natural to mural painting are an important element in the success and popularity of group work in painting murals both in the past and today. To some extent, it explains how murals painted by many hands with unequal degrees of skill can attain a consistent style and high aesthetic quality.

Style

Siqueiros wrote:

> The inescapable problem for us was to express ourselves with a figurative art capable of saying things which were important to our people. . . . non-figurative art did not serve our purpose. . . . If you do not want to paint figurative art, find it in your own artistic ideology, with your own names, symbols, and essential abstract elements, but try to say something of the past of your people and of your concept of what its future should be.[2]

Basically, we would agree with Siqueiros in affirming the natural affinity between muralism and the image of humanity; most of today's muralists have chosen to speak in a figurative manner. However, some have chosen to work in a nonfigurative mode, and those who have followed Siqueiros's dictum of drawing from the past and present of their people, their essential symbols and abstract elements, have been able to communicate successfully. Mario Castillo is a case in point (fig. 4). Others who have done murals in this more abstract vein include Leonard Castellanos, Charles Felix, Mario Galán, Carlos Barrera, and Gary Rickson.

Contemporary painting norms have affected not only the abstract branch of the mural movement but also the figurative schools. To confuse current figurative murals with academic realism would be a serious error. These murals are rarely a rehash of socialist realism or the heroic regionalism of the WPA. In fact, the two major categories of figurative murals, the more poster-influenced murals and the more meditative painterly-thematic walls, derive from other more contemporary sources. Painterly styles used by individual muralists

[2] David Alfaro Siqueiros, "Lectures to Artists," *New University Thought* (Winter 1962).

draw on such recent mural and canvas traditions as the Mexican mural movement, Cubism (and/or the African sculptural tradition on which Cubism drew), Surrealism, etc. The work of Mitchell Caton, for example, shows how an African-Cubist artistic influence can be transformed into a new and highly individual style. In regard to his approach, Caton has commented: "Early in my life as an artist, I had the idea of finding a technical approach which would enable me to capture what especially interested me in the city. The threading traffic, its lights, the river of humanity chartered and flowing through and around itself, imposed limitations. Who knows consciously what they are doing when creating?"[3] Surrealism has influenced the styles of such community muralists as Willie Herrón, Don Pellett, Castillo, and Rickson. Many muralists use surrealist-related approaches to composition, "discovering" images in the wall (e.g. Herrón), or in abstract linear networks of freehand rhythmic line, or in constructed perspective lines. Only rarely has a single style influence been copied in a mechanical fashion. More often, the ongoing developments in contemporary art have been combined with other sources and shaped to the demands of the mural form.

William Walker has achieved a fully developed personal art that extends the classical tradition of Rivera. His sensitivity to architecture and site can be seen in the interior and exterior murals of Stranger Home MBC, formerly the Saint Marcellus Church. In the interior murals (figs. 87 and 88), the beams of the roof of the small church have been repeated in the painting to form ordered spaces in front and behind the structures in which the scenes of the painting are both separated and connected to each other and the architecture. In the lower sections, the brick of the church has been carried into the mural above; the bricked-in window has been optically reopened and emphasized as a basic structure.

The outdoor environment provides relatively little in the way of architectural "clues" or support. Walker's originality is most clearly revealed in his compositional use of the surrounding environment, of wall textures, his adaptation of palette to available light and

[3] Chicago Mural Group Report to National Endowment for the Arts, 1972.

surrounding color. In *Peace and Salvation* (pl. 9), the emphasis on the brick texture and the use of painted brick tie the painting to the building and to the surrounding environment, creating a shifting back and forth between real wall and painted wall. A photograph cannot capture the powerful impact of this mural, either in its compositional and textual detail or in its larger, immense space. The painted posters on the lower left-hand side of the mural integrate and repeat the forms of the real signs on the street beyond. The radical use of reverse perspective and the integration of emblematic symbolic elements are typical techniques of Walker's muralism. The four hands, the confrontation faces, the four figures with interlocking faces, the chess game, the unity march—each appears in four different murals by Walker between 1967 and 1975.

The publication of photos of Siqueiros's work in the popular press and in Chicano publications brought this master's work to the attention of many who do not read art journals. In general, muralists searching for guidance and training in the early years of the movement made use of the available illustrated books of the Mexican murals and took from them what they needed. This influence most often was not so much a direct take-over of symbols or design elements as it was knowledge of the constructive principles employed by the Mexicans. Sometimes, local murals painted by the Mexicans in the United States were a more direct source.

The work of Artes Guadalupanos de Aztlán combines quotations and adaptations of Siqueiros's great mural in La Raza Hospital, Mexico City (the perspective grid background, the heroic worker), with pre-Columbian, traditional folk art and artisanal tourist elements transformed into a very recognizable and coherent group style. They use doorways, windows, corners, etc., metaphorically as active elements of imagery. A similar delight in ingenious transformations of architectural accident is found in other artists influenced by Siqueiros, e.g. Ray Patlán, Mark Rogovin.

Patlán has steadily developed from Siqueiroesque beginnings toward a more personal, complex, and metaphorical style. Like that of certain other Chicano muralists, his work often combines flat pre-

98. Ray Patlán: *Rising Sun of Justice* (detail). 1974. Mount Carmel Chapel, Joliet, Illinois.

99. Mark Rogovin, director: *Break the Grip of the Absentee Landlord.* 1972–73. Chicago.

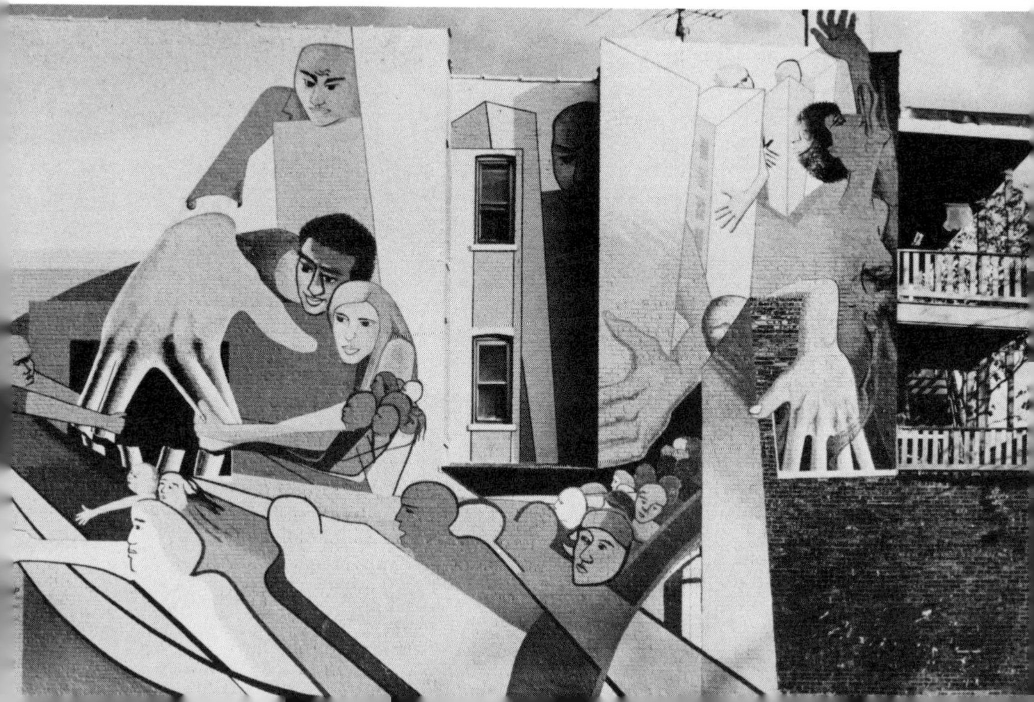

Columbian designs with fully modeled figures. Dewey Crumpler in San Francisco and Esteban Villa in Sacramento are two other highly distinctive artists in the dramatic tradition of Siqueiros and Orozco. Rogovin's relation to Siqueiros is somewhat different, dating from the graphic style of Siqueiros's workshop for the Polyforum in Mexico City in which Rogovin participated. The simplified forms of Rogovin's "direct impact" murals are based on an analysis of the moving viewers' "polyangular perspective." One of the innovations in Rogovin's *Break the Grip* is the use of the bare brick compositionally as a "wall" in the mural.

The late-Siqueiros influence toward graphic, simplified form and strong directional movements, as in the murals of Rogovin (and Lucy Mahler in New York City), is combined with a tendency toward quite flat color, which gives these murals a posterlike look. For those like Rogovin who paint "aimed art" directed at specific local issues, the carrying power of a flat graphic style provides an effective vehicle because of its high legibility and dramatic impact. *Break the Grip* deals with an urgent local problem, absentee landlordism and its social consequences; in fact, the mural faces the office of the local alderman.

Other muralists have been influenced by event-oriented *topical* posters. The idea of using walls as giant posters or billboards has produced certain consciously temporal murals. The Walls of Respect and Truth are a case in point. This national precedent was reinforced by the example of the Chilean brigades in the early 1970s. The Chileans' rapid collective method of work, Légeresque rhythmic designs, and concern for temporality were widely publicized within the mural movement. Not only the Chilean idea of poster-function murals, but also their style has had an influence. The use of floating forms, a heavy black outline, and pure flat color—so well suited to a long horizontal format and group work with semiskilled artists—can be seen in the work of the People's Painters, John Weber's ACLU billboard (fig. 8), and a series of Puerto Rican murals painted to advertise the massive pro-Independence rally in Madison Square Garden, October 1974.

Traditional poster-art techniques, especially serigraphy, have also provided a direct style influence. The 1960s saw a tremendous revival in politically oriented silk-screen posters: Cuban, French, antiwar, and psychedelic posters became common wall decorations not just in movement offices but also in middle-class homes. Cooperative silk-screen workshops sprang up in many cities, often with close relations to mural workshops. Because the kinds of simplifications of forms used in graphic work are similar to those necessary in murals, similar methods have often been used. The depiction of faces with a solid single-color shadow area common in photo–silk-screen is also common in murals. For example, the Grove Street campus of Merritt College in Oakland, California (later phased out), blossomed with a number of such faces. A similar technique appears in Cityarts' *History of Chinese Immigration* mural in Chatham Square (fig. 93). Multicolor silk-screen posters, which often juxtapose areas of bright, unmixed color, have a counterpart in the type of color use employed by San Francisco's Mujeres Muralistas (pls. 6 and 17), as well as in certain ethnic-design and emblematic murals elsewhere in the nation.

Another important graphic influence is that of comix and cartoons. Comix-derived graphic styles were important in the early Raza murals in San Francisco. One style was based on the underground comix of Robert Crumm, who collaborated with the artists on a mural at the Mission Rebels youth center in 1972. The other comic-book style, based on standard teen romances, can be seen in the Jamestown mural in the type of color, line, and the use of thought balloons. The reinvented pre-Columbian idols, which, like a Greek chorus, echo and comment on the action, are an additional narrative touch. More recent work in San Francisco, especially following the Bank of America mural (fig. 83), shows a shift from popular influences toward a more constructed, Riveraesque look.

Both collage and photomontage are two other poster-related styles in common use, especially for group work. Although the scale shifts involved in this style have a tradition in Mexican and WPA mural design, the current montage murals tend toward a more

100. Consuelo Méndez: Jamestown mural (detail). 1972. Jamestown School and Recreation Center, San Francisco.

graphic look. The possibilities for combining a whole series of different ideas into a coherent mural design through photomontage methods are optimally manifested in the mural at Bialystoker House in New York City (fig. 34). The mural incorporates the whole spectrum of feelings within the Jewish community about their identity and heritage.

Most collective youth murals use flat poster-related styles because they provide a simple vehicle for introducing untrained persons to mural art. Techniques especially developed for figurative murals with beginning groups—photomontage and drawing montage used with projection, silhouette projection, and rhythmic line—have helped create this large body of work. The varicolored overlapping silhouettes typical of the silhouette-projection technique have a distinctive look in that the flat patterns and shallow space implied by the figures demand an equally patterned and abstract background. The free rhythmic-line method often leads to bold graphic and poetic juxtapositions reminiscent of Chilean murals. As groups work on more than one mural, they generally begin to experiment with more complex thematic and visual ideas. Systematic techniques for modeling (e.g. all forms modeled from left to right, or from full-intensity color to white) allow an entire group to work in the same style and are often used to produce 3-D effects. As the same group of artists continue to work together, they tend to move from this kind of rigid stipulation to a more informal blending of styles.

Groups formed by artists with developed individual styles usually modify their individual styles to develop a group style that is harmonious. Sometimes, however, stylistic harmony is achieved by a consistency of color intensity, or a division of the format into distinct areas that are stylistically different yet related—e.g. figurative scenes within supergraphic frameworks.

The diversity of mural styles that now exists is a reflection of the diverse bases of the movement and the actual diversity of American society. There is no homogeneous American society: Why should the art historians and critics search for an "American" style?

Nor is there a class style, although there is a class *content*. It was the Zhdanovist confusion between style and content that led to the senseless imposition of an outworn academism as a standard for socially committed art. Today's muralists have become committed to serving the people "through the process of going into their very midst."[4] This raises the question of popularization versus raising of standards. Today's established critics have, for the most part, alternately deprecated public art in general as "poor art for poor people," ignoring in bad faith the masterpieces of this young movement or, adopting a romantic pose, have patronized "naïve" graffiti.

The issue of popularization and raising of standards is a developing, living one, which can only be answered by addressing the question: *whose* standards? Our concern is first of all the com-

[4] Mao Tse-tung, "Talks at the Yenan Forum on Literature and Art" (May 1942) in *Selected Works* 3: 78.

munity audience. In establishing intelligible styles, what is truly popular cannot be viewed as static and rooted only in the past. Although contemporary muralists have legitimately drawn from poster art, film, comix, precolonial symbols, and folk designs, such elements mechanically repeated and divorced from the context of change and struggle can rapidly be adapted as commercial cliché formulas for the anodyne picturesque. Artists such as Siqueiros and poet and playwright Bertolt Brecht were resolutely modernist and functional. In his essay "The Popular and the Realistic," Brecht is perfectly clear about the purpose of his art: "There is only one ally against the growth of barbarism: the people on whom it imposes these sufferings. Only the people offer any prospects. Thus it is natural to turn to them and more necessary than ever to speak their language."[5] But Brecht is equally clear that "to speak their language" does not mean to play down to a lowest common denominator of the familiar. "Besides *being popular* there is such a thing as *becoming popular*. If we want a truly popular literature, alive and fighting, completely gripping reality, then we must keep pace with reality's headlong development."[6]

The possibility of developing a genuine people's art is verified by the types of criticism emerging directly from the communities in which today's murals are created. Many muralists have spoken of the frank and uninhibited criticism they receive from local residents. Dana Chandler of Boston comments: "Then I discovered that my best critics and most important people were the people to whom it was directed. . . . [Art] critics don't understand what I am doing. First of all, they don't understand why the images remain simple and don't become complex. Black people have no qualms about criticizing . . . when it isn't right, they'll tell me."[7] As shown in the narratives in chapters 4 and 5, criticism from the community emerges on different levels as people watch the mural progress. As

[5] Bertolt Brecht, *Brecht on Theatre, 1933–1947*, ed. John Willet (New York: Hill & Wang, 1964), p. 107.

[6] *Ibid.*, p. 112.

[7] Dana Chandler, interview with Eva Cockcroft, 1974.

the wall nears completion, the type of criticism becomes more astute. People not only question the content of images but advise the artist on the drawing, talk in terms of the relation of one figure to another, and compare the handling of different elements within the mural.

As a series of murals go up in an area, neighborhood critics, like any other critics, tend to compare the relative merits and meaning of a mural with previous murals by the same artist, as well as with other murals. People's close observation of a mural in process, of the changes an artist makes and the reasons for them, develops their sensibility to craftsmanship, symbolism, and imagery. The creative act is demystified, and people come to respect the work, skill, and art involved in mural painting. Their aesthetic standards are raised. In the case of neighborhood youths who help paint a mural, the experience sometimes turns them toward intensive study of art. We have already noted how several graffitists have been moved, under the influence of murals, toward higher levels of artistic expression. This new grass-roots interest in art extends far beyond actual participants in mural projects. As early as 1971, it was possible to hold seminars on mural painting in Chicago's Cabrini-Green public housing projects. Anyone who has done any type of organizational work will easily appreciate the level of interest represented by over two hundred people, adults and children, crowding in to see slides and discuss mural painting. Brecht's words sum this up: "I speak from experience when I say that one need never be frightened of putting bold and unaccustomed things before the proletariat, so long as they have to do with reality. There will always be educated persons, connoisseurs of the arts, who will step in with a 'the people won't understand that.' But the people impatiently shoves them aside and comes to terms directly with the artist."[8]

Raising the level of popular taste was also an aim of the Chilean mural brigades. In a mural painted for Fabrilana, a textile factory in Santiago, the Brigada Ramona Parra did not ask the workers what they wanted as a mural; they felt that the workers, because of a lack

[8] Brecht, *Brecht on Theatre,* p. 111.

of knowledge of the possibilities, would probably want some heroic figures of laborers. Rather, they toured the factory and then painted a semicubist representation of the great dye vats, looms, and skeins of yarn. In the mural (fig. 95), the looms were portrayed as rectangular forms. Other machines were abstracted into their circular components. The colors of the wool flowed throughout the mural, becoming hands, smoke, hair, flags. "In fact," Brigada members explained, "the painting represents the workers' reality of looms and wool, a reality that flows directly out of the workers' experience." When the mural was finished, the textile workers recognized that it reflected their experience, more so than would a Soviet-style depiction of some heroic worker figures.[9]

The experience of the Chilean mural brigades, working in a semi-industrialized country where the level of education and literacy in the working class is far lower than in the United States, strengthens our conviction in a similar process that is occurring here. Both in Chile and in the United States, people without extensive education can understand complex artistic styles when the experience represented in the mural reflects their common feelings and the reality of their lives. It is not style but content that determines the acceptance of a mural in a community. "Abstract" styles are not per se bad. They have been used in decorative art since the beginning of time. It is the harmony between style and content and the appropriateness of a particular form of expression to its content, not the style as such, that gives a work its validity.

Conservative Tendencies

As the mural movement has matured, artists have begun applying some of their newly acquired knowledge of earlier mural movements. Some of the murals have begun to look more accomplished, but also more like older murals. Some of the innovations, e.g. cartoon and graphic manners and other Pop possibilities, are insuffi-

[9] Eva S. Cockcroft and James D. Cockcroft, "Murals for the People of Chile," *TRA—Towards Revolutionary Art*, no. 4 (1973): 14.

ciently explored, as murals begin to take on a more conventional figurative look.

This problem of conservative tendencies is compounded by that of cliché imagery. A message in a mural is generally presented by a single representative image, a positive-negative sequence, a narrative progression, or a montage of elements. Negative images, which often draw on personal experience and strong feeling, are rarely clichés. Positive images present a more serious problem, because they are often idealizations with little reality behind them. Because positive images often become role models for children and young people living in mural neighborhoods, it is important that the artist try to create positive images that have experiential validity. Certain images—a fist breaking chains, hands clasped in brotherhood—arose validly out of the common visual vocabulary of a certain time. They can, however, rapidly become empty clichés if repeated mechanically and outside of the historical context of struggle that gave them meaning. Contrary examples are Caryl Yasko's heroic figures in the Logan Square mural (fig. 32), which seem to move between past and future in an original and *concrete* vision; or Alan Okada's *Chi Lai—Arriba—Rise Up!* (pl. 12), where the positive crowning image develops with convincing visual logic from the images of the past.

Graffiti

Graffiti are a completely different question. Graffiti as such are not purely negative gestures. On the one hand, they are an attack on property, but on the other, they are a positive assertion of identity. In the East Los Angeles *barrio*, graffiti artists have developed their own styles of calligraphy and small cult of admirers. David Kahn, who has worked with some of the young Chicano muralists, writes about these gang graffiti:

> Gangs formed by both sexes have over the years in some ways alleviated the problem of identity, at least for the young Chicanos who have belonged to them. The territory of each

> gang is defined by the use of its graffiti or gang writing. Each gang, and sometimes each member within a gang, has a particular style of writing, a code formed of distortions and substitutions of the roman alphabet. . . . For the individual, his name means he exists. For the gang member who writes his name in coded script on a wall, he owns that part of the wall and his "soul" is there.[10]

In the late 1960s, a group of young blacks made a brief bid to make Philadelphia "The Graffiti Capital of the World." Using imaginative names such as Cool Earl, Cold Duck, and Cornbread, King of the Walls, they sprayed their way to notoriety. For these individualists, graffiti were an alternative to gang life, not a part of it. As the most renowned of the wall writers, Cornbread, has said: "When you live where we do, you either gang war or you're a junkie. We just wrote on walls."[11] Although, from this point of view, graffiti writing is a step up from killing or selling dope, it remains a narrow and essentially antisocial form of self-assertion, reflecting an antisocial society.

> I'm a product of this community, not a part of it. I'm lost in a society that cares more about its economy and buildings than its youth. . . . Walls that house me in projects, walls in schools that stifle me with a dull education, walls that keep me from getting a job, billboards on walls that scream get it all now—cars, money, things—now. Walls with signs everywhere, signs advertising . . . where to get buried cheaply. The boxed-in walls of television brainwash me day after day. So I write a message, advertise the easy way, get famous the easy way. I write on walls.[12]

The plague of graffiti visited on the New York City subways by a small group of Latin "graffiti masters" in the early 1970s was essen-

[10] David Kahn, "Chicano Street Murals: People's Art in the East Los Angeles Barrio," *Aztlán* 6, no. 1 (Spring 1975): 2.

[11] Cited in Sandy Rubin and Bob Rivera, *A Primer for Community Graffiti Workshops* (Philadelphia: Graffiti Alternatives Workshop, 1972), p. 6.

[12] *Ibid.*, p. 2.

tially similar to the Philadelphia phenomenon in its individualism, with the difference that in New York official semitoleration allowed the graffitists to develop elaborate, multicolor, large-scale inscriptions. Despite the obvious and inventive decorative qualities, the message, whether candy-striped or polka-dotted, remained simple self-promotion.

Certain gallery artists, whose murals have been heavily defaced, have claimed that the graffiti "improved" their murals. We find such statements a devastating admission of bankruptcy. Furthermore, to deny the obvious implied criticism, to deny that the alteration of their work was evidence of disrespect, is really to patronize the audience. Even more patronizing (à la Norman Mailer) is the implication that the community and the graffitists can *only* participate in this way. The community muralists consider the emergence of distinctive calligraphic graffiti not as an end in itself but as proof of tremendous pent-up creative energies and talent, which need only an opportunity, encouragement, and direction to develop more complete means of expression.

Permanence and Technique

In the early days of the Mexican mural movement, the muralists turned to the Indian artists of Cholula, who still used fresco techniques in their work, and to the *pulquería* painters, who decorated popular saloons with realistic murals of popular scenes (toreadors, beautiful women, portraits of the twin volcanos in whose shadows Mexico City rests).[13] In working to reinvent the lost fresco technology, they sought out these popular artists to learn their craft. We are luckier than the Mexicans were, because we have their experience on which to build. Yet, at the beginning of the current mural movement, artists once again faced the problem of finding techniques suitable for painting on brick and other common exterior city wall surfaces.

[13] Jean Charlot, *The Mexican Mural Renaissance, 1920–1925* (New Haven and London: Yale University Press, 1963), p. 37.

Like the Mexicans, today's muralists, too, turned to popular craftsmen—sign painters—for help and learned from them how to deal with brick surfaces. From sign painters they learned about tuck-pointing, how to recognize saltpetering and chemical decomposition of the wall, and how to minimize the problems of moisture and chemical leaching, which cause the paint to peel within a few years. They learned to prepare the wall, to clean it well and use a resin sealer and undercoat of masonry paint, before laying out their design. Sign painters' enamels became a preferred medium in Chicago and New York. The techniques developed by today's muralists have been a mixture of things learned from sign painters, house painters, the Mexican muralists, and a good deal of guesswork and rule-of-thumb common sense.

Direct painting with sign paints and water-base polymers has remained the preferred technique, allowing great flexibility in making compositional changes on the wall. Indoors, such paints are substantially permanent, but outdoors, even on an excellent, well-prepared wall, their life-span hardly exceeds a decade. In many urban areas, such a life-span is quite acceptable and although certain colors (yellows, purples) are unstable in direct sunlight, the effect of the faded wall, gradually blending back into its surroundings, is not at all unpleasant. Early peeling, a less acceptable situation, has sometimes created a serious problem. Often, artists have had no choice but to paint on walls in deplorable condition, e.g. retaining walls or party walls exposed by the tearing down of adjoining buildings. Whether the result of improper wall preparation, moisture in the wall from a leaky roof or foundation, or the serious saltpetering caused by years of neglect, peeling becomes an embarrassment to artist and sponsor.

Many of the early Chicago murals that have become landmarks have been conscientiously retouched and repainted by the artists. In 1974, for example, Mitchell Caton repainted and changed his mural *Universal Alley;* John Weber reworked *Unidos para Triunfar;* and Bill Walker regularly retouches the *Peace and Salvation, Wall of Understanding*. The necessity for such retouching could, however, rapidly become a limiting factor; most of an artist's summer would be occupied maintaining existing murals rather than creating new ones. The use of polyurethane varnish has been found to lengthen the life of a mural. Still, there exists a desperate need for funding for restoration of major murals.

These problems are spurring concern with permanent media—concrete, metal, tile, mosaic—and the development of new, more permanent paints and paint techniques. Such permanent media will demand a higher level of funding, although the mosaics of Harold Haydon and the plaza projects of Cityarts Workshop show that nonprofessional volunteer labor can be successfully used if the project is properly designed and supervised. What has been lacking is architects who plan buildings with public art in mind. Jean Charlot's ceramic-tile murals for the Public Service Workers' Hall in Honolulu, Hawaii, represent an encouraging example.

The rediscovery of the fresco medium was an important contribution by the Mexican muralists. Yet, just as important for the current mural revival has been the spirit of continuing experimentation with more contemporary materials: the use of spray guns and plastic-based paints, and experiments with concrete and sculptural murals. This kind of ongoing experimentation is an essential part of the continuing development of the mural form.

The problem of permanence is not wholly a question of technique. Some murals have been destroyed when the buildings on which they were painted changed ownership, or they were demolished by urban-renewal wrecking crews. Sometimes, simply a change in tenants is sufficient, as when the building in the heart of Santa Fe's *barrio* that had housed the Clínica de la Gente was rented to a religious group who then covered over the Aztec god figures on the exterior (fig. 78) with a coat of adobe-brown paint.

Occasionally, however, a mural outlives its community and remains as a relic of a one-time Puerto Rican or black presence in the area. In some rapidly changing areas, as Robert Sommer points out, the short life-span of a mural may not be as limited as it appears: "A five-or-ten-year existence may not seem like a long time measured against a 500-year-old indoor painting, but it can be a significant term in the life of an individual or community. . . . It is difficult to describe something as impermanent or ephemeral when it outlasts the conditions that gave rise to it."[14] The fact that many early murals were not seen as permanent led the artists to deal with timely immediate issues in a more direct fashion than they might have done in more permanent locations. Since then, a genre of intentionally temporary murals, often on portable panels, cloth, or billboards, has developed that deals with current events. On the other hand, permanent murals more and more deal with themes that will be with us for a long time.

Because of the prevalence of photography in all strata of society, an ironic parallel between the murals and conceptual art exists. Both become permanent through the recording of the moment on film, and the lost masterpieces (the clinic painted by Artes, the Walls of Respect and Truth, the Dana Chandler–Gary Rickson wall in Boston) often are easier to see, through slide shows and magazine reproduction, than are existing walls and more recent projects. As photographers and commercial slide-distribution enterprises (e.g. Environmental Communications[15]) sell photographs of the murals to an audience that does not bother to go into the mural neighborhoods, the ability, so highly developed in our time, to commercialize the unsellable comes forward, raising the danger that, as in conceptual art, the photograph becomes more real than the act, and the act (mural) simply an excuse for the photograph.

A Question of Relevance

A mural's effectiveness may depend on factors relatively extrinsic to traditional aesthetic criteria but more closely related to the coin-

[14] Robert Sommer, *Street Art* (New York: Quick Fox, 1975), p. 62.

[15] Environmental Communications, 64 Windward Avenue, Venice, California 90291.

cidence of the mural with community struggle. Arnold Belkin calls this quality of some murals a "sense of historic moment."[16] Since murals are *public* acts, what they say and how they affect existing social situations are highly relevant to any aesthetic evaluation. Those murals that embody the essence of a specific historical moment, that fall on the cutting edge of a particular social movement, that work to build community or mobilize people to action, that become engraved in the minds of people even when the wall itself has been destroyed—they have an importance that corresponds to their impact.

Judgments about such murals are always made from a specific point of view. This is inevitable and legitimate. That the *Wall of Respect* became a focus for the struggle against urban renewal does matter. On the other hand, a decorative mural in a current gallery style might, in a neighborhood being nibbled away by real-estate speculation, actually accelerate those forces destroying family housing and pushing minority residents out. To ignore the social impact of a public artwork would be irresponsible.

Quality is the code word for much of the adverse criticism of today's murals. In fact, these works cannot be adequately discussed within the terminological confines of contemporary art criticism.

> Any valid criticism of community murals must deal with a number of supposedly "non-artistic" factors. For example: impact on the community, degree and type of community participation, development of individual and group aesthetic consciousness. . . . One of the most important of emerging criteria for a meaningful criticism of the mural movement is that of political and revolutionary significance, since in the minds and hearts of growing numbers of people these murals do in fact constitute not only significant artistic expression but also essential weapons in the struggle to be free.[17]

[16] Arnold Belkin, "Public Art & People's Art," *Art Workers Newsletter* 2, no. 8 (1972): 4.

[17] Eva S. Cockcroft and James D. Cockcroft, "Cityarts Workshop—People's Art in New York City," *Left Curve/art and revolution*, no. 4 (Summer 1975): 14–15.

All art is political and speaks to particular social classes or serves social ends, whether intentionally or not. Public artists must accept responsibility for the meaning and effect of their murals. A formally excellent mural, showing great virtuosity and skill in the solution of technical problems yet without deep meaning for its audience, falls short of the mark, just as would a thematically powerful mural that ignores the plastic problems involved in mural design. As Charlot states, "Whatever axe the painter grinds, it is his job to grind it fine."[18]

[18] Jean Charlot, "Public Speaking in Paint," *American Scholar* 10 (1941): 468.

12

Continuations and Perspectives

> What is needed is to return art to the people as a means of expression of their lives. The people have been robbed of this —the power to formulate their own view of the world, including the power to give visual form to the world. To be revolutionary in art today is to act to return the right to culture to the people.
>
> —John Weber, "Two Letters on Revolutionary Art."

The mural movement's continuation, like its birth and development into a vital force, relates strongly to larger developments in society as a whole. The early 1970s witnessed the phenomenological breakup of the New Left, civil-rights, and antiwar organizations of the 1960s. The repression of militant organizations, co-optation of select leaders, and changing patterns of salient issues have all contributed to a seeming quiescence of the mass direct-action movements. This quiescence, no doubt, is temporary. It cannot be compared to those reverses of history that literally crush, or else set severe historical limits on, movements for radical change (e.g. post-coup Chile). An understanding of each historical conjuncture is crucial. Murals alone cannot change the world; social movements, changes in government policies, and underlying economic forces constitute determining factors that condition any effort toward a people's art.

In late 1973, economic issues moved to the forefront of social struggle, as the United States entered a depression. The gross national product declined over ten percent in the first quarter of 1975 while unemployment climbed to nine percent (by official figures). More than fifty thousand workers marched on Washington, April 26, 1975, protesting the manner in which the government and the corporations were handling the crisis. Few could deny the economic indicators that showed that society's ruling circles were passing the costs of defeat in Southeast Asia and world economic crisis on to the masses—through job layoffs, cutbacks in essential services, and higher prices. At the same time, a reactionary, ideological offensive moved into high gear. A new computerized racism was promoted and encouraged in high places in an attempt to combat the heightened cultural and political awareness of the 1960s, which had become diffused through larger and larger layers of the population. The military-political defeat in Indochina; the revelations of corruption, cover-up, and illegal behavior surrounding Watergate; and the passing on of economic hardship to the majority of the population contributed to a generalized discontent with the status quo and to widespread public distrust of those governing society and the economy.

These larger developments in the mid-1970s coincided with a maturing process in the mural movement. To an extent, this maturation included some predictable conservative tendencies: a certain "domestication" of murals as they became more acceptable, even fashionable, or as some muralists consented to paint less controversial themes in exchange for wall permissions or funding; a gaining of command of the mural medium; a broadening of themes, imagery, and style, which often included less aggressive or militant communication than that manifested in the late 1960s; and a desire to study Mexican and other traditional mural techniques in order to perfect one's craft.

At the same time, this maturing process witnessed the spreading of murals from urban slums to stable working-class, petit-bourgeois, and even suburban neighborhoods. A number of factories, workshops, labor unions, and related organizations began sponsoring or seeking murals as a means of transmitting the history of working-class struggle. Housing projects, at one time extremely difficult for muralists to enter, have become more common as mural sites. The interest in murals thus continued to grow at the grass-roots level—a reflection both of the vitality of the mural movement and of the gradual spreading of progressive consciousness among the people. The mural movement also matured in the sense of its consolidation, self-confidence, and steady growth and dedication to good painting and craftsmanship during the early 1970s, precisely when many other progressive forces appeared to be in momentary disarray.

Economic Support: On Whom Do You Rely?

The question of economic support for the growing number of muralists reaching maturity, and the even larger number of younger artists who have joined the mural movement, is qualitatively different from what it was in the late 1960s. Not only does economic support involve greater numbers of practicing muralists and higher costs of materials, it also includes a broader range and depth of mural art. The economic question now includes the question of permanence of murals, their preservation, and the size and scope of future murals (including the possibility of more elaborate materials, sculptural, collage, and other combinations of art forms).

Will there be new sources of government funding for muralists? There is discussion of a new WPA for artists. This prospect seems remote so long as there is no large-scale work relief for the unemployed. The Comprehensive Employment Training Act (CETA) of 1973, which was to provide three hundred thousand jobs for a one-year period, has given employment to artists in only a few places.

Despite a resolution passed in January 1975 by the U.S. Conference of Mayors to "provide employment to the individual creative artist . . . through CETA," only a few cities have acted. San Francisco, where about eleven percent of the jobs are going to the arts, is the only city that has employed muralists to any extent. Most other cities have preferred to use the meager CETA salaries to maintain services and patronage in nonart areas.

Will there be a federal one percent for art? The existing law, dating from the 1930s, according to which one-fourth of one percent of all federally sponsored construction funds is to be spent for art, is rarely observed. At least two cities, Boston and Baltimore, have enacted their own one-percent laws applying to all construction on lands taken by eminent domain. Major commissions, especially for sculpture, have resulted. As might be expected when commissions are awarded by competitions, decorative pieces by well-known New York artists have been favored. The one-percent-for-art program has been applied primarily to private developers and only occasionally to city buildings, such as schools or hospitals. In the rest of the country, few artists of any sort receive commissions to create permanent murals for buildings. The National Endowment for the Arts Visual Arts Program has deemphasized the inner city, although it still funds a few programs and has given small individual fellowships to a few community muralists. To be eligible for the NEA's Expansion Arts funding, a program must have been in existence for at least three years, which automatically disqualifies individual muralists and younger programs. Nonetheless, artists might fight for increased government funding for public art and mobilize public support for proposals such as artists-in-residence in schools and public housing.

Can a great muralism flourish without the opportunity of major commissions and high-level patronage? As in the first years of the Mexican mural movement, a number of very accomplished muralists have emerged. There exist today at least a dozen American figurative muralists of exceptional skill, power, and energy. The fundamental question is whether the government, private agencies, corporations, and art connoisseurs ever will (or really want to) support the best, most representative, and most dynamic in American public art.

For the muralists, the question of adequate funding is not limited to the area of official patronage. Such patronage can have unexpected negative consequences, such as the setbacks suffered when official funding is cut off. Veteran black muralists, such as Dana Chandler in Boston, have found themselves excluded from municipal decoration programs, while the cutbacks in Neighborhood Youth Corps, college work-study loan and scholarship programs, and the like, have made it more difficult for nonwhite and working-class youth to pursue art. A number of artists are determined to continue in the direction they have set, regardless of commissions or the vicissitudes of government funding. They are relying on the local community, where there are signs of growing interest among labor unions, merchant organizations, and schools in sponsoring mural activities. Several muralists are prepared, if necessary, to "return to the beginnings": smaller-scale work based solely on local community requests and support, or even to self-sponsored, semilegal work on isolated or abandoned walls.

Future of Groups and Programs

Artist groups tend to dissolve and art movements have historical limits, rarely lasting the lifetimes of their originators. The struggle for a genuine democratic culture goes on, nonetheless. We believe that groups have played a crucial role in the contemporary mural movement and, in fact, give the recent upsurge in public art its character as a movement. Like other alternative institutions that have their roots in the late 1960s, the mural groups are facing a difficult struggle to survive in the economic hard times of the mid-1970s.[1] Most of the mural collectives, like other participatory collec-

[1] A distinct problem arises with possible success and recognition during periods of relative social stability—the establishment of set patterns and the dominance of a few artists who become widely known, making continued in-

tives, have rarely lasted more than two years, and larger cooperative groups are continually beset with internal problems. Of the many paid-staff programs and workshops, only a limited number will be able to stabilize their funding in the period ahead.

Some veteran muralists, fatigued with the uncertain hand-to-mouth existence of most inner-city mural programs, are seeking more stable employment. A few have found positions in university art departments or ethnic-studies programs. They are hired as "resident radical" artists in response to student demands, just as showcase radicals were hired by other departments a few years back (even while younger, less prestigious radicals were being fired). The establishment of university-based mural-painting programs reflects a dramatic change in attitudes toward public art, as well as toward socially involved and figurative art. A few of the muralist-academics, like Nelson Stevens at the University of Massachusetts, Amherst, have been able to use a college base effectively to train young muralists and produce exciting public art in nearby urban areas. One wonders, nonetheless, about the long-term co-optive tendencies involved in the academization of what began as a rebellious in-the-streets movement. One also wonders how long these new university mural programs will last, in the face of general cutbacks and next year's fad idea.

In 1974 and 1975, in part perhaps because of the recent institutionalized teaching of mural art, we have observed the appearance of scores of young artists attempting murals. These new muralists, many without a point of view, seem somewhat different from those who came to mural painting earlier out of the civil-rights and anti-war movements and through apprenticeships on the street, but it is impossible to tell how many of them will continue after the dense clouds of Bicentennial commercialism have cleared away.

Problems of instability in voluntary groups, whether collectives or

novation and the entry of new artists difficult. Rising costs and technical expectations with the use of permanent media may also raise the ante for new artists and remove them from a base in their impoverished communities. This can be observed, for example, in the problems experienced by the younger generation of socially oriented muralists in Mexico.

cooperatives, tend to become highly exacerbated during economic hard times. Yet during prolonged economic crises, while many individuals and groups go under, others emerge stronger or new ones are created in response to new political developments or sudden upsurges in mass struggle or protest activity. The essential point is that economic hard times make it less possible to "muddle through" and more necessary than ever for mural groups and programs to work toward eliminating sources of disunity and resolving internal squabbles. For it is precisely during such times that tensions created by unequal levels of skill, aesthetic understanding, political consciousness, and commitment are most likely to overflow into irrational individualism and factionalism. No group, including one with a paid staff, can consolidate or advance without facing up honestly and frankly to these problems.

Murals as Revolutionary Art Activity

Characteristic of the community-based mural movement has been an emphasis on activism, on relating theory to practice, on developing theory and strategy out of action. To a certain degree, our beginnings were spontaneous and even antihistorical in character. Today's mural movement has taken as its definition: work with the oppressed, with the working class. There has been little room for self-indulgence, and the hard work involved has discouraged opportunism. The basis for successful community murals has been: respect for people, respect for self, respect for art. These "Three Respects" have proven more valuable as a guide and touchstone of experience than any merely verbal position on art or politics.

But with its maturation, the mural movement has discovered both the advantages and defects of its having undergone this essentially organic development with the people. There has grown up an informal network of mural groups, contacts, and practicing muralists from coast to coast, including communication with older-generation muralists. Within this network, there is active discussion and exchange of experience. A few small conferences of muralists have taken place, and larger ones are planned for the future. For many, it is a time of summing up accumulated experience, taking the longer view, and better preparing for the prolonged struggle ahead.

At least one attempt is underway to formulate parts of this informal network into an artists' front: the International Front of Cultural Workers (Frente Internacional de Obreros Culturales). Although it is too early to ascertain what will become of this particular front, it is significant that such an organizing endeavor is attempted. So far, only a few muralists have committed themselves to the Front, mainly on the West Coast. But the very presence of such a phenomenon introduces once more the question of an artists' front, and of partisan art.[2]

We affirm the proposition that artists can transform themselves and their viewpoint, that artists can take a partisan stance and be partisan in practice. Moreover, they can do this without sacrificing either their artistic integrity or their aesthetic evolution. There is no necessary contradiction between the aesthetic, expressive, and didactic aspects of art. Currently, the American mural movement is more eclectic than any earlier mural movement in history; it is less dependent on any single source of funding, moral support, or style inspiration. It has its own characteristic aesthetics, which is still developing, based primarily on the interrelationship between artist and audience, with a rich diversity of style and range of authentic directions. Right now, this movement has the potential for daring innovations in mural art. It is imperative that muralists fulfill this potential, daring to seek the cutting edge—in quality, in theme, in class struggle.

The experience of the mural movement constitutes a partial basis for the formulation of a revolutionary programme in culture. As the muralists have discovered, only cultural work with the people—the true character of mass work—can provide such a basis for programme and can test programme. In our examination of this experi-

[2] The First National Murals Conference, sponsored by Cityarts Workshop, was held in New York City, April 30–May 2, 1976.

ence, the interested reader will have found many ideas of radicals of the past confirmed, but others questioned, refuted, or ignored as irrelevant.

The Question of Relationship to the Left

The actual relationship between murals and organized leftist groups has been tangential, sporadic, problematic. Radical and alternative newspapers have reported on and praised the mural movement on much the same basis as have the regular local papers. In private, however, some artists have been urged to abandon mural painting in favor of graphics and more regular organizing. While most veteran community muralists are deeply committed to their people and to the people's struggles, there is no general consensus on "correct line" or on the need to relate to political organization. Among those few muralists who have worked directly with political organizations (making banners, posters, etc.), some have found their mural work subjected to criticism without opportunities for open discussion or study of cultural questions. *Individualism, opportunism, reformism, social pacifism, cultural nationalism,* and *sexism* have been a few of the epithets. No doubt there has been some basis for all of these terms being used. But the artists have often been left with the impression that categories were being applied according to preconceived ideas of what art *should* look like, and also that there has been very little willingness to examine the variables of time, place, and condition. Implicit in these philistine, mechanistic, and a priori views is a basic disrespect not only for art but also, and more importantly, for people. We make these observations, not in order to pander to anticommunist hysterics, but fraternally as committed individuals, to call on the political movement to reexamine its positions on culture.

We do not mean to imply that the Left is unaware of, or uninterested in, culture. Currently, there is renewed talk of "revolutionary" culture and of art "as a weapon." What seems to be meant are banners, emblems, posters, leaflets, newspaper graphics, songs, skits, even short films if they can be used at a rally or meeting. All these things are, in fact, necessary, and muralists as much as any artists have been involved in providing them on demand. But, as one muralist commented, "a lot of people on the Left simply want us to be commercial artists for the movement—we are asked to do poster after poster 'like the one before,' but there is no interest in our development." At the moment, it seems that the interest of Leftist organizations in culture hardly goes further than having artists serve their immediate organizational needs.

The desire of the masses for culture goes far beyond the immediate tactical horizon of the organized Left, and beyond the slogans of a given moment. Our experience has shown us that plain people want a partisan culture, but one that is expressive as well as agitational. Art is a weapon to the degree that it is rooted in people's struggles. The reappropriation of culture by the people is about the restoration to the people of a fully human image and creative possibility. As a kind of midwife to the rebirth of a socially committed public art, the human process of murals has reconfirmed the people as the ultimate source of energy and change in culture. The mural that affirms *Hay Cultura en Nuestra Comunidad*—"There Is Culture in Our Community"—affirms human dignity and, thereby, also the possibility of winning a future of justice and peace.

Select Bibliography

Manuals

Abramson, Joan, and Woodbridge, Sally B. *The Alvarado School-Community Art Program.* San Francisco: The Alvarado Workshop, 1973.

Arai, Tomie, ed. *Into the Streets: Statements from the National Murals Movement.* New York: Cityarts Workshop, 1975.

Caruso-Green, Susan; Friedman, Ben; and Miller, Susan. *Public Art on Public Schools: A Guide to Community Mural Making.* New York: Cityarts Workshop, 1975.

Morrison, Rhoda; Peugh, Karen; and Rogovin, Mark. *Silhouette Murals.* Chicago: Public Art Workshop, 1976.

Rogovin, Mark; Burton, Marie; and Highfill, Holly. *Mural Manual.* Edited by Tim Drescher. Boston: Beacon Press, 1975.

Rubin, Sandy, and Rivera, Bob. *A Primer for Community Graffiti Workshops.* Philadelphia: Center for Alternative Graffiti Workshop, 1972.

Mexican Murals and WPA

Bernstein, Barbara. "Federal Art: Not Gone, Just Forgotten." *Chicago Tribune Magazine* (December 2, 1973): 80–88.

Charlot, Jean. *The Charlot Murals in Georgia.* Athens, Ga.: University of Georgia Press, 1941.

———. *The Mexican Mural Renaissance, 1920–1925.* New Haven and London: Yale University Press, 1963.

———. "Public Speaking in Paint." *American Scholar* 10 (1941): 455–468. First chapter of *The Charlot Murals in Georgia.*

Enciso, Jorge. *Design Motifs of Ancient Mexico.* New York: Dover Publications, Inc., 1953.

Goldman, Shifra M. "Siqueiros and Three Early Murals in Los Angeles." *Art Journal* 33, no. 4 (Summer 1974): 321–327. *Art Journal* is a publication of the College Art Association of America.

McKinzie, Richard D. *The New Deal for Artists.* Princeton, N.J.: Princeton University Press, 1972.

O'Connor, Francis V. *Art for the Millions.* Greenwich, Conn.: New York Graphic Society, 1973.

———. *Federal Support for the Visual Arts: The New Deal and Now.*

Greenwich, Conn.: New York Graphic Society, 1969.
———. "New Deal Murals in New York." *Artforum* (November 1968): 41–49.
———, ed. *The New Deal Art Projects: An Anthology of Memoirs.* Washington, D.C.: Smithsonian Institution Press, 1972.
Plenn, Jaime, and Plenn, Virginia. *A Guide to Modern Mexican Murals.* Mexico City: Ediciones Tolteca, 1963.
Reed, Alma. *The Mexican Muralists.* New York: Crown Publishers, 1960.
Refregier, Anton. "Governmental Sponsorship of the Arts." Reprinted by Public Art Workshop, Chicago, from *Public Ownership in the U.S.A.* New York: Peace Publications, 1961.
Rodríguez, Antonio. *A History of Mexican Mural Painting.* New York: G. P. Putnam's Sons, 1969.
Siqueiros, David A. "Lectures to Artists." *New University Thought* (Winter 1962): 17–26. Reprinted by Public Art Workshop, Chicago.
Suárez, Orlando. *Inventario del Muralismo Mexicano: Siglo VII 1968.* Mexico City: Universidad Nacional Autónoma de México, 1972.

Contemporary

Alloway, Lawrence. "Art." *The Nation,* September 21, 1970; September 25, 1972; and August 3, 1974.
Amalgamated Meatcutters and Butcher Workmen of America, AFL-CIO. *Cry for Justice.* Chicago: 1972. Illustrated booklet on Chicago murals.
Art in America, May–June 1974. Issue devoted to public art, but almost nothing on murals.
Arts in Society 12, no. 1 (Spring–Summer 1975). Issue on community arts.
Art Workers News (formerly *Art Workers Newsletter*) 3, no. 7 (October 1973). Issue on public art; other numbers include occasional articles on murals in Chicago, New York, Chile, etc.
Belkin, Arnold. "Public Art & People's Art." *Art Workers Newsletter* 2, no. 8 (1972): 4. Personal statement.
Bloom, Janet. "Changing Walls." *The Architectural Forum* 138, no. 4 (May 1973): 20–27.
Bright, Mura. *L.A. Chicano Street Art.* Los Angeles: Environmental Communications, 1974. Text accompanying slide collection of L.A. Chicano art, sold by Environmental Communications, 62 Windward Avenue, Venice, California 90291.
Brunazzi, Ceci. "Murals in the Mission." *Common Sense* 2, no. 6 (May 1975): 8.
Castellanos, Leonard. "Chicano Centros, Murals, and Art." *Arts in Society* 12, no. 1 (Spring–Summer 1975): 38–43.

Charbit, Esther. "Toward a More Relevant Public Art: The Community Mural Movement." *Investigart,* no. 5 (Spring 1975): 1–8. *Investigart* is a biannual publication of the Art Education Program, Concordia University, Montréal, Québec.

"The City Is Their Canvas." *City* (May–June 1971): 38–40. Early Los Angeles murals.

Cockcroft, Eva S. "Coup Topples Chile Walls." *Art Workers News* 3, no. 8 (November 1973): 1.

Cockcroft, Eva S., and Cockcroft, James D. "Cityarts Workshop—People's Art in New York City." *Left Curve/art and revolution,* no. 4 (Summer 1975): 3–15.

———. "Murals for the People of Chile." *TRA—Towards Revolutionary Art,* no. 4 (1973), pp. 3–11. Condensed in *Art Workers Newsletter* 3, no. 1 (March 1973): 1, 10–11.

Cockcroft, Eva S., and Lippard, Lucy. "The Death of a Mural Movement." *Art in America* 62, no. 1 (January–February 1974): 35–37.

Del Oemo, Frank. "Murals Changing Face of East L.A." *Los Angeles Times,* December 3, 1973, sec. II, p. 1.

Ebony, December 1967, pp. 48–50. Dedication of *Wall of Respect.*

Franco, Jean. *The Modern Culture of Latin America, Society and the Artist.* Baltimore: Penguin Books, 1970, p. 157.

Garber, Susan, and Miller, Susan. "An Historical Summary of Public Art in Boston." Mimeographed. Boston: Institute of Contemporary Art, May 1974. Prepared for ICA symposium "Arts Renewal: Boston's Visual Environment, 1974–1984."

Garcia, Rupert. *Raza Murals and Muralists: An Historical View.* San Francisco: Galeria de la Raza, 1974.

Harding, David. *Glenrothes' Town Artist, David Harding.* Glenrothes Development Corporation, Glenrothes House, Glenrothes Central, Fife, Scotland KY7-5PR, 1974.

Haydon, Harold. "A New American Art—by the People, for the People." *The 1975 Compton Yearbook.* Chicago: F. E. Compton Company, 1975, pp. 30–45.

———. "The Walls Have Tongues." *PTA Magazine* (March, 1973): 12–17. Children's murals.

Holtz Kay, Jane. "Artists as Social Reformers." *Art in America* (January–February 1969): 44–47. Early article on Boston's murals.

Hoyt, Roger. "The Explosion of a Dormant Art Form: Chicago's Murals." *Chicago History* 3, no. 1 (Spring–Summer 1974): 28–35.

Kahn, David. "Chicano Street Murals: People's Art in the East Los Angeles Barrio," *Aztlán* 6, no. 1 (Spring 1975): 3–8. *Aztlán* is a publication of the Chicano Center, UCLA.

Kohl, Herbert. *Golden Boy as Anthony Cool.* New York: Dial Press, 1972. Graffiti & early murals.

———. "The Writing's on the Wall–Use It." *Learning* (May–June 1974).

Kroll, Eric. "Folk Art in the Barrios." *Natural History* 82, no. 5 (May 1973): 56–65. Reprinted as "Murals in New Mexico." *Artforum* (September 1973): 55–57.

Lee, Feelie. "The People's Art Gallery." *San Francisco Sunday Examiner and Chronicle, California Living Magazine,* March 11, 1973, pp. 20–23.

Lewis, Samella. "The Street Art of Black America." *Exxon USA* 12, no. 3 (1973): 2–9.

Lewis, Samella, and Waddy, Ruth. *Black Artists on Art.* 2 vols. Los Angeles: Contemporary Crafts, 1971. Includes statements by muralists.

Mangurian, David. "Revolutionary Art: The Murals of Chile Awake a Nation." *Clipper* (September 1972): 5–8. *Clipper* magazine is published by Pan Am.

"Mural in East Harlem." *Street,* no. 13 (Fall 1974): 14–16. Story of Hank Prussing's mural.

"Object Diversity." *Time,* April 6, 1970, p. 80. Early black murals in Boston and black art in general.

"Painting the Town." *Life,* July 17, 1970, pp. 60–63. Picture story on nation's murals.

Patlán, Ray, and Weber, John. "A Wall Belongs to Everybody." *Youth* 23, no. 9 (September 1972): 58–66. *Youth* is published by United Church Press, 1505 Race Street, Philadelphia, Pennsylvania 19102.

Quintero, Victoria. "A Mural Is a Painting on a Wall Done by Human Hands." *El Tecolote* 5, no. 1 (September 13, 1974): 6, 7, 12. Story about Mujeres Muralistas. *El Tecolote*'s address is 1292 Potrero, San Francisco, California 94110.

Quirarte, Jacinto. "The Murals of El Barrio." *Exxon USA* 13, no. 4 (1974): 2–9.

Romotsky, Jerry, and Romotsky, Sally R. "Barrio School Murals." *Children Today* 3, no. 5 (September–October 1974): 16–20.

Rosenberg, Lilli Anne Killen. *Children Make Murals and Sculpture.* New York: Reinhold Book Corp., 1968.

Schmidt-Brümmer, Horst. *Venice, California: An Urban Fantasy.* New York: Grossman Publishers, 1973.

———, and Lee, Feelie. *Die Bemalte Stadt.* Berlin: DuMont Aktuell, 1973.

Schneider, Betty. "Mural Movement." *Community* 29, no. 4 (Summer 1970): 8–13. Early Chicago murals.

Solorzano, Julio. "Pintando, las minorías ganan la calle." *Revista de Revistas, Excelsior,* no. 20 (October 18, 1972): 24–29. Interview with John Weber.

Sommer, Robert. *Street Art.* New York: Quick Fox, 1975.

———. "Peoples Art." *Natural History* 80, no. 2 (February 1971): 40–45.

Stevens, Elizabeth. "Black Arts Centers." *Museum News* (March 1975): 19–24.

"Street Art Explosion." *Sunset* (April 1973): 110–113.

Taylor, Robert. "Wall-to-Wall Boston." *Boston Sunday Globe,* October 26, 1969.

———. "In Four Years, 72 Hub Public Murals." *Boston Sunday Globe,* August 13, 1972.

Thompson, Rich, and Alexander, Ron. " 'Public Art'—The Aesthetics of the People." *DRUM* 6, no. 1 (Winter 1975): 19–24. An interview with Nelson Stevens. *DRUM's* address is 426 New Africa House, University of Massachusetts, Amherst 01002

U.S., Department of Housing and Urban Development. *National Community Arts Program.* Washington, D.C.: Government Printing Office, n.d. Photographs.

Wagner, Kathie, and LuJan, Lori. "Public Works: San Francisco and Beyond the City." *San Francisco Sunday Examiner and Chronicle, California Living Magazine,* September 21, 1975, pp. 26–30; and September 28, 1975, pp. 26–34.

Walker, William; Weber, John; Eda, Eugene; and Rogovin, Mark. *The Artists' Statement.* Chicago: Museum of Contemporary Art, 1971. Written for the "Murals for the People" exhibit, February–March 1971. Excerpted as "The Chicago Muralists." *American Dialog* 7, no. 2 (1972): 23–25.

Weber, John. "Chicago Mural Movement." *TRA—Towards Revolutionary Art,* no. 2 (1972): 4–8.

———. "Chicago's Wall Paintings: An Artist Sounds Off." *Chicago Daily News, Panorama,* March 15 and 16, 1975, p. 17. Reprinted as "A Muralist Answers: 'Chicago Murals, Are They Our Best Public Art?' " *New Art Examiner,* April 1975, p. 13.

———. "Murals as People's Art." *Liberation* 16, no. 4 (September 1971): 42–46.

———. "Two Letters on Revolutionary Art." *TRA—Towards Revolutionary Art,* no. 2 (1972): 7.

Wilson, William. "The L.A. Fine Arts Squad: Venice in the Snow and Other Visions." *Art News* 12 (Summer 1973): 28–29.

Select List of Mural Information, Resource and Workshop Centers (by city)

(For more complete listings of mural resource centers, write to the groups given here.)

Boston
Institute of Contemporary Art
955 Boyleston St.
Documentation*

Mayor's Office of Cultural Affairs
City Hall
Documentation

Chicago
Chicago Mural Group
2261 North Lincoln Ave.
Artist group. Workshops; artists for mural projects; documentation; exhibits

Public Art Workshop
5623 West Madison St.
Artist group. Workshops; artists for mural projects; documentation (nationwide); reprints

Los Angeles
Citywide Mural Project & Resource Center
3970 South Menlo
Artists for mural projects; documentation

Goez Gallery
3757 East 1st St.
Artist group. Artists for mural projects

New York
Cityarts Workshop
58 Ludlow St., Manhattan
Workshops; artists for mural projects; documentation; exhibits

Philadelphia
Dept. of Urban Outreach (DUO)
Philadelphia Museum of Art
Workshops; artists for mural projects; documentation, exhibits

Graffiti Alternatives Workshop
Community Services Center
University of Pennsylvania
4025 Chestnut St., 4th floor
Assistance in setting up graffiti workshops

San Diego
Centro Cultural de la Raza
Balboa Park
P.O. Box 8096
Artist group. Artists for mural projects

* Documentation, unless otherwise stated, refers only to the named city, and includes lists of murals, collections of clippings, slides, etc.

San Francisco

Alvarado Art Workshop, Inc.
2340 42nd Ave.
Information on setting up school art programs

Galeria de la Raza
2851 24th St. (at Bryant)
Artist group. Artists for mural projects; documentation; exhibits

Neighborhood Arts Program
San Francisco Arts Commission
165 Grove St.
Information and assistance in community arts

Index

Boldface type indicates illustrations.